The Digital Transformation of Healthcare

Health 4.0 is a term that has derived from the Fourth Industrial Revolution (Industry 4.0), as it pertains to the healthcare industry. This book offers a novel, concise, but at the same time, broad picture of the challenges that the technological revolution has created for the healthcare system.

It offers a comprehensive view of health sector actors' interaction with the emerging new technology, which is disrupting the status quo in health service delivery. It explains how these technological developments impact both society and healthcare governance. Further, the book addresses issues related to key healthcare system stakeholders: the state, patients, medical professionals, and non-governmental organizations. It also examines areas of healthcare system adaptiveness and draws its conclusions by analysing recent health policy changes in different countries across the Americas, Europe, and Asia. The authors offer an innovative approach to the subject by identifying the critical determinants of successful implementation of the Fourth Industrial Revolution's outcomes in practice, on both a macro- and microlevel. The macrolevel analysis is focused on essential factors of healthcare system adaptiveness for Health 4.0, while the microlevel relates to patients' expectations with a particular emphasis on senior citizens.

The book will appeal to academics, researchers, and students, across a wide range of disciplines, such as health economics, health sciences, public policy, public administration, political science, public governance, and sociology. It will also find an audience among healthcare professionals and health and social policymakers due to its recommendations for implementing Industry 4.0 into a healthcare system.

Marek Ćwiklicki is a Professor of Business Studies and Public Management and Head of Chair for Public Management at the Cracow University of Economics in Poland.

Mariusz Duplaga is a Professor at Jagiellonian University Medical College and is currently Head of the Department of Health Promotion and e-Health.

Jacek Klich is an Associate Professor at the Cracow University of Economics, Department for Management of Public Organisations.

Routledge International Studies in Health Economics
Edited by **Charles Normand**, *Trinity College Dublin, Ireland* and **Richard M. Scheffler**, *School of Public Health, University of California, Berkeley, USA*

Health, Economic Development and Household Poverty
From Understanding to Action
Edited by Sara Bennett, Lucy Gilson and Anne Mills

Efficiency Measurement in Health and Healthcare
Bruce Hollingsworth and Stuart J. Peacock

Reconfiguring Global Health Innovation
Padmashree Gehl Sampath

Public Policy and the Public Interest
Lok Sang Ho

Economics and HIV
The Sickness of Economics
Deborah Johnston

Medical Innovation
Science, Technology and Practice
Edited by Davide Consoli, Andrea Mina, Richard R. Nelson and Ronnie Ramlogan

Politics, Hierarchy, and Public Health
Voting Patterns in the 2016 US Presidential Election
Deborah Wallace and Rodrick Wallace

Equity and Healthcare Reform in Developing Economies
The Case of Turkey
Songül Çınaroğlu

The Digital Transformation of Healthcare
Health 4.0
Edited by Marek Ćwiklicki, Mariusz Duplaga and Jacek Klich

The Digital Transformation of Healthcare

Health 4.0

Edited by Marek Ćwiklicki, Mariusz Duplaga, and Jacek Klich

Routledge
Taylor & Francis Group
LONDON AND NEW YORK

First published 2022
by Routledge
2 Park Square, Milton Park, Abingdon, Oxon OX14 4RN

and by Routledge
605 Third Avenue, New York, NY 10158

Routledge is an imprint of the Taylor & Francis Group, an informa business

British Library Cataloguing-in-Publication Data
A catalogue record for this book is available from the British Library

Library of Congress Cataloging-in-Publication Data
A catalog record has been requested for this book

ISBN: 978-0-367-70050-8 (hbk)
ISBN: 978-0-367-70053-9 (pbk)
ISBN: 978-1-003-14440-3 (ebk)

DOI: 10.4324/9781003144403

Typeset in Bembo
by KnowledgeWorks Global Ltd.

Contents

Figures

Tables

Editor biographies

Marek Ćwiklicki – Prof., Dr. hab. in management sciences, PhD, a Professor of Business Studies and Public Management and Head of Chair for Public Management at the Cracow University of Economics in Poland. He researches, writes, and lectures on organisation theory, business research methodology, and public management. He is a habilitated doctor of Economics within the discipline of management science and holds PhD in Economics science within the field of Management Science, both obtained in Cracow University of Economics in Poland.

Mariusz Duplaga – Dr. hab. in health sciences, PhD in medicine, MD with specialities in internal medicine and pulmonary medicine, University Professor at Jagiellonian University Medical College, currently Head of the Department of Health Promotion and e-Health. His research interests focus on e-health and telemedicine, public health and health promotion, and health and e-health literacy. Participated in several national and international research and development projects (fifth, sixth, seventh Framework Programmes, EU Health Programme). From 2003 serving as an expert in consecutive EU Framework Programmes and from 2008 in Ambient Assisted Living Programme. Author or co-author of 120 full papers and 130 conference submissions.

Jacek Klich – PhD in economics, habilitation in economics, and PhD in political sciences. An Associate Professor at the Cracow University of Economics, Department for Management of Public Organisations. He researches on healthcare management and health policy and runs courses on strategic management in healthcare, health policy, and social entrepreneurship. He took part in various projects connected with healthcare system both on national (Polish Ministry of Health, The Polish Agency for Health Technology Assessment and Tariff System) and international (the World Bank, USAID, Project HOPE, Harvard-Jagiellonian Consortium for Health, Erasmus, Leonardo da Vinci, Socrates, EU/TACIS, and the European Agency for Reconstruction) level.

Contributors

Rosa De Angelis – Department of Business and Quantitative Studies, University of Naples "Parthenope", Italy. BSc (Business Economics and Administration, Parthenope University of Naples, 2019). Currently she is pursuing a master's program in Innovation at the Parthenope University of Naples.

Gaetano Cafiero – Entrepreneur, founder, and CEO of Kelyon. Prior to this, he worked as consultant and then as sales manager for a number of multinational and SME ICT companies. Currently he serves as board member of Campania Bioscience District on Life Sciences, Unione Industriali Napoli and Compagnia delle Opere Campania - two main associations representing manufacturing and service companies based in Napoli and Campania, respectively, and other associations in the field of open innovation and open source.

Alicja Domagała – Dr. hab. in health sciences, Associate Professor at the Department of Health Policy and Management, Institute of Public Health Jagiellonian University Medical College. Her research interests focus on health workforce, healthcare systems, and human resources management. One of her areas of expertise is capacity planning of human resources for health. She is a member of the European Health Workforce Planning and Forecasting Expert Network. She worked as a consultant for several projects run by the National Science Centre Poland, World Bank, and World Health Organization (e.g. EVIPNET Poland – Situation Analysis on Evidence-Informed Health Policy Making). Currently she is the leader of the Polish partner within the European Union's Health Programme: A Roadmap out of medical deserts into supportive health workforce initiatives and policies (2021–2024). Author and co-author of more than 100 full-text publications.

Szczepan Jakubowski – Master of Public Health, research and teaching assistant in the Department of Health Promotion and e-Health, Institute of Public Health, Jagiellonian University Medical College in Krakow (Poland). He is preparing a doctoral dissertation on drug policy and clinical trials for orphan medications. He mainly lectures on information systems, e-health, health promotion, and health education. His research interests include digital health, telemedicine, and medical informatics. Co-author of several scientific articles in the field of electronic health systems and security of patient data.

Norbert Laurisz – PhD (Economics); Assistant Professor, Department of Public Management, Cracow University of Economics (Poland). Research interests include public policies, social policy, social economy, social innovation, co-creation and social participation, labour market, and labour market policy.

Ambroży Mituś – Department of Regulatory Policies, Cracow University of Economics (Poland). Author of several dozen publications on public administration and its socio-economic environment, particularly in the field of local government, management control, public procurement, and the economy. Research interests: purpose of public administration and purpose of legal-administrative regulations.

Agnieszka Pacut – PhD (Economics); Assistant Professor, Department of Public Management, Cracow University ofEconomics (Poland). Completed postgraduate studies in Management of Non-governmental Organisations (Collegium Civitas, Poland) and Management in Public Administration (Cracow University of Economics, Poland). Research consultant for Statistics Poland. Her research interests include social entrepreneurship, social economy, non-governmental organisations, cooperatives, public policies, entrepreneurship, and project management. She is an expert in European, national, regional scientific and implementation projects on social economy, and entrepreneurship.

Kamila Pilch – Research assistant in the Department of Management of Public Organisations, Cracow University of Economics. She holds an MA in Sociology (Economy and Market Research) and completed postgraduate studies in Public Relations at the Jagiellonian University. She has experience in conducting qualitative and quantitative research projects. Her research interests include methodology of marketing, social research, and public policy analysis.

Michela De Rosa – BSc (Economics and Business Management, University of Salerno, 2015) and MSc (Economics, the University of Salerno, 2017). In 2017, she started her Industrial PhD Program in Big Data Management at the University of Salerno. Research interests: e-health management through innovative solutions with a focus on the marketing strategy of enterprises operating in the health sector.

Francesco Schiavone – Associate Professor (Management), Parthenope University of Naples, Italy (since 2016). PhD in Network Economics and Knowledge Management (Ca' Foscari University of Venice, 2006). Affiliated Professor at Emlyon and Paris School of Business. In April 2017, following his habilitation, he received the title of Full Professor in Management from MIUR (Italian Ministry of Education and Research). Current main research areas: technology management, strategic innovation, digital transformation, healthcare management, and innovation. Since 2021, Director of VIMASS (research lab in healthcare innovation and management, the University of Naples Parthenope).

Stefano Tagliaferri – Technical Director of Kelyon. MSc (Computer Science), senior international IT expert in biotechnology and life sciences in a variety of positions across several European countries. For the last 15 years, he has successfully managed and coordinated the development of complex innovative software solutions in collaboration with marketing and medical teams of big pharma companies together with scientific societies, universities, and research centres. Supervises ICT projects in biomedical and bioinformatics areas, especially in the field of medical devices software (ISO 13485 compliant).

Michał Żabiński – PhD (Economics), Assistant Professor, Department of Public Organisations Management. Expert in numerous research and implementation projects in the field of local government, including quality management in local government administration and public policy analysis. Author and co-author of scientific publications in the field of public management, local administration, and quality management in local administration. Co-creator of the Institutional Development Planning method.

List of abbreviations

3D	three-dimensional
3DP	three-dimensional printing
4IR	Fourth Industrial Revolution
AAL	Ambient Assisted Living
AI	Artificial Intelligence
AR	augmented reality
BD	Big Data
BIT model	Behavioural Interventional Technology model
C2C	consumer-to-consumer
C2P	consumer-to-professional
CAGR	compound annual growth rate
CC	cloud computing
CFC	cloud and fog computing
CHESS	Comprehensive Health Enhancement Support System
COPD	chronic obstructive pulmonary disease
CPS	Cyber-Physical Systems
DHT	Digital Health Technologies
DL	deep learning
EHR	Electronic Health Records
EM RAM	Electronic Medical Record Adoption Model
EPHO	essential public health operation
FG	Fog Computing
FP	Framework Programmes
GDP	Gross Domestic Product
GP	general practitioner
GPRS	general packet radio service
GPS	global positioning system
HAL	Hybrid Assistive Limb
HCPS	Health Cyber-Physical Systems
HE	human enhancement
HIMSS	Healthcare Information and Management Systems Society
HIPAA	Health Insurance Portability and Accountability Act

HTA	Health Technology Assessment
ICDs	implantable cardiovascular defibrillators
ICT	Information and Communication Technologies
INAHTA	International Network of Agencies for Health Technology Assessment
IoHT	Internet of Health Things
IoMT	Internet of Medical Things
IoNT	Internet of Nano Things
IoT	Internet of Things
ITU	International Telecommunication Union
LPWA	Low-power wide area
MBps	megabits per second
MICT	Medical Information and Communication Technologies
m-IoT	Internet of mobile health Things
MIS	minimally invasive surgery
ML	machine learning
NASA	National Aeronautics and Space Administration
NGS	next generation sequencing
NIST	National Institute of Standards and Technology
OECD	Organisation for Economic Co-operation and Development
OOP	out-of-pocket
P2C	professional-to-consumer
P2P	professional-to-professional
P4 medicine	predictive, preventive, personalised, and participatory medicine
PDA	personal digital assistants
PE	patient empowerment
PeOPLe	Person-centred Open Platform for Wellbeing
PHR	personal health records
POCUS	point-of-care ultrasonography
TEMPiS	Telemedic Pilot Project for Integrative Stroke Care
TRCs	Telehealth Resource Centres
USSR	Union of Soviet Socialist Republics
VR	virtual reality
WHO	World Health Organization
WIoT	Wearable Internet of Things

Preface: The Fourth Industrial Revolution and healthcare

Marek Ćwiklicki, Mariusz Duplaga, and Jacek Klich

The Fourth Industrial Revolution (4IR) unfolding before our eyes is the driving force behind changes that directly and indirectly affect all the spheres of human life. Its sweeping impact is vividly illustrated by the nested interactive graph prepared by the World Economic Forum (WEF1). It is quite significant that in the seven impact areas of the 4IR highlighted in its inner ring (Technology Access and Inclusion, Technology Innovation, Frontier Technologies, Ethics and Identity, Agile Technology Governance, Agency and Trust, and Demanding New Skills) no mention is made of health. Moreover, as regards Frontier Technologies, only one of its 10 links (to the groups of issues flagged in the outer ring) is directly related to health (Precision Medicine). It is even more surprising that the category most closely aligned with health, i.e. the Future of Medicine and Healthcare, links only to Ethics and Identity (WEF2). In consequence, one may be left with the impression that the impact of the 4IR (via new products, devices, technologies, or artificial intelligence [AI], i.e. the groups of factors highlighted in the interactive graph cited above) on health is relatively small.

The authors of this book set out to demonstrate that the 4IR has a large and growing impact on the healthcare system, public health, and individual health; moreover, it not only triggers structural changes in the healthcare system as such but also represents a turning point in the history of humans as a species.

The main concepts and technologies shaping the 4IR find their way into healthcare and medicine, gradually changing the way healthcare services are delivered and medical products are manufactured. The cyber-physical systems (CPSs) as well as the Internet of Things (IoT), cloud computing (CC) and big data (BD) analytics are listed as the main technologies that shape the landscape of Industry 4.0.

The CPSs are perceived as a technology that permits the integration of computation and physical processes; in other words, it links the virtual cybernetic world with the world of physical reality (Lhotska, 2020). Health CPSs (HCPS) are a subtype of CPSs that rely on intelligent communication between medical devices and computers (Jain et al., 2021). The examples of currently available HCPS solutions include electronic medical records, applications to support daily living, monitoring the patients' health status, or controlling the intake of prescribed medications (Haque et al., 2014).

The IoT, perceived as one of the pillar technologies of Industry 4.0, brings great opportunities to the delivery of modern healthcare services. Essentially, the IoT is a huge network of interconnected objects, both devices and people, which can communicate with one another (Lakhwani et al., 2020). Wireless sensors capable of monitoring various signals originating from the human body or from the surrounding environment are particularly important for the development of innovative solutions for healthcare. Progress in the domain of e-health resulted in the implementation of telemonitoring systems which usually relay a limited set of biosignals or other parameters needed to track the course of specific diseases. The rise of mobile health technologies associated with progress in smartphones, smart bands, and other kinds of wearables equipped with a whole array of embedded sensors has led to more complex ways of monitoring people's health status and their activity regardless of where they may be during their daily routine. The potential of the IoT relies on its capacity to integrate a considerable amount of data coming not only from devices carried by individuals but also from sensors embedded in the furniture and equipment used at homes (e.g. refrigerators) and from devices used to monitor the external environment, such as those that measure air pollution levels. Depending on its main aims, several terms have been proposed for a system used in healthcare and based on the IoT technology, including general ones, such as the Internet of Health Things (IoHT) or the Internet of Medical Things (IoMT), and several more specific ones, such as the Wearable Internet of Things (WIoT), the Internet of mobile health Things (m-IoT), or even the Internet of Nano Things (IoNT) (Hiremath et al., 2014; Istepanian et al., 2011; Omanović-Mikličanin et al., 2015; Terry, 2016). The fact that so many terms apply to health-related IoTs certainly results from a concatenation of advanced technologies and reflects a high interest of technical and medical communities in the development of services that benefit from them.

The CC is another pillar technology for Industry 4.0 which transforms the way healthcare services are delivered. It is defined as "a system that enables ubiquitous, convenient, on-demand network access to a common pool of configurable computing resources" (Mell & Grance, 2011). The CC is essentially a new model of accessing hardware, software, and data in order to run proprietary applications. The user - a healthcare institution - accesses the IT infrastructure and is charged only for the actual usage of the resources (Sultan, 2014). The CC facilitates access to advanced IT solutions for healthcare providers; however, this can be subject to special restrictions due to legal requirements applicable to the health sector (Gia et al., 2015).

The expectations associated with the exploration of BD in medicine and healthcare are also quickly rising. Healthcare generates significant amounts of heterogeneous data which, once processed, promise to deliver advanced diagnostic capacities and the ability to deliver individualised therapies.

Furthermore, AI combined with machine learning (ML) and deep learning (DL) is perceived as the key strategy for analysing BD sets in medicine and healthcare services.

Apart from the pillar technologies mentioned above, there are many other areas of technical progress that profoundly affect the healthcare system. Progress in robotic surgery, leading to daring projections about automatic procedures (Bhandari et al., 2020), is well aligned with the integration of virtual and physical worlds offered by the CPS. From the very first applications of robots in surgery in 1980s, substantial advances have been made in the ergonomics of systems offered to surgeons (Jain et al., 2020), the support for human interactions with robotics tools, and the use of augmented reality (AR) to guide surgeons during procedures (Makhataeva & Varol, 2020). The growing abilities of equipment have led to a renewed interest in the use of AR in medical imaging diagnostics, surgical planning, and navigation (Sutherland et al., 2019). Specific niches for therapeutic interventions based on AR and virtual reality are also emerging, among others, in psychiatry (Sutherland et al., 2019).

The exploration of BD sets generated by Internet users gave rise to a new area called infodemiology (Eysenbach, 2009). It is based on the observation that a large proportion of information supply and demand has a health-related context. Unstructured user contributions in social media and on other websites may also be used to implement the so-called infoveillance algorithms which make it easier to anticipate emerging epidemic threats or assess the most pressing health needs of a given population. The analysis of these using AI is expected to have a significant impact on the strategies of monitoring population health, including during pandemics (Bragazzi et al., 2020; Dolley, 2018).

The concept of precision medicine (as shown in the cited WEF graph) draws on the functionalities provided by three-dimensional printing (3DP), including patient-specific implants, controlled delivery of medication, or patient-specific *in vitro* models for assessing the response to pharmaceutical agents (Prendergast & Burdick, 2020). Although the most common real-life applications of 3DP in healthcare include 3D models printed for educational purposes and to some extent, 3D implants, the opportunities resulting from the increasing availability of body parts printed with biological materials, or even viable cells, seem to be the most anticipated (Kačarević et al., 2018).

This broad discussion of the impacts of the 4IR on health explains why the term Health 4.0 appears in the title of this book. Given the enormous scope of the 4IR's effect on the healthcare system, it seems reasonable to take a broader perspective to review the factors that emerge from the 4IR to shape the organisational and financial aspects of the healthcare system now and in the near future.

In the current literature, the technological angle prevails with the healthcare system and its main actors - society and policymakers - being afforded only cursory treatment. In our study, we intend to focus on patients, societies, and governments. The application of systemic and macro approaches allows us to combine individual studies into a fresh perspective on Health 4.0.

This book consists of 15 chapters. Chapter 1, The Fourth Industrial Revolution and the Healthcare System, depicts the 4IR phenomenon in the context of the challenges it poses to healthcare systems. The list of these challenges includes new medicines and medical technologies, new medical devices, nanotechnology and genetic engineering, implants, telemedicine and e-health, AI, and human enhancement. The concept of Health 4.0 is also defined and its four components are discussed. Throughout, Chapter 1 introduces the issues to be addressed in more depth in subsequent chapters.

Chapter 2, entitled The Transition from Telemedicine and e-Health to Health 4.0, charts the evolution from telemedicine to Health 4.0. It explores from a historical perspective telemedicine and telehealth, e-health and m-health, and the transition from Health 1.0 to Health 3.0, to end with Health 4.0 as part of the 4IR.

Technologies that underlie Health 4.0 are the focus of Chapter 3 (Technologies Enhancing Health 4.0). It serves as an introduction to the areas mentioned above: CPSs, the IoT, cloud and fog computing (CFC), big data analysis and AI, blockchain technology, robotic systems, virtual reality and AR, and 3D printing.

While the previous chapter provides a general description of the technologies in question, Chapter 4 (The Landscape of Health 4.0 – Areas of Application) presents examples of their practical use in the healthcare system including the concept of 4P medicine, remote monitoring, ambient assisted living, robotic surgery, and the issues of public health and epidemic surveillance especially relevant in the context of the SARS-CoV-2 pandemic.

Patient empowerment (PE) in the healthcare system is one of the four components of the concept of Health 4.0 discussed in this book. This issue is dealt with in Chapter 5 (Patient Empowerment in Health 4.0). Apart from defining PE, it explores the relationship of PE to Health 4.0 and discusses modelling the impact of ICT on PE, technologies for PE, personal health records, remote monitoring, electronic patient-physician communication, and participating in online patient communities.

New information technologies and applications brought about by the 4IR can improve the quality of life for people with disabilities, an issue addressed in Chapter 6 entitled People with Disabilities in the Information Society. After defining the relevant concepts, the authors briefly review the current disability models and go on to discuss the unfulfilled promises of digital inclusion as well as the benefits and risks associated with the Internet use.

Along with people with disabilities, senior citizens comprise the second group that may benefit from the achievements of the 4IR. They are discussed in Chapter 7 (Health 4.0 for the Elderly: New Challenges and Opportunities for a Smart System) and include the issues associated with the ageing population and digital transformation from a societal perspective, the factors that need to be taken into account when introducing the digital transformation into senior care as well as the author's original proposal for a new paradigm of a senior citizen–friendly healthcare system.

Chapter 8, entitled Co-creation in Health 4.0, follows up on the contents of Chapter 5. It introduces and develops the theme of active patient participation in product creation, identifying the stages of planning, design, implementation/delivery, and maintenance, along with references to the current trends in healthcare. The chapter ends with a presentation of models of consumer value co-creation in healthcare.

Chapter 9 (The Implementation of New Technologies in Health 4.0 in Selected Countries) discusses the ranking of the top 10 countries using the World Index of Healthcare Innovation 2020, followed by more detailed profiles of four countries (USA, Germany, Japan, and Australia) in terms of their achievements in the area in question. The chapter concludes with a review of the four key success factors in implementing Health 4.0 as well as the risks and problems associated with it.

The issues associated with implementing Health 4.0 in practice are addressed in Chapter 10, entitled The Key Factors of the Healthcare System's Adaptiveness for Health 4.0. It proposes six factors considered important in this regard - human capital, information and communication technologies, social capital, financial resources, governance, and legal regulations - and briefly characterises each of them.

Finance, one of the factors mentioned in the previous chapter, is dealt with in more detail in Chapter 11 (Financing Health 4.0). It looks at healthcare spending in OECD countries in 2000-2019 and outlines the prospects for change in healthcare financing in connection with the implementation of Health 4.0. The author argues that even though in post-socialist countries the share of out-of-pocket (OOP) expenses in total health spending is already significant, the rapid progress in the introduction of new medicines, medical devices, and technologies, but above all human enhancement services, is likely to increase even further. This may widen the already large gaps in access to health services and destabilize not only the healthcare system in the foreseeable future.

Chapter 12, entitled Law and Health 4.0, takes up and expands on the second of the six factors identified in Chapter 10 that affect the implementation of Health 4.0, i.e. the legal regulations. The author focuses on the legal framework for the use of AI, nanotechnology, genomics, and genetic engineering.

The next chapter (Human Capital vs. Health 4.0) explores the issue of social capital, the third factor identified in Chapter 10. The author addresses the key challenges posed by the 4IR to selected stakeholders in the healthcare system, i.e. patients (the demand side) and health professionals (the supply side), especially in the context of the virtually unlimited access to information on the Internet. The authors demonstrate how Health 4.0 technologies (including telemedicine) can improve the utilisation of staff resources and help alleviate its shortfalls. The determinants and barriers to the use of modern devices and applications, including AI, are also discussed. In the authors' opinion, the curricula of medical schools (as the key health professionals) must be updated with a view to developing communication, or more broadly, soft skills, and digital skills among physicians and nurses.

Chapter 14, The Role of Civil Society Organisations in Health 4.0 Service Delivery: Examples from Poland, refers to the fourth constitutive feature of Health 4.0 highlighted in Chapter 1, i.e. PE in the healthcare system and the development of civil society. It presents the findings of a pilot study conducted among six non-governmental organisations in Poland, which lead to the identification of a range of key issues associated with the implementation of Health 4.0 principles.

Chapter 15 (Recommendations for Implementing Industry 4.0 in the Healthcare System) offers guidelines for the major stakeholders in the healthcare system, i.e. government (state authorities), patients, health professionals, and non-governmental organisations.

The contents outlined above are addressed to a broad readership, ranging from central and regional health policymakers, healthcare providers (managers and health professionals), health science, and medical students, to individuals interested in technological progress and innovation in the healthcare system. We also hope that the book will be of interest to students, scholars, and practitioners working in health and social policy, political science, public management, and governance.

The publication was co-financed from the subsidy granted to Cracow University of Economics.

References

Bhandari, M., Zeffiro, T., & Reddiboina, M. (2020). Artificial intelligence and robotic surgery: current perspective and future directions. Current Opinion in Urology, 30(1), 48–54.

Bragazzi, N. L., Dai, H., Damiani, G., Behzadifar, M., Martini, M., & Wu, J. (2020). How big data and artificial intelligence can help better manage the COVID-19 pandemic. International Journal of Environmental Research and Public Health, 17(9), 3176. https://doi.org/10.3390/ijerph17093176

Dolley, S. (2018). Big data's role in precision public health. Frontiers in Public Health, 6, 68. https://doi.org/10.3389/fpubh.2018.00068

Eysenbach, G. (2009). Infodemiology and infoveillance: framework for an emerging set of public health informatics methods to analyze search, communication and publication behavior on the Internet. Journal of Medical Internet Research, 11(1). https://doi.org/10.2196/jmir.1157

Gia, T. N., Jiang, M., Rahmani, A., Westerlund, T., Liljeberg, P., & Tenhunen, H. (2015). Fog computing in healthcare Internet of Things: a case study on ECG feature extraction. 2015 IEEE International Conference on Computer and Information Technology; Ubiquitous Computing and Communications; Dependable, Autonomic and Secure Computing; Pervasive Intelligence and Computing, 356–363. https://doi.org/10.1109/CIT/IUCC/DASC/PICOM.2015.51

Haque, S. A., Aziz, S. M., & Rahman, M. (2014). Review of cyber-physical system in healthcare. International Journal of Distributed Sensor Networks, 10(4), 217415. https://doi.org/10.1155/2014/217415

Hiremath, S., Yang, G., & Mankodiya, K. (2014). Wearable Internet of Things: concept, architectural components and promises for person-centered healthcare. 2014 4th International Conference on Wireless Mobile Communication and Healthcare - Transforming Healthcare Through Innovations in Mobile and Wireless Technologies (MOBIHEALTH), 304–307. https://doi.org/10.1109/MOBIHEALTH.2014.7015971

Istepanian, R. S. H., Hu, S., Philip, N. Y., & Sungoor, A. (2011). The potential of Internet of m-health Things "m-IoT" for non-invasive glucose level sensing. 2011 Annual International Conference of the IEEE Engineering in Medicine and Biology Society, 5264–5266. https://doi.org/10.1109/IEMBS.2011.6091302

Jain, M., Cohen, K., & Shouhed, D. (2020). Enhancing Safety and Efficiency in Robotic Surgery. In Human Factors in Surgery (pp. 107–115). Cham: Springer.

Jain, R., Gupta, M., Nayyar, A., & Sharma, N. (2021). Adoption of Fog Computing in Healthcare 4.0. In S. Tanwar (Ed.), Fog Computing for Healthcare 4.0 Environments: Technical, Societal, and Future Implications (pp. 3–36). Springer International Publishing. https://doi.org/10.1007/978-3-030-46197-3_1

Kačarević, Ž. P., Rider, P. M., Alkildani, S., Retnasingh, S., Smeets, R., Jung, O., Ivanišević, Z., & Barbeck, M. (2018). An introduction to 3D bioprinting: possibilities, challenges and future aspects. Materials, 11(11), 2199. https://doi.org/10.3390/ma11112199

Lakhwani, K., Gianey, H. K., Wireko, J. K., & Hiran, K. K. (2020). Internet of Things (IoT): Principles, Paradigms and Applications of IoT. Bpb Publications. https://vbn.aau.dk/en/publications/internet-of-things-iot-principles-paradigms-and-applications-of-i

Lhotska, L. (2020). Application of Industry 4.0 concept to healthcare. Studies in Health Technology and Informatics, 273, 23–37. https://doi.org/10.3233/SHTI200613

Makhataeva, Z., & Varol, H. A. (2020). Augmented reality for robotics: a review. Robotics, 9(2), 21.

Mell, P., & Grance, T. (2011). The NIST Definition of Cloud Computing (NIST Special Publication (SP) 800-145). National Institute of Standards and Technology. https://doi.org/10.6028/NIST.SP.800-145

Omanović-Mikličanin, E., Maksimović, M., & Vujović, V. (2015). The future of healthcare: nanomedicine and Internet of Nano Things. Folia Medica Facultatis Medicinae Universitatis Saraeviensis, 50(1), Article 1. http://www.foliamedica.mf.unsa.ba/index.php/FM/article/view/33

Prendergast, M. E., & Burdick, J. A. (2020). Recent advances in enabling technologies in 3D printing for precision medicine. Advanced Materials, 32(13), 1902516. https://doi.org/10.1002/adma.201902516

Sultan, N. (2014). Making use of cloud computing for healthcare provision: opportunities and challenges. International Journal of Information Management, 34(2), 177–184. https://doi.org/10.1016/j.ijinfomgt.2013.12.011

Sutherland, J., Belec, J., Sheikh, A., Chepelev, L., Althobaity, W., Chow, B. J. W., Mitsouras, D., Christensen, A., Rybicki, F. J., & La Russa, D. J. (2019). Applying modern virtual and augmented reality technologies to medical images and models. Journal of Digital Imaging, 32(1), 38–53. https://doi.org/10.1007/s10278-018-0122-7

Terry, N. P. (2016). Will the Internet of Things transform healthcare. Vanderbilt Journal of Entertainment & Technology Law, 19, 327. http://dx.doi.org/10.2139/ssrn.2760447

WEF1. Fourth Industrial Revolution. World Economic Forum. https://intelligence.weforum.org/topics/a1Gb0000001RIhBEAW?tab=publications [accessed: 27 April 2021]

WEF2. Future of Health and Healthcare. World Economic Forum. https://intelligence.weforum.org/topics/a1Gb00000038u3nEAA?tab=publications [accessed: 27 April 2021]

1 The Fourth Industrial Revolution and the healthcare system

Jacek Klich

Introduction

The Fourth Industrial Revolution (4IR) profoundly affects not only service production and provision but also business, governments, people, and the entire social sphere (Schwab, 2016a). The aim of this chapter is to explore the phenomenon and nature of the 4IR (the first part of the chapter) in the context of the challenges it poses (and will pose) to the health system (the second part). The concept of Health 4.0 is then used to interpret these challenges (the third part). The author sets out to demonstrate that the 4IR has initiated a new stage in human development, which will require far-reaching changes in the organisation and financing of the healthcare system.

The Fourth Industrial Revolution and its dimensions

The concept of the Fourth Industrial Revolution

The 4IR is understood here as an economic and social phenomenon driven, among others, by the development of artificial intelligence (AI; Dahl, 2019), robotics, the Internet of Things (IoT), autonomous vehicles, 3D printers, nanotechnology, additive manufacturing, neurotechnology, biotechnology, materials engineering, energy storage, quantum computers, etc. Although the 4IR is *in statu nascendi*, it is rapidly developing and is subject to intensive research. Research findings show that it is having an increasing impact on all the dimensions and aspects of human life, including the healthcare system (Nadella, 2018, p. 9). As Karl Schwab puts it, we will have to "understand and shape the new technology revolution, which entails nothing less than a transformation of humankind" (Schwab, 2016a, p. 7). The phrase "transformation of humankind" is by no means an exaggeration in this context.

The 4IR entails far-reaching and system-wide changes due to its three essential characteristics: (a) high pace; (b) breadth and depth; and (c) a sweeping impact on all the spheres of human life. These changes result in, among other things, "a fusion of technologies that is blurring the lines between the physical, digital, and biological spheres" (Schwab, 2016b). The interpenetration of

DOI: 10.4324/9781003144403-1

these three worlds with sophisticated technologies can be considered as the specific difference between the 4IR and the previous three industrial revolutions. In such a context, of key importance are the consequences of these processes, including, in particular, the gradual disappearance of the boundary between man and machine. This is a two-way process, which involves, on the one hand, equipping machines with functions and characteristics inherent to humans (using AI) and, on the other, equipping humans with a range of devices (including implants) and/or applications that expand their physical and cognitive capabilities to an unprecedented degree, known in the literature as human enhancement (HE).

The impact of the Fourth Industrial Revolution on the environment and human life

The 4IR leads to profound changes in the environment and human life.[1] Its impact on industry and industrial relations (Badri et al., 2018; Martinez et al., 2019; Schwab, 2016a; Schwab, Davis, 2018), trade (Kaur, Kaur, 2018), and education (Gleason, 2018) has been intensively studied, and its scope as an object of research is constantly expanding.

The World Economic Forum identifies eight areas through which the 4IR affects economies and societies: ethics and identity, agile technology management, inequality, business disruption, labour market disruption (including worker skills), security and conflict, innovation and productivity, and technology connectivity/interpenetration. Each of these areas is subsequently associated with more narrowly defined fields and phenomena (based on functional relationships and dependencies). Their list is quite long (currently, it consists of 31 items and is growing as our knowledge develops) and is comprised of, among others, values, biotechnology, global governance, justice and judicial infrastructure, cybersecurity, drones, circular economy, the future of economic growth, mental health, advanced materials, 3D printing, information technology, entrepreneurship, international security, public finance and social protection, and geopolitics (World Economic Forum, 2019).

It is noteworthy that relatively little attention (as emphasised by e.g. Schwab, 2016a; WHO, 2011) is devoted to tracking and analysing the current and expected future impacts of the 4IR on health or, more broadly, on the healthcare system. This book aims to contribute to filling this research gap.

The impact of the Fourth Industrial Revolution on health

The recently published research findings on the impact of the 4IR on health have made it possible to identify its five key aspects, namely "the impact on healthcare efficiency and effectiveness, the impact on government action, the impact on human resources, the impact on health system organisation, and the financial impact on the health sector" (Castro e Melo and Faria Araújo, 2020). Given the current status of the 4IR as an emerging phenomenon,

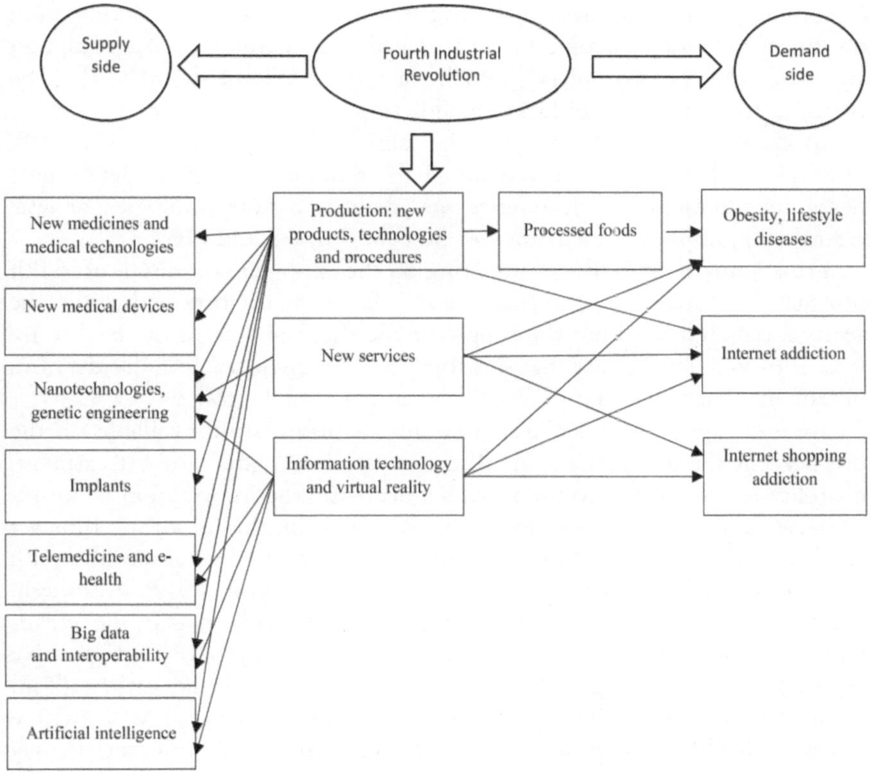

Figure 1.1 Directions of impact of the Fourth Industrial Revolution on healthcare system.

Source: Own study based on Klich (2021).

research on how it affects public health and the healthcare system is only gaining momentum. In Figure 1.1, the author identifies the directions of the 4IR's impact on health as part of the still modest current of cross-sectional studies[2]aimed to classify and categorise these issues. The following have been singled out as direct effects of the 4IR: new products, technologies and procedures, new services and information technologies, and virtual reality. These effects can then be associated with the supply and demand side of the healthcare system, and then in each of these areas, we can try to identify sample categories which stem from the highlighted direct impacts of the 4IR, as shown in Figure 1.1.[3]

The supply side comprises new medicines, medical devices and technologies, new medical devices and technologies, nanotechnology and genetic engineering, implants, telemedicine, big data, and AI.

The demand side includes a range of categories, such as obesity (which in this context is associated with media and electronic gadget addiction and the consumption of highly processed foods), lifestyle diseases, and stress and depression (broadly defined, including stress and depression resulting from job loss as a result of people being replaced by machines and/or computer applications in the workplace), which, in the context of the 4IR, shall be treated as the derivatives of Internet addiction.

This book focuses exclusively on the supply side of the impact of the 4IR on health, and only selected elements shall be discussed in more detail: new medicines and medical technologies, new devices, nanotechnologies, genetic engineering, implants, telemedicine and e-health, AI, and HE.

At this point, it is worth commenting on the exponential growth of health information available on the Internet as it has a dual nature and cannot be clearly attributed to either the supply or the demand side of the healthcare system. In view of the fact that this topic will be discussed in more detail in subsequent chapters, it is only briefly remarked upon below.

Easy and rapid access to large amounts of information available on the Internet encourages patients at all stages of illness (diagnosis, treatment, rehabilitation, recovery) to use it, which decreases the information asymmetry between them and their physicians. Research on the use of the Internet has shown that it has become an influential mass media source of health information in Northern Europe (Kummervold, Wynn, 2012). Although, admittedly, access to health-related sites is not difficult, it is by no means unproblematic. Advice sourced from the Internet may have both positive and negative (i.e. outright dangerous) consequences for the patient (Tan, Goonawardene, 2017). The former includes a greater awareness of disease processes, health promotion, and preventive healthcare. However, it may easily become harmful when patients acquire information that is unproven, incomplete, or even contradicts medical science and may go on to use it to self-diagnose themselves and/or challenge their physician's findings/recommendations, which may have a negative effect on therapeutic relationship and outcomes (see Chapter 13).

Challenges posed by the 4IR to the healthcare sector

The phenomena illustrated in Figure 1.1 can be interpreted in terms of challenges posed by the 4IR to the healthcare sector[4]. They are only briefly remark on here since they are discussed in more detail in subsequent chapters of the book.

The challenges that the 4IR poses to the health sector should be analysed in the context of the most pressing issues facing global health policy. In 2019, before the outbreak of the SARS-CoV-2 pandemic,[5] they included problems arising from malnutrition and living in areas of armed conflict and natural disasters (including the endemic presence of the Ebola virus), the spread of HIV, antibiotic-resistant microorganisms (e.g. gonorrhoea strains), family planning methods (including modern contraceptives), provision of nursing care at present and in the near future, and more broadly defined issues affecting health, such as the relationship between health and AI, dynamic changes in the natural world and their impact on humans, and problems of using big data (Nathe, 2019). Francesca Scassellati-Sforzolini (2018), when drawing up her list of the five most significant challenges faced by European health systems, emphasised the need for innovation and effective promotion of vaccination, apart from making the patient the central part of the system. Thus, the considerations above strongly suggest that innovation and AI represent the challenges common to global health policy and individual health systems.

For the purposes of this book and in the spirit of the World Health Organization (WHO) definition, a health system is understood as all the interrelated institutions, organisations, and resources whose primary purpose is to preserve and improve health by responding to the legitimate needs of patients and protecting them against the cost of ill health (WHO, 2020).

It is also worth emphasising that an important actor/stakeholder in the healthcare system is households, which provides unpaid care to sick and/or disabled relatives and thus makes an important contribution to the financing of the healthcare system by committing their own resources (see Chapter 11). This important role of households in the healthcare system is also worth noting from the perspective of strengthening the position of the patient in the system (see Chapter 5), who is increasingly becoming a partner in the process of diagnosis and treatment.

According to Weber et al. (2010), the key elements of any healthcare system include the financing of the system (including the position and role of the payer), legal regulations providing for the cooperation between the public and private sector in the system, governance, health insurance, logistics, payment for health services, incentives for providers and employees, information system, well-trained staff, basic infrastructure, and delivery (Weber et al., 2010, p. 4).

Below, the selected effects or challenges posed by the 4IR to the healthcare sector are discussed by area of impact: new medicines and medical technologies, new devices, nanotechnologies, genetic engineering, implants, telemedicine and e-health, and AI. HE is mentioned at the end - it has been deliberately left out of Figure 1.1 as it is viewed as an outcome of the revolution's impacts on health presented there and mainly includes the achievements of nanotechnology, genetic engineering, and AI.

New medicines and medical technologies

The global medicine market is rapidly growing. As at the end of 2019, its volume in terms of sales revenue was estimated at USD 1,250.4 billion[6] compared to USD 390.2 billion in 2001 (Mikulic, 2020a). The pharmaceutical industry is one of the most knowledge-intensive sectors of the economy. In 2019 alone, global R&D expenditures in this sector were estimated at USD 186 billion (Mikulic, 2020b).

The largest global pharmaceutical markets are the United States and Europe. Despite the pandemic, in the United States, 53 new medicines were approved in 2020, of which 21 (40%) were first-in-class substances (New Drug Therapy Approvals, 2020). It is worth remembering that in the United States, the number of newly registered drugs has shown an upward trend since 2008.

In Europe, in 2020, the European Medicine Agency (EMA) recommended 97 new drugs and 39 new active substances for marketing authorisation (Human Medicines Highlights, 2020). As is the case in the United States, there is an increasing trend in the number of new medicines and active substances authorised in the Europe. The growing supply of new and innovative pharmaceuticals results in higher costs for healthcare systems and, given their high share in household health spending, has an adverse effect on their financial position (these issues will be addressed in Chapter 11).

Another distinct category worth mentioning when discussing the impact of the 4IR on the market for new pharmaceuticals and health technologies is the individualisation of treatment. Thanks to advances in genomics, among other things, personalised medicines are becoming more widely available. Using sophisticated tools and techniques, targeted individual therapies are being identified for individual patients at the right time in a consistent and standards-based manner. Such developments are made possible, thanks to the fact that large amounts of information (big data) can be extracted and used to create more accurate patient profiles. A good example of personalisation is the innovative *CAR-T* cell therapy - to date, the most advanced and personalised technology used in haemato-oncological treatment, which consists in producing a medicine for each patient based on their own lymphocytes (Stelmach, 2019).

New medical devices

New medical devices and appliances constitute such a diverse and broad-ranging category that they certainly warrant separate (and extensive) book treatment. At this point, it is only possible to draw attention to this area and illustrate it with a handful of examples.

The medical devices and equipment market is large and rapidly growing. According to the findings of Precedence Research, the global value of the medical devices and equipment market in 2019 totalled USD 447.63 billion, and it is estimated to grow to USD 671.49 billion in 2027 (Globe Newswire, 2020).

Prime examples of high-tech medical devices and equipment include innovative patient monitoring devices already in use (e.g. underwear capable of taking blood pressure and pulse) or being prepared for production. The latter group comprises digestible microchips that signal whether the patient has taken the prescribed medication and technologies capable of tracking a patient's gastric pH and transmitting relevant data (using the Bluetooth technology) to his/her mobile phone and then to the monitoring centre, the attending physician or nurse. Another sophisticated measuring device is contact lenses for diabetics equipped with sensors that measure glucose levels in tears and relay this information to a smartphone and from there to a monitoring centre, etc. A south-Korean medical start-up offers Rapael Smart Glove, equipped with sensors controlled by dedicated software and intended as an aid to improve upper limb function in stroke patients (Robotics Business Review, 2015).

These examples show that the impact of new technologies on medicine has been and will remain very strong. The progressive technicisation of medicine is now a well-recognised phenomenon as the technical and technological advances themselves occur at an increasing pace, especially in surgery (Klipfel, 2017).

The issues mentioned here are discussed in more depth in Chapter 3 on technologies and Health 4.0, and in Chapter 4 that addresses the individual areas of application of modern technologies in Health 4.0.

Nanotechnologies and genetic engineering

Nanotechnology and emerging new materials underpin what constitutes the *differentia specifica* of the 4IR, namely the blurring of the boundaries between man and machine. Although the applications of nanotechnology may be diverse, it is not without reason that the literature sees human health and the health sector as nanotechnology's most important domains (Jha et al., 2014).

The achievements of nanotechnology are already significant. Raffa et al. (2010) classified current and future nanomaterials and found 11 current medical uses of nanotechnology. Their list includes nanovectors (used in targeted gene delivery to selected disease sites), nano- (used in electrostimulation therapies), cell movement control (cell therapy for regeneration and tissue engineering, islet cell transplantation, and anti-metastatic tumour therapy), magnetic drug delivery (controlled release targeted drug delivery), magnetic resonance imaging (MRI) contrast agents (tumour imaging and molecular imaging), nanohyperthermic ablation (*in situ* destruction of tumours as an alternative or adjunct to surgical excision), antimicrobial agents (antiseptic agents, control of antibiotic-resistant bacteria, infection-resistant bioimplants, stents, and prostheses), electrochemotherapy (low-voltage, noncontact electrochemotherapy of tumours avoids the use of external electrodes), nano-bio-generators (dispense with the need for power supply in powered implants), nano-biosensors (*in vitro* and *in vivo* diagnostics), and nano-scaffoldings (regenerative medicine and tissue engineering; Raffa et al., 2010, p. 134).

Thanks to the advances in nanotechnology, it is now possible to treat cardiovascular diseases, cancer, musculoskeletal disorders, neurodegenerative and psychiatric disorders, diabetes, and bacterial and viral infections more effectively.

It appears that the greatest opportunities for nanotechnology to cross the boundary between man and machine may come from nanosystems and molecular nanosystems, nano-bio-generators, and nano-scaffoldings.

One practical example of nanotechnology-based therapy is the eMacula - a system tailored to the needs of visually impaired individuals who benefit from both vision correction using lenses as well as magnified and digitally enhanced views of their surroundings. This system consists of two key components: glasses with an integrated screen and a new-generation 'smart' contact lenses that enable the wearer to see their surroundings clearly and to view digital information delivered from high-resolution microchips mounted at the centre, thanks to which they can focus on digital content provided by near-eye microdisplays mounted within the glasses. The lens is 'smart' in the sense that it separately processes the actual view from the displayed media and does so without the need for any form of electronics. These systems are passive in nature and "will meet expectations that wearers will have for a comfortable, disposable contact lens" (Hastings, 2019).

Genetic engineering continues to play an important role in the personalisation of therapy and in HE. Recent years have seen breakthrough discoveries and advances in this field. In China, in November 2018 (at the time, it was a closely guarded secret), two girls nicknamed Lulu and Nana were born, whose genome had been edited using the CRISPR technology (Clustered Regularly-Interspaced Short Palindromic Repeats). These births sparked widespread discussion about the medical and ethical aspects of the procedure (Musunuru, 2019).

Several successful landmark interventions have also been reported in recent years, including the correction of a defective gene in a patient with Hunter syndrome (mucopolysaccharidosis Type II - a genetic disorder caused by a deficiency of the enzyme iduronate 2-sulfatase (I2S), the genetic alteration of T-lymphocytes in cancer patients to prime them to attack and kill cancer cells. For the first time ever, a genetically modified bacteriophage was used to treat a bacterial infection in an antibiotic-resistant individual. A completely new form of DNA was also obtained, called hachimoji DNA, which consists of four natural and four synthetic nucleobases. Animal research has also entered a new phase, as a pig-monkey chimeras (pigs with a proportion of monkey cells) were created in 2019.

These are just a few examples illustrating the dynamic progress in genetic engineering, which will set new trajectories for science and for medical practice.

Implants

Implants meet the criteria for medical devices and should therefore be subsumed under the heading of *New medical devices* above. The reason why they are discussed in a separate section reflects their growing importance in blurring the boundary between man and machine. It is not about simple dental implants - which continue to claim the largest share of the implant market - but extremely advanced ones, including those created using nanotechnology.

The global medical implants market is driven by the rising incidence of chronic diseases, improvements in surgical techniques and outcomes, patient acceptance of advanced medical implants, and an ageing population worldwide.

According to Allied Market Research, the global medical implants market was estimated to be worth USD 86.38 billion in 2019 and is expected to grow at a compound annual growth rate (CAGR) of USD 147.46 billion by 2027 (Allied Market Research, 2020), which reflects its high potential. North and South America account for almost half (49.18%) of the global implant market, followed by Europe (27.45%) and Asia (Market Research Future, 2019).

In the context of the 4IR, high-tech implants are particularly noteworthy. This group of medical devices includes the above-mentioned eMacula system, technologically advanced cochlear implants aligned with speech recognition/processing software (Cosetti, Waltzman, 2011), and the Gliadel Wafer intracranial implant (Ashby et al., 2016), which is a controlled release formula for carmustine delivery directly into the space left after surgery to remove a portion of the brain. This new mode of delivery is expected to work better than other forms of carmustine and have fewer side effects.

Telemedicine and e-health

The 4IR brings not only products that are used in the treatment process but also changes and enhances the service delivery process itself. In the latter case, the most important area is telemedicine, which is becoming a focus of intensive research.[7]

Paraphrasing the definition of the WHO, we can say that telemedicine is the performance of health services from a distance by health professionals using information technology and the exchange of information to treat and educate patients in order to improve the quality of healthcare. A constitutive feature of telemedicine is the extensive use of information and communication technology (ICT) and the Internet.

Advances in ICT have led to the creation of the concept of e-health, which covers an increasingly wide range of services and procedures in the health sector.

According to the WHO, e-health is an umbrella term that covers a wide range of health and care services delivered through ICTs in the health sector for clinical, educational, research, and administrative purposes, for the provision of services both on-site and remotely. The issues mentioned here will be discussed in more depth in Chapter 2.

Artificial intelligence

Although issues related to the use of AI in medicine were addressed in research as early as the 1990s (Miksch et al., 2005), it is only in recent years that they have significantly accelerated and are being carried out in a number of centres, universities, and institutes, with healthcare occupying a prominent position among the contexts where AI is used (alongside cars, human-AI collaboration, and the use of AI for social purposes; cf. Nadella, 2018, p. 9).

AI is beginning to play an increasingly significant role in modern therapy, including in the treatment of psychiatric conditions (Watson, 2017), where virtual reality technologies are used (Rizzo et al., 2014). It is also gaining traction in rehabilitation (Dockx et al., 2016) and in pain management (Keefe et al., 2012). The technology's achievements in diagnostics demonstrate that it is at least as effective as man, and in some cases (e.g. in the area of psychiatry and diagnosing suicidal intentions) it is even more accurate than a physician (Loh, 2018). AI is on par when it comes to making diagnoses in radiology (Esteva et al., 2017) and pathology (Gargeya, Leng, 2017). Some researchers go as far as to say that AI will replace physicians in the foreseeable future (Loh, 2018).

AI can assist in data collection, processing, and use, including the identification of correlations which are notoriously difficult to capture using standard data and methods. This, in turn, can be of great importance, e.g. in epidemiological research, personalisation of medicinal products, and therapies.

In this context, the complete computer-generated genome of a bacterium known as *Caulobacter ethensis 2.0* can be considered as the beginning of a new chapter in human history. Work is currently underway to create a synthetic organism based on this blueprint. If we add to this the fact that at InSilico Labs AI has already created six completely new inhibitors of the *DDR1* gene with potential applications in the treatment of, among others, pulmonary fibrosis (the first experiments on mice have shown great promise; cf. Motyka, 2019), it can be argued that we are entering a completely new stage in the evolution of *Homo sapiens*.

Human enhancement

The outcomes of the 4IR outlined above can be used in various combinations for HE. The idea of HE has a nearly 40-year institutional history and military roots, as it was the US Army Research Institute that originally requested the National Research Council of the National Academy of Sciences to establish an institute to study HE (Druckman, Bjork, 1994, p. vii). Over the years, reflection on HE has become more mainstream and has been discussed from a variety of scientific perspectives (Bateman et al., 2015; Koops et al., 2013), including bioethics (Buchanan, 2011a), religion (Mercer, Trothen, 2015; Trothen, Mercer, 2017), but above all ethics and philosophy (Clarke et al., 2016; Forsberg et al, 2017) represented by philosophical anthropology, philosophy of technology, and philosophy of risk (Coeckelbergh, 2013).. The number of studies aimed at a wider audience than just the academic circles has also increased (Buchanan, 2011b; Moore, 2008).

Due to the multidimensionality of HE, there is no single, universally accepted definition of this phenomenon (Moore, 2008). The term tends to be associated with a wide range of devices and systems from smart pills, plastic surgery, genetic selection, computer brains, clones, and chimeras to fully computer-controlled robots (Koops, 2013, p. 184).

For the purposes of this book, we have adopted a definition of HE using the elements of Anders Sandberg's proposal as cited by Pete Moore (Moore, 2008, p. xi) and Allen E. Buchanan (Buchanan, 2011b, p.5). Thus, HE is an intervention - a human action of any kind - in the biology or psychology of a person that either increases species-typical normal functioning above the statistically typical levels or produces a new capacity that normal human beings do not possess. Or in simpler terms, HE can be seen as synonymous with biomedical enhancement.

HE cannot be identified with therapy (i.e. actions aimed at curing a disease or protecting against one); for this reason, hearing aids, vision restoration technologies, or artificial organs are not considered HEs since they serve to restore the features/functions lost due to illness/accident, rather than augment them.

HEs can be classified according to the type of ability/feature they are intended to improve or the intervention and technology used to that end. Biomedical enhancements can improve motor traits, such as physical strength, speed, and endurance[8] as well as cognitive ones, cognitive ability, mood, temperament, emotional capacity, or longevity (Buchanan, 2011b, p. 5). These traits can be enhanced through the ingestion of chemicals, exposure to a special device, or by surgical intervention.

Debates on HE, although mostly focused on its benefits, do not ignore the attendant threats, which include the widening gap between the rich and the poor, and corruption (Buchanan, 2011b).

This brief presentation of selected examples of ultra-new human achievements and the 4IR in the context of the transhumanist movement can be concluded by invoking Kurzweil's question concerning human transgression of the limits of biology and the times of the singularity (Kurzweil, 2017). This, in turn, entails a different outlook on health and the healthcare system, where the concept of Health 4.0 has recently come to play a major role.

The concept of Health 4.0

Any serious response to the challenges posed by the 4IR must include a new approach to organising the healthcare system, which can be called Health 4.0[9] for short.

Health 4.0 is a concept rooted in advanced information technologies (Karboub et al., 2019), and is treated in this book as a system possessed of the following four constitutive elements:

1 Widespread use of modern information technologies, increasingly sophisticated medical devices (including those supported by AI), genetic engineering, nanotechnology, robotics, and extensive databases (big data) interlinked to form a single system which ensures a smooth flow of information and data in real time.

2. Far-reaching (and progressive) personalisation/customisation of products, devices, and services, accompanied by increased patient participation in healthcare financing (cost sharing).
3. Growing supply of health services, an increasing proportion of which can be classified as HE.
4. System-wide empowerment of the patient as a key stakeholder in the healthcare system. Patient empowerment is understood in its broad sense, which also includes issues related to the involvement of patients in the development of new technologies, applications, and devices used in therapy or rehabilitation (discussed in Chapter 8 on co-creation) and, in a slightly broader context, activities undertaken by the civil society for Health 4.0 (referred to in Chapter 14 devoted to NGOs in Health 4.0).

Health 4.0 is thus a vision of the future healthcare system. Admittedly, it is not a distant image at all, as its elements are already present today and are steadily becoming more sophisticated. The key components of Health 4.0 will be discussed in more detail in subsequent chapters of this book.

Conclusions

The foregoing observations make it perfectly clear that the 4IR has a large and growing impact on the healthcare system. The ways in which it affects health are increasingly being researched, and the findings should become the subject of keen interest (and sound analysis) not only for the primary stakeholders in the health system - providers, patients, and payers - but also for health policymakers, legislators, and the manufacturers of pharmaceuticals, medical equipment, and devices. Research on the 4IR in the context of public health and the healthcare system must be intensified, as both the 4IR and Health 4.0 are in the early development stages.

In considering the impact of the 4IR on the healthcare system, special attention should be paid to HE, as the interpenetration of the physical and biological world with the digital one constitutes the specific difference of the 4IR. The added value of this chapter is that it identifies the main directions of impact of the 4IR on the health sector in the context of the emerging concept of Health 4.0.

Notes

1. The discussion below is based on excerpts from Klich, J. (2021).
2. For example, the cited study by Castro e Melo and Faria Araújo (2020) was based on 10 interviews with experts from the United States, Brazil, Belgium, the United Kingdom, and Portugal associated with the health sector and representing industry, the public sector, the World Health Organization, government, and academic circles.
3. A detailed description of the categories and terms used in Figure. 1.1 can be found in Klich (2021).

4 This section is based on extracts from Klich (2021).
5 The painful experience of 2020-2021 has shown that the efforts to effectively combat the pandemic caused by the rapidly mutating SARS-CoV-2 virus constitutes a serious challenge to all health systems.
6 Just one top-selling drug in 2019, AbbVie's Humira, brought in an estimated USD 19.2 billion in revenue.
7 Telemedicine has a dedicated scientific journal, the *International Journal of Telemedicine and Applications*.
8 These three characteristics constitute the combat value of a soldier, which partly explains the military origins of the institutional development of human enhancement in the United States of America.
9 The term Health 4.0 is used in the literature to describe the target state towards which the current healthcare system is progressing (Karboub et al., 2019; Chute and, French, 2019), and this is the perspective from which it is discussed in this book in order to emphasise the qualitative change that can be experienced by people in the near future (which falls within the scope of HE) in relation to their physicality.

References

Allied Market Research (2020). *Medical Implant Market Size to Reach $147.46 Billion by 2027*, https://www.globenewswire.com/news-release/2020/12/07/2140609/0/en/Medical-Implant-Market-Size-to-Reach-147-46-Billion-by-2027.html, accessed 26.02.2021.

Ashby, L.S., Smith, K.A., Stea, B. (2016). Gliadel wafer implantation combined with standard radiotherapy and concurrent followed by adjuvant temozolomide for treatment of newly diagnosed high-grade glioma: A systematic literature review. *World Journal of Surgical Oncology*, 14, 225, https://doi.org/10.1186/s12957-016-0975-5.

Badri, A., Boudreau-Trudel, B., Souissi, A.S. (2018). Occupational health and safety in the industry 4.0 era: A cause for major concern? *Safety Science*, 109, 403–411.

Bateman, S., Gayon, J., Allouche, S. (Eds) (2015). *Human Enhancement: Interdisciplinary and International Perspectives*. Basingstoke: Palgrave Macmillan.

Buchanan, A. E. (2011a) Beyond Humanity?: The Ethics of Biomedical Enhancement. New York: Oxford University Press.

Buchanan, A.E. (2011b). *Better Than Human. The Promise and Perils of Enhancing Ourselves*. New York: Oxford University Press.

Castro e Melo, J., Faria Araújo, N.M. (2020). Impact of the Fourth Industrial Revolution on the Health Sector: A qualitative study. *Healthcare Informatics Research*, 26(4), 328–334. https://doi.org/10.4258/hir.2020.26.4.328.

Chute, C., French, T. (2019). Introducing Care 4.0: An integrated care paradigm built on Industry 4.0 capabilities. *International Journal of Environmental Research and Public Health*, 16(12), 2247. https://doi.org/10.3390/ijerph16122247.

Clarke, S., Savulescu, J., Coady, C.A.J., Giubilini, A., Sanyal, S. (Eds) (2016). *The Ethics of Human Enhancement: Understanding the Debate*. Oxford: Oxford University Press.

Coeckelbergh, M. (2013). *Human Being @ Risk. Enhancement, Technology, and the Evaluation of Vulnerability Transformations*. Philosophy of Engineering and Technology 12. Dordrecht: Springer.

Cosetti, M.K., Waltzman, S.B. (2011). Cochlear implants: current status and future potential. *Expert Review of Medical Devices*, 8(3), 389–401.

Dahl M. (2019). Niemcy jako europejski i światowy ośrodek badań i rozwoju sztucznej inteligencji, *Studia Europejskie – Studies in European Affairs*, 2, 153–162.

Dockx, K., Bekkers, E.M.J., Van den Bergh, V., Ginis, P., Rochester, L., Hausdorff, J.M., Mirelman, A., Nieuwboer, A. (2016). Virtual reality for rehabilitation in Parkinson's disease. *Cochrane Database of Systematic Reviews*, 12. doi: 10.1002/14651858.CD010760.pub2.

Druckman, D., Bjork, R.A. (1994). *Learning, Remembering, Believing. Enhancing Human Performance*. Washington, DC: National Academy Press.

Esteva, A., Kuprel, B., Novoa, R.A., Ko, J., Swetter, S.M., Blau, H.M., Thrun, S. (2017). Dermatologist-level classification of skin cancer with deep neural networks. *Nature*, 542, 115–118. https://doi.org/10.1038/nature21056.

Forsberg, E-M., Shelley-Egan, C., Thorstensen, E., Landeweerd, L., Hofmann, B. (2017). *Evaluating Ethical Frameworks for the Assessment of Human Cognitive Enhancement Applications*. Springer Briefs in Ethics. New York: Springer International Publishing.

Gargeya, R., Leng, T. (2017). Automated identification of diabetic retinopathy using deep learning. *Ophthalmology*, 124, 962–969. doi: 10.1016/j.ophtha.2017.02.008.

Gleason, N.W. (ed.). (2018). *Higher Education in the Era of the Fourth Industrial Revolution*. https://doi.org/10.1007/978-981-13-0194-0.

Globe Newswire (2020). *Medical Devices Market Size Worth Around US$671.49 Bn by 2027*. Ottawa, Nov. 11, 2020, https://www.globenewswire.com/news-release/2020/11/11/2124829/0/en/Medical-Devices-Market-Size-Worth-Around-US-671-49-Bn-by-2027.html, accessed 26.02.2021.

Hastings, C. (2019). eMacula augmented reality for vision impaired: interview with Steve Willey, CEO of Innovega. *Medgadget*, June 19, http://www.medgadget.com/2019/06/emacula-augmented-reality-for-vision-impaired-interview-with-steve-willey-ceo-of-innovega.html, accessed 27.08.2019.

Human Medicines Highlights 2020, https://www.ema.europa.eu/en/documents/report/human-medicines-highlights-2020_en.pdf, accessed 23.02.2021

Jha, R.K., Jha, P.K., Chaudhury, K., Rana, S.V.S., Guha, S.K. (2014). An emerging interface between life science and nanotechnology: present status and prospects of reproductive healthcare aided by nano-biotechnology. *Nano Reviews*, 5(1), 22762.

Karboub, K., Tabaa, M., Dellagi, S., Dandache, A., Mountaouakki, F. (2019). Toward Health 4.0: Challenges and Opportunities. *8th International Conference on Innovation and New Trends in Information Systems*, INTIS'2019, 20–21 December 2019, https://www.researchgate.net/publication/338117498_Toward_Health_40_Challenges_and_Opportunities, accessed 6.04.2021.

Kaur, J., Kaur, P.D. (2018). CE-GMS: A cloud IoT-enabled grocery management system. *Electronic Commerce Research and Applications*, 28, 63–72. https://doi.org/10.1016/j.elerap.2018.01.005.

Keefe, F.J., Huling, D.A., Coggins, M.J., Keefe, D.F., Rosenthal, M.Z., Herr, N.R., Hoffman, H.G. (2012). Virtual reality for persistent pain: A new direction for behavioral pain management. *Pain*, 153(11), 2163–2166. doi: 10.1016/j.pain.2012.05.030.

Klich, J. (2021). *Kreowana i rzeczywista odpowiedzialność państwa. Studium sektora ochrony zdrowia państw postsocjalistycznych* (Created and Actual State Responsibility. A Study of the Healthcare Sector of Post-socialist Countries). Warszawa: Wydawnictwo Naukowe Scholar.

Klipfel, A. (2017). La technicisation de la chirurgie représente-t-elle un danger? Entre regret et perspectives d'avenir. *Journal international de bioéthique et d'éthique des sciences*, 2(28), 131–143.

Koops, B-J. (2013). Conclusion: The debate about human enhancement. In: Koops, B-J., Lüthy, C.H., Nelis, A., Sieburgh, C., Jansen, J.P.M., Schmid, M.S. (Eds). *Engineering the Human. Human Enhancement Between Fiction and Fascination*. Heidelberg: Springer.

Koops, B-J., Lüthy, C.H., Nelis, A., Sieburgh, C., Jansen, J.P.M., Schmid, M.S. (Eds) (2013). *Engineering the Human. Human Enhancement Between Fiction and Fascination*. Heidelberg: Springer.

Kummervold, P.E., Wynn, R. (2012). Health information accessed on the internet: the development in 5 European countries. *International Journal of Telemedicine and Applications*, 2012, 297416. https://doi.org/10.1155/2012/297416.

Kurzweil, R. (2017). *Nadchodzi osobliwość. Kiedy człowiek przekroczy granice biologii*. Warszawa: Kurhaus Publishing.

Loh, E. (2018). Medicine and the rise of the robots: a qualitative review of recent advances of artificial intelligence in health. *BMJ Leader*, 2, 59–63.

Market Research Future (2019). *Medical Implants Research Report – Global Forecast till 2023*, http://www.marketresearchfuture.com/reports/medical-implants-market-2806, accessed 27.08.2019.

Martinez, B., Cano, C., Vilajosana, X. (2019). A square peg in a round hole: The complex path for wireless in the manufacturing industry. *IEEE Communications Magazine*, 57(4), 109–115. https://doi.org/10.1109/MCOM.2019.1800570.

Mercer, C., Trothen, T.J. (Eds) (2015). *Religion and Transhumanism. The Unknown Future of Human Enhancement*. Santa Barbara: Praeger, An Imprint of ABC-CLIO, LLC.

Miksch, S., Hunter, J., Keravnou, E. (eds.) (2005). *Artificial Intelligence in Medicine. 10th Conference on Artificial Intelligence in Medicine Proceedings*, Aime 2005, Aberdeen, UK, July 23-27. Berlin: Springer-Verlag.

Mikulic, M. (2020a). *Pharmaceutical Market: Worldwide Revenue 2001-2019*, May 25, 2020, https://www.statista.com/statistics/263102/pharmaceutical-market-worldwide-revenue-since-2001, accessed 23.02.2021

Mikulic, M. (2020b). *Total global pharmaceutical R&D spending 2012-2026*, Sep 4, 2020, https://www.statista.com/statistics/309466/global-r-and-d-expenditure-for-pharmaceuticals, accessed 23.02.2021

Moore, P. (2008). *Enhancing Me. The Hope and the Hype of Human Enhancement*. Chichester: John Wiley & Sons.

Musunuru, K. (2019). Opinion: We need to know what happened to CRISPR twins Lulu and Nana, *MIT Technology Review*, December 3, 2019, https://www.technologyreview.com/2019/12/03/65024/crispr-baby-twins-lulu-and-nana-what-happened, accessed 25.02.2021

Motyka, P. (2019). Genetycznie modyfikowani ludzie, pierwsze zdjęcie czarnej dziury i cyklokarbon. Największe odkrycia naukowe 2019 r. *Onet. Wiadomości*, http://https://wiadomosci.onet.pl/nauka/najwieksze-odkrycia-naukowe-2019-roku/ze2zrsw, accessed 4.01.2020.

Nadella, S. (2018). *Foreword*. In: Schwab K., Davis N.(Eds), *Shaping the Future of the Fourth Industrial Revolution. A Guide to Building a Better World (pp.* 8–10). New York: Currency.

Nathe, M. (2019). *10 Global Health Issues to Watch in 2019*, IntraHealth International, Pozyskano z: https://www.intrahealth.org/vital/10-global-health-issues-watch-2019, accessed 8.09.2019.

New Drug Therapy Approvals 2020. Impact Innovation Predictability Access. FDA's Center for Drug Evaluation and Research January 2021, https://www.fda.gov/drugs/new-drugs-fda-cders-new-molecular-entities-and-new-therapeutic-biological-products/new-drug-therapy-approvals-2020, accessed 23.02.2021

Raffa, V., Vittorio, O., Riggio, C., Cuschieri, A. (2010). Progress in nanotechnology for healthcare. *Minimally Invasive Therapy & Allied Technologies*, 19(3), 127–135.

Rizzo, A., Hartholt, A., Grimani, M., Leeds, A., Liewer, M. (2014). Virtual reality exposure therapy for combat-related posttraumatic stress disorder. *Computer*, 47(7), 31–37. doi: 10.1109/MC.2014.199.

Robotics Business Review (2015). *Smart Glove: The Low-Cost Disruptor for Hand Therapy*, June 4, https://www.roboticsbusinessreview.com/health-medical/smart_glove_the_low_cost_disruptor_for_hand_therapy, accessed 20.01.2020.

Scassellati-Sforzolini, F. (2018). *5 Key EU Health Policy Challenges*. Incisive Health, 31st August 2018, Public Health, https://www.incisive-health.com/5-key-eu-health-policy-challenges, accessed 9.09.2019.

Schwab, K. (2016a). *The Fourth Industrial Revolution*. Geneva: World Economic Forum.

Schwab, K. (2016b). *The Fourth Industrial Revolution: What It Means, How to Respond*, https://www.weforum.org/agenda/2016/01/the-fourth-industrial-revolution-what-it-means-and-how-to-respond, accessed 9.04.2021.

Schwab, K., Davis, N. (2018). *Shaping the Future of the Fourth Industrial Revolution. A Guide to Building a Better World*. New York: Currency.

Stelmach, M. (2019). *Po raz pierwszy w Polsce zastosowano innowacyjną terapię CAR-T*, Termedia, http://www.termedia.pl/mz/Po-raz-pierwszy-w-Polsce-zastosowano-innowacyjna-terapie-CAR-T,36223.html, accessed 3.12.2019.

Tan, S.S.-L., Goonawardene, N. (2017). Internet health information seeking and the patient-physician relationship: A systematic review. *Journal of Medical Internet Research*, 19(1), e9. doi: 10.2196/jmir.5729.

Trothen, T.J., Mercer, C. (Eds) (2017). *Religion and Human Enhancement. Death, Values, and Morality*. Palgrave Studies in the Future of Humanity and its Successors. Cham: Palgrave Macmillan.

Watson, J. (2017). The digital doctor: Revolutionary technologies reshaping healthcare. *Medscape*, July 12, http://www.medscape.com/slideshow/digital-doctor-6008897, accessed 26.08.2019.

Weber, S., Brouhard, K., Berman, P. (2010). *Synopsis of Health Systems Research Across the World Bank Group from 2000 to 2010* (Draft Report), November, The World Bank.

World Economic Forum (2019). *Strategic Intelligence*, https://intelligence.weforum.org/topics/a1Gb0000001RIhBEAW?tab=publications, accessed 14.08.2019.

WHO (2011). *Health system strengthening: current trends and challenges: report by the Secretariat*, World Health Organization, http://www.who.int/iris/handle/10665/3250, accessed 18.08.2019.

WHO (2020). *Health system. Health systems strengthening glossary*, World Health Organization, https://www.who.int/healthsystems/hss_glossary/en/index5.html, accessed 2.03.2020.

2 The transition from telemedicine and e-health to Health 4.0

Mariusz Duplaga

Introduction

The progress in information and communication technologies (ICT) made in recent years has provided new opportunities for the provision of health services. It has become apparent that the traditional face-to-face consultations between patients and physicians could, in many cases, be replaced or supported by technical tools. Despite the initial resistance of professional communities and patients, the growing access to innovative ICTs, the expansion of the Internet, and the omnipresent wireless networks have led to a radical transformation of how health services can be delivered.

The first opportunities for medical care to be delivered to remote locations, based on the use of inventions enhancing human communication, such as the telegraph, the radio, or the telephone, were referred to as telemedicine. For many years, telephone-based communications were the most common form of telemedicine, even though the users rarely considered that they were participating in telemedicine. Although examples of solutions and systems facilitating telemedicine were observed throughout the 20th century, really significant progress has been achieved only in recent decades. This may be attributed to the rapid developments in computer technologies and telecommunication. In the 1990s, the Internet quickly became the prime tool used for communications, which triggered new forms of commerce, social interactions, and service provision. The exploitation of the opportunities for health and medicine offered by the Internet resulted in the concept of e-health, a complex environment of digital service provision to patients, the general population, and healthcare providers. Further development of the Internet and related technologies was accompanied by new developments in the digital health. The ability to create one's own content and social interaction, in addition to accessing information (Health 2.0), was the first step, followed by exploiting the potential of the semantic web for health-related applications (Health 3.0). The concept of Health 4.0, which goes far beyond the achievements of the Internet and the interactions possible between healthcare stakeholders described as Health 2.0 and Health 3.0, has now emerged. Health 4.0 is dependent on the Fourth Industrial Revolution and incorporates the

DOI: 10.4324/9781003144403-2

technologies perceived as key components of Industry 4.0, which include the cyber-physical systems, the Internet of Things (IoT), cloud computing (CC), and Big Data (BD) analytics. In the domain of Heath 4.0, virtualisation leading to the personalisation of health services has become the leading theme.

Telemedicine and telehealth

Initially, the term "telemedicine" was used to describe the provision of medical services to a patient located at a distance from the healthcare provider. Although the first concepts of telemedicine systems originated in the latter part of the 19th century, the first definition of telemedicine was formulated in the early 1970s. The definition proposed by Kenneth Bird in 1971 mentions the practising of medicine without the traditional contact between a physician and a patient using an interactive audio-visual system (Bird, 1971). As Bird was interested in using television systems for medical interactions, his definition did not refer to communication or computer technologies. A few years later, Rashid Bashshur defined telemedicine as a system fulfilling a set of criteria including the geographical distance between the centres or persons exchanging information; the use of information technology instead of direct interaction; the employment of the medical and technical staff supporting the interactions; the availability of appropriate organisational structures; and finally, the use of clinical protocols and standards regulating the activities of medical personnel and administrative staff in relation to the quality of care and confidentiality (Bashshur, 1975).

The inventions enhancing communication that occurred in the 19th century (Sosa-Iudicissa et al., 1998) led to the idea that medical services could be available without face-to-face contact between a patient and a physician. Radio, telegraph, and telephone communication were soon adopted for medical use. For many years, the telephone was the main method used for contacts between remotely located patients and medical doctors. Consequently, telephone telemedicine was the dominant form of telemedicine for many decades in the 20th century (Wootton, 2006). Paradoxically, in many countries, the COVID-19 pandemic has resulted in the widespread use of telephone communication for remote medical services (Ministerstwo Zdrowia & Narodowy Fundusz Zdrowia, 2020).

The first examples of telephone use for medical support originated in 1870. Some authors repeat the anecdote that one of the first telephone contacts between Alexander Graham Bell and Thomas Watson, his assistant, on March 10, 1876, could be perceived as a telemedicine contact (Aronson, 1977). In the 1870s, an anonymous author reported in the Lancet that a general practitioner, after listening to a child's cough by telephone, excluded the possibility of croup (Aronson, 1977). In 1910, the Lancet reported on the invention of an electric stethoscope enabling the transmission of heart sounds by the telephone (Anonymous, 1910). The same year Willem Einthoven used the telephone for the transmission of an electrocardiogram from a hospital to his laboratory

(Hjelm & Julius, 2005). Wilhelm Röentgen was awarded the 1901 Nobel Prize in Physics for the discovery of X-ray. Already in the late 1920s, the telegraph was used for the transmission of X-ray dentition images (Kells, 1926).

From the 1920s, radio communication was used for providing medical support for liner passengers and crews during long cruises (Goethe, 1984). Later, the service was made available for airline crew needing to help or treat passengers. At that time, the expectations that radio communication could be used in medical practice were quite common and in 1924, and the "Radio News" journal showed the image of a "prototype" equipment for maintaining communications between a patient and a physician on the cover of one of its issues (Gernsback, 1924). Although the concept could not be realised at the time because of technical limitations, the general functionality of the device corresponded with telemedical teleconferencing stations, which became available several decades later. Another interesting concept was presented in 1925. A device named "teledactyl" was supposed to enable the remote physical examination of a patient with the use of manipulators coupled with radio transmission (Gernsback, 1925). Again, it was not technically feasible in the 1920s; however, it could be treated as the vision of robotic manipulators, which became available for surgery at the end of the 20th century.

In the 1940s, Austin Cooley worked on a system to transmit X-ray images using telephone and radio connections. The solution incorporating a facsimile machine was used for 2 years to connect hospitals in Philadelphia and Chester Country in the USA (Gershon-Cohen & Cooley, 1950). In the late 1950s, further progress was made by Albert Jutras, who developed a system based on concentric cables which enabled fluoroscopic images to be transmitted between two hospitals in Montreal (Jutras & Duckett, 1957).

The development of more mature television systems led to considerable progress in telemedicine. In the late 1950s, Cecil Wittson of the Nebraska Psychiatric Institute used a closed-circuit television system for consultations between general practitioners and psychiatrists, and tele-education (Wittson & Benschotter, 1972). The same Institute maintained a television-based connection with Norfolk State Hospital located 180 km away during the 1960s.

Also, in the 1960s, satellite communication was first utilised for telemedicine purposes. The National Aeronautics and Space Administration (NASA) and the U.S. Public Health Service implemented the Space Technology Applied to Rural Papago Advanced Health Care project. The project made use of mobile diagnostic units in the Papago Indian settlements located in Arizona. By the 1970s and 1980s, several telemedicine projects were established in Alaska, Canada, and Australia (Bashshur & Shannon, 2009a; Brown, 1995).

It appears that for a major part of the 20th century, the USA instigated the main innovations in telemedicine. In the 1980s, telemedicine networks to provide specialised care were operating in several states in the USA. Telemedicine gained worldwide publicity in 1988 when cooperation between the USA and the Union of Soviet Socialist Republics (USSR) enabled telemedicine consultations, using the satellite bridge established by

NASA (Istepanian & Nikogosian, 2000) to be provided for the survivors of the disastrous earthquake in Armenia.

In Europe, the use of information and telecommunication technologies in healthcare has been advanced by successive European Union Research and Development Framework Programmes (FP). The priority theme titled "Computer for Doctors" was funded from 1989 to 1990 and "Networks for Healthcare Professionals" from 1990 to 1994 in the following FPs (Iakovidis, 2014). Research and development initiatives using ICT for the delivery of healthcare services created considerable interest in the medical, research, and industrial communities. This triggered further actions to explore the use of telemedicine, which has led to the emergence of the e-health community. It must be recognised that telemedicine was of significant interest to international organisations, including the World Health Organisation (WHO) and the International Telecommunication Union (ITU), which perceived telemedicine as a means for providing medical support in developing countries (Wright, 1998).

In their book *History of Telemedicine*, Bashshur and Shannon identified four stages in the development of telemedicine: the genesis of telemedicine (from about 1870 to 1954), the pioneering era (until the early 1970s), the emergence and subsequent hiatus of telemedicine (from early 1970s to late 1980s), and finally, the maturation stage (since the late 1980s; Bashshur & Shannon, 2009b). The first stage was characterised by isolated experiments by individual pioneers in the USA, Canada, and Europe. During the second stage, several pilot programmes were organised and implemented, mainly in the USA. The third stage was characterised by the federal government in the USA initiating many telemedicine programmes; however, they soon ceased having exhausted the funding. According to the authors who published the book mentioned above, in 2009, the maturation stage was still existing and was leading to the transformation of telemedicine from relatively straightforward solutions based on connectivity to intelligent systems supporting clinical decision-making.

e-Health and m-health

According to the 1999 definition by John Mitchell, e-health is a term used to describe the use of electronic communication and information technology in the health sector (Mitchell, & John Mitchell & Associates, 1999). It also means the use of digital data in healthcare for various purposes: clinical, educational, and administrative at local sites and at a distance. Eysenbach (2001) defined e-health as "an emerging field in the intersection of medical informatics, public health and business referring to health services and information delivered or enhanced through the Internet and related technologies". Interestingly, one of the early definitions of e-health made a clear reference to public health. However, it appears that the public health communities only recently began to appreciate the importance of digital technologies (Odone et al., 2019). The term "e-health" has quickly gained considerable popularity and, in its broad meaning, refers to the use of ICTs for the delivery of health-related services. Such a broad understanding of e-health is in line with the definition included in the document accompanying the 58th World Health Assembly of WHO as "the cost-effective and secure use of information and communications technologies in support of health and health-related fields, including health-care services, health surveillance, health literature, and health education, knowledge and research" (WHO, 2005).

Although the term "e-health" is now commonly used in scientific literature and policy papers, some authors adhere to the term "telemedicine" as the general umbrella for the use of ICT in health and medicine. According to Bashshur et al (2011), e-health and m-health are "neologisms introduced to reflect technological innovations" advanced by business and industry. However, even though the origins of the term "e-health" are associated with e-commerce, it seems that its current understanding is broader than telemedicine. It appears that the "commercial" flavour of e-health, which may be repulsive for authors involved in the development of telemedicine, is currently one of its many dimensions.

From the onset, the perception of e-health was very broad. Nykänen (2006) indicated three categories of e-health applications (citing findings from the European MEDITRAV project completed in 2003): the delivery of care to patients by healthcare professionals, education and dissemination of health-related information and knowledge, and trading health products. According to this classification, hospital systems and primary and home care systems were included in the first category. The second category encompassed web portals and specific health-related websites, virtual hospitals, and Internet-based consultation services. The third category referred to e-commerce or the e-trading of medical and health-related products, pharmaceuticals, and medical devices.

Following the report of Ruotsalainen et al. (2003), Nykänen classified e-health applications based on their functionality and identified the following groups:

- Regional health information networks
- Hospital systems, clinical systems, diagnostic systems and hospital management systems
- Telemedicine and teleconsultation systems
- Insurance, cards, or systems that "present the payer's view on health service"
- Citizen-centred systems, patient-centred systems, and health information portals
- Home care systems and health-related fitness systems

According to Pagliari et al. (2005), the areas which dominated e-health included professional clinical informatics, electronic patient/health records, healthcare business management, and consumer health informatics. These authors also treated e-health as a part or equivalent to medical or clinical informatics. The key applications belonging to professional clinical informatics would include decision aids, clinical management tools, e.g. electronic health records, educational tools, electronic tools for clinical communication, electronic networks, discipline- or disease-specific tools, and telemedicine applications. The issues identified in the context of electronic patient/health records were record linkage, a universal patient indicator, databases and population registers, multi-professional access, data protection and security issues, and patients' access and control. The principal healthcare business management systems encompassed those for billing and quality assessment. Finally, consumer health informatics covered decision-making aids for patients, online information, clinician–patient communication tools, access and equity issues, the quality of online health information, and "virtual" health communities (Pagliari et al., 2005).

The classifications in the e-health domain may differ in accordance with the perspective of different authors. However, it is obvious that the domain goes beyond the definition of telemedicine as a system that makes use of ICT tools to enable communication and interaction between patients and physicians or between healthcare professionals. The participation of citizens and patients, as the consumers of diversified health-related services, mainly because of the growth of the Internet, is another important feature of the e-health environment.

It should be emphasised that from the time of the first use of the term "e-health" in the late 1990s, the e-health domain has experienced an accelerating evolution induced by the emergence of new technologies, particularly those associated with wireless communication and sensors. By the early 2000s, the potential of wireless connectivity, combined with the expansion of the Internet, led to the development of a new model of healthcare that foresaw the broad participation of patients and the general population (Laxminarayan & Istepanian, 2000). It anticipated flexible and rapid access to specialised advice in healthcare facilities, support for interactive consultations, the transmission of medical videos and images, the management of healthcare in areas having limited access to medical services, and finally, the improvement of emergency medicine (Laxminarayan & Istepanian, 2000). Only a few years after the first definition of e-health, the term "m-health" was applied to refer the use of mobile and wireless systems for the delivery of healthcare services (Istepanian & Lacal, 2003). In 2004, m-health was defined as the application of mobile data processing, medical sensors, and communication technologies in healthcare (Istepanian et al., 2004). The growth of m-health was associated with the successive generations of mobile communication (general packet radio service [GPRS], 3G, 4G, 5G) as well as the increasing use of Bluetooth technology and global positioning systems (GPS) (Mechael & Sloninsky, 2008). The key attributes of m-health systems, indicated in the context of improvements to healthcare services, include interactivity, multidirectional communication, personalisation, absence of time boundaries, context awareness, accessibility, and omnipresence (Siau & Shen, 2003). The growth of m-health is associated with the strong emphasis on the personalisation of health-related service, patient empowerment, and shared care. According to the 2011 WHO report, the main activities performed by m-health systems included

- communications between citizens and healthcare facilities (helplines),
- communication between healthcare institutions and citizens and patients (adherence to therapy, reminders, society mobilisation, and health promotion),
- consultations between healthcare providers (called in the report as mobile telemedicine),
- intersectoral communication in emergencies,
- monitoring and control of health status, and
- access to information for healthcare providers at the point of care.

According to Ali et al., there have been three periods in the development of the m-health domain (Ali et al., 2016). During the first period, until 2006, personal digital assistants (PDA) were the dominant type of mobile device. The period 2007–2012 was characterised by the use of the basic functions available on mobile phones. The use of smart devices, smartphones, and tablets is the feature of the third period, which commenced in 2013 (Ali et al., 2016). Currently, the use of wearable devices is one of the most prominent features of m-health systems. Wearable technologies are defined, in the context of health, as intelligent, low-cost, ultra-low-power sensor networks developed to collect large quantities of biomedical data and provide support to dependent persons (Alrige & Chatterjee, 2015). Some authors have proposed more inclusive definitions of wearables, stating that they are those technologies, electronics, or otherwise, with the primary functionality that requires them to be connected to a patient's body (Gouge & Jones, 2016).

From Health 1.0 to Health 3.0

The use of specific terms to identify the successive stages in the development of medicine, healthcare, and health-related ICT has led to confusion in the nomenclature. Firstly, some authors have identified the consecutive stages of medical practice as Medicine 1.0, Medicine 2.0, etc. to refer to progress in the use of medical technologies. Wolf and Scholze (2017) proposed that the term Medicine 1.0 should be used in relation to the time in which medical practice depended principally on the knowledge of highly trained doctors who could use a limited number of drugs based on natural substances (Wolf & Scholze, 2017). Medicine 2.0 would mean the period involving the use of antibiotics and the application of X-rays for diagnosis. Medicine 3.0 was characterised by the use of microsystems and electronics, resulting in applications such as navigated surgery, image recognition, and robotics. Finally, Medicine 4.0 is related to advanced ICTs, electronics, and microstructure technologies, leading to a higher level of efficient, innovative, and therapeutic modalities.

However, the terms from Health 1.0 to Health 4.0 are applied to the domains of health-related applications available on the Internet. Consecutive stages from 1.0 to 4.0 would correspond to functions resulting from progress on the World Wide Web. Nevertheless, the term Health 4.0 or Healthcare 4.0 is now applied to reflect the innovations corresponding with features of the Fourth Industrial Revolution transferring to medicine and healthcare. Although solutions attributed to Web 4.0 are certainly part of Industry 4.0, an understanding of Health 4.0 as being in parallel with "Industry 4.0" would necessitate the inclusion of many other innovative technologies in Health 4.0, including cyber-physical systems, IoT, BD analytics, and artificial intelligence (AI).

The World Wide Web is the part of the Internet that was designed to enable humans to interact with technological networks. The stages of World Wide Web development can be considered as Web 1.0, 2.0, 3.0, and 4.0. Web 1.0 was synonymous with the read-only web, called a web of cognition. It was characterised by a unidirectional model of communication as it was mainly an information place for commercial entities providing information to customers. In this stage, users had limited interaction. Users could mainly search for, find, and read information, analogically as in the traditional mass media.

The term Web 2.0, introduced at the end of the 1990s, is also known as the read-write, participative or social web (Musser & O'Reilly, 2006). This stage of Web development offered, in addition to content, the options for social interaction. O'Reilly defined Web 2.0 as "a set of economic, social and technology trends that collectively form the basis for the next generation of the Internet, a more mature, distinctive medium characterised by user participation, openness and network effects" (O'Reilly, 2005). In Web 2.0, a user can simultaneously receive and produce information. The difference between authors and consumers of information was blurred. Because of tools like blogs and discussion fora, anyone could publish on the Internet, and, as a result, the Internet became a type of social platform supporting interactivity and the personalisation of content. The expansion of social media is a prominent characteristic of this stage of web evolution.

Web 3.0, or the semantic web, is characterised by the provision of machine-readable contents as an attempt to reduce human tasks and enable them to be carried out by machines (Berners-Lee et al., 2001). The term Web 3.0 was first introduced in 2006 to refer to the attempts to enhance Web 2.0 by employing AI mechanisms based on semantic solutions. Web 2.0 uses smart solutions to facilitate access to the required information in accordance with the preferences of users. Consequently, Web 3.0 may be treated as the response to the challenge of indiscriminate information pouring from the Internet.

Web 4.0, called the read-write-execution-concurrency web, or the web of integration, was expected to provide intelligent interactions (Aghaei et al., 2012). According to some authors, Web 4.0 combines the attributes of Web

2.0 and Web 3.0 to become truly ubiquitous, whilst others associate it with the concept of IoT (Almeida, 2017).

The term Health 1.0 is rarely found in the literature. By analogy to Web 1.0, it referred to the use of health-related information available online (Van Der Vaart & Drossaert, 2017). One of the most popular tools applied to assess e-health literacy, the eHealth Literacy Scale (eHEALS), developed by Norman and Skinner in 2006, focuses mainly on the skills required in Health 1.0 – searching for and accessing the information on the Internet (Norman & Skinner, 2006).

In general terms, Health 2.0 extends the use of the Internet beyond these basic activities. It should be recognised that in addition to the term Health 2.0, Medicine 2.0 is used in a similar context. In 2010, a systematic review of the definitions of Health 2.0 and Medicine 2.0 was published (Van De Belt et al., 2010). They found 42 definitions for Health 2.0 and 2 definitions for Medicine 2.0., and their analysis confirmed that there were 7 main recurrent topics in those definitions. The reference to patients, or consumers of healthcare, was found in 35 definitions. Increased patient participation or empowerment, apart from a general mention of their involvement, was used frequently in the context of addressing the role of patients (or consumers). In many definitions, there was a reference to Web 2.0, an obvious association. The other topics included the motives for social networking, changes to healthcare, collaboration, and health information or content. The analysis by Van De Belt et al. (2010) also showed that Health 2.0 could be perceived in two ways: as the next stage of technological developments embedded into healthcare and as the new generation of healthcare.

An analysis by Kordzadeh and Warren (2013) identified two major types of actors within Health 2.0 websites and distinguished six main Health 2.0 collaboration platforms. They included health blogs, physician ratings, medicine ratings, online health social networks, health discussion boards, and ask-a-doctor platforms. There are four types of interaction, depending on the main participants: professional-to-professional (P2P), professional-to-consumer (P2C), consumer-to-consumer (C2C), and consumer-to-professional (C2P).

By an analogy to Web 3.0, Health 3.0 would involve the wider use of the semantic web, AI, and machine-readable contents in a health context. However, another interpretation of Health 3.0, as "mobile social networking", was proposed (Nash, 2008). In 2012, Gagnon defined it as a philosophy of management and a set of organisation and delivery mechanisms of care and services that promote new patient–clinician relationships, assisted by communication and self-managed health technologies, to foster patients' autonomy, especially for those patients with chronic diseases (Gagnon & Chartier, 2012). Chen et al. (2013) proposed a Health 3.0 care model based on the application of knowledge management and semantic technologies. They postulated that this model requires cooperation between the emergency care services, insurance companies, hospitals, pharmacies, governments, specialists, academic researchers, and patients (Chen et al., 2013).

In 2007, Giustini anticipated that Web 3.0 would have a major effect on medicine, enabling the processing of larger amounts of data through built-in semantic relations (Giustini, 2007). In turn, Coughlin (2011) believed that a goal of Health 3.0 would be "digital healing", meaning the reassurance, support, and validation obtained by patients from other contacts in social media. Other features predicted for Health 3.0 included improved access to health-related information on the web, based on semantic and network resources; supportive virtual communities, enabling a better understanding of health-related issues; personalised social networking resources; and virtual reasoning tools (Beggelman, 2008; Nash, 2008).

The borders between the successive stages from Health 1.0 to Health 4.0 are not clearly visible, and the way in which these terms are defined depends on the author. In a post from 2008 placed on the "Health Management Rx" blog, McCabe (2008) tried to clarify the definitions of consecutive "dot-o" stages of health by proposing the following attributes (McCabe, 2008):

- Health 1.0 = content
- Health 2.0 = content + community
- Health 3.0 = content + community + consumer-centric commerce
- Health 4.0 = content + community + working commerce models + coherence (connectors)

According to Karboub et al., Health 1.0 relied on computers and administrative software tools as the main technology; Health 2.0 relied on CC, Health 3.0 on big data, wearables devices, and optimisation systems; and Health 4.0 uses IoT, AI, and data analytics (Karboub et al., 2019). These authors proposed that the transition from Health 1.0 to Health 4.0 involves the change of focus from automation, through connections, then communication with patients, and finally to prediction and diagnosis supported by AI.

As it is not fully apparent what Web 4.0 means, defining the concept of Health 4.0 by reference to the stage of global web development may be difficult. This is because earlier attempts to classify the Health x.0 stages frequently stemmed from an e-commerce perspective, but more recent approaches identify more clearly the use of new concepts and technologies, e.g. AI or IoT. Furthermore, currently, the concepts of Health 4.0 or Healthcare 4.0, built in relation to the Fourth Industrial Revolution, seem to prevail in the literature.

Health 4.0 as part of Fourth Industrial Revolution

Industry 4.0 anticipates that the industry will develop its manufacturing potential by using all the benefits of advanced technology but will progress to providing services characterised by a high level of personalisation depending on client needs and preferences. The concept of Health 4.0 or Healthcare 4.0, inspired by the Fourth Industrial Revolution 4.0, can benefit from the application of many innovative technologies such as AI, BD analytics, cyber-physical systems, IoT, robotics, and CC. Health 4.0 is perceived as being related to many terms and applications associated with the use of ICTs in healthcare, e.g. telemedicine and e-health, smart health, wireless health, mobile health, even health or medical informatics, or simply digital health (Jayaraman et al., 2020). The rather broad connotations mean that it is difficult to define precise borders for the Health 4.0 domain.

The widespread use of digital technologies on which Health 4.0 is founded is expected to result in more effective and individualised health services (Thuemmler & Bai, 2017). It is expected that the personalisation of healthcare will be achieved by the virtualisation of the spatial–temporal matrix and by employing the core components of Industry 4.0, such as cyber-physical systems, IoT, BD tools, and software building blocks (Thuemmler & Bai, 2017).

Conclusions

The chapter describes the evolution of the use of ICT in healthcare and medicine. It opens with the presentation of the first attempts to enhance healthcare services using the early tools for improving and accelerating human communications, e.g. telephone and telegraph. The advanced telemedicine projects and initiatives are also delineated. The transformation of healthcare services resulting from the use of the Internet and mobile technologies leading to e-health and m-health environments is also presented. The progress in Web-related technologies and their application to the healthcare domain has been aligned with the consecutive phases from Health 1.0 to Health 4.0. However, Health 4.0 means much more than relying only on the next stage of Internet development. It has become a term used for associating the transformation of healthcare and medicine with the technologies seen as the hallmarks of the Fourth Industrial Revolution, which, in addition to CPS, include the IoT, CC, and BD analytics.

References

Aghaei, S., Nematbakhsh, M. A., & Farsani, H. K. (2012). Evolution of the World Wide Web: from Web 1.0 to Web 4.0. *International Journal of Web & Semantic Technology*, 3(1), 1–10.

Ali, E. E., Chew, L., & Yap, K. Y. (2016). Evolution and current status of mhealth research: a systematic review. *BMJ Innovations*, 2(1), 33–40.

Almeida, F. (2017). Concept and dimensions of Web 4.0. *International Journal of Computers and Technology*, 16(7), 7040–7046. https://doi.org/10.24297/ijct.v16i7.6446

Alrige, M., & Chatterjee, S. (2015). Toward a taxonomy of wearable technologies in healthcare. In B. Donnellan, M. Helfert, J. Kenneally, D. VanderMeer, M. Rothenberger, & R. Winter (Eds.), *10th International Conference DESRIST 2015, New Horizons Design Science: Broadening the Research Agenda* (pp. 496–504). Cham, Heidelberg, New York, Dordrecht, London: Springer.

Anonymous. (1910). The telephone as an aid to diagnosis. *The Lancet*, 175(4523), 1284. https://doi.org/10.1016/S0140-6736(01)74654-5

Aronson, S. (1977). The Lancet on the telephone 1876-1975. *Medical History*, 21, 69–87.

Bashshur, R., Shannon, G., Krupinski, E., & Grigsby, J. (2011). The taxonomy of telemedicine. *Telemedicine and E-Health*, 17(6), 484–494.

Bashshur, R.L. (1975). Telemedicine and medical care. In R.L. Bashshur, P. Armstrong, & Z. Youssef (Eds.), *Telemedicine: Exploration in the Use of Telecommunications in Healthcare*. Springfield, IL: Charles C. Thomas Publishers.

Bashshur, R.L., & Shannon, G. (2009a). Telemedicine comes of age. In R.L. Bashshur & G. Shannon (Eds.), *History of Telemedicine. Evolution, Context and Transformation* (pp. 187–235). New Rochelle, NY: Mary Ann Liebert Inc.

Bashshur, R.L., & Shannon, G. (2009b). The Genesis of Telemedicine, 1870 to 1955. Introduction. In R.L. Bashshur & G. Shannon (Eds.), *History of Telemedicine* (p. 131). New Rochelle, NY: Mary Ann Liebert, Inc.

Beggelman, M. (2008). Virtual reasoning redefining healthcare through Health 3.0. *White Paper.*

Berners-Lee, T., Hendler, J., & Lassila, O. (2001). The semantic web. *Scientific American*, 284 (5), 34–43. https://doi.org/10.1038/scientificamerican0501-34

Bird, K. (1971). *Teleconsultation: A New Health Information System. Third Annual Report* (Vol. 201). Boston, MA: Massachusetts General Hospital.

Brown, N. (1995). A brief history of telemedicine. *Telemedicine Information Exchange*, 105, 833–835.

Chen, T. F., Ko, C. H., & Cheng, F. C. (2013). Knowledge management and semantic technology in the health care revolution: Health 3.0 model. *Advanced Materials Research*, 680, 633–638. https://doi.org/10.4028/www.scientific.net/AMR.680.633

Coughlin, J. F. (2011). Health 3.0: Baby Boomers, Social Media & the Evolution of Digital Healing. *Big Think*. https://bigthink.com/disruptive-demographics/health-30-baby-boomers-social-media-the-evolution-of-digital-healing

Eysenbach, G. (2001). What is e-health? *Journal of Medical Internet Research*, 3(2), e20.

Gagnon, S., & Chartier, L. (2012). Health 3.0 – The patient-clinician "Arabic spring" in healthcare. *Health*, 4(2), 39–45. https://doi.org/10.4236/health.2012.42008

Gernsback, H. (1924). *Radio News Magazine* (Cover). Experimenter Publishing Company, April.

Gernsback, H. (1925). *The Radio Teledactyl*. Science Invention, February.

Gershon-Cohen, J., & Cooley, A. (1950). Telognosis. *Radiology*, 55, 582–587.

Giustini, D. (2007). Web 3.0 and medicine. *British Medical Journal*, 335, 1273–1274.

Goethe, W. (1984). Medical care on ships without a doctor. Radio medical advice. In W. Goethe, E. Watson, & D. Jones (Eds.), *Handbook of Nautical Medicine* (pp. 53–65). Berlin, Heidelberg, New York, Tokyo: Springer.

Gouge, C., & Jones, J. (2016). Wearables, wearing, and the rhetorics that attend to them. *Rhetoric Society Quarterly*, 46(3), 199–206. https://doi.org/10.1080/02773945.2016.1171689

Hjelm, N., & Julius, H. (2005). Centenary of tele-electrocardiography and telephonocardiography. *Journal of Telemedicine and Telecare*, 11(7), 336–338.

Iakovidis, I. (2014). European eHealth Agenda, 1990-2010. In M. Rosenmoller, D. Whitehouse, & P. Wilson (Eds.), *Managing eHealth. From Vision to Reality* (1st Edition, pp. 26–36). Palgrave Macmillan. https://www.palgrave.com/gp/book/9781137379429

Istepanian, R., & Lacal, J. (2003). Emerging mobile communication technologies for health: some imperative notes on m-health. Proceedings of the 25th Annual International Conference of the IEEE Engineering in Medicine and Biology Society. (IEEE Cat. No. 03CH37439; Vol. 2, pp. 1414–1416). Cancun, Mexico: IEEE.

Istepanian, R., & Nikogosian, H. (2000). Telemedicine in Armenia. *Journal of Telemedicine and Telecare*, 6, 268–272.

Istepanian, R.S., Jovanov, E., & Zhang, Y.T. (2004). Guest editorial introduction to the special section on m-health: beyond seamless mobility and global wireless health-care connectivity. *IEEE Transactions on Information Technology in Biomedicine*, 8(4), 405–414.

Jayaraman, P.P., Forkan, A.R.M., Morshed, A., Haghighi, P.D., & Kang, Y.B. (2020). Healthcare 4.0: a review of frontiers in digital health. *WIREs Data Mining and Knowledge Discovery*, 10(2), e1350. https://doi.org/10.1002/widm.1350

Jutras, A., & Duckett, G. (1957). Distant radiodiagnosis, telefluoroscopy & cinefluorography. *L'Union Medicale Du Canada*, 86(11), 1284–1289.

Karboub, K., Tabaa, M., Dellagi, S., Dandache, A., & Moutaouakki, F. (2019). Toward Health 4.0: challenges and opportunities. *8th International Conference on Innovation and New Trends in Information Systems*, INTIS'2019, 20-21 December 2019.

Kells, C. (1926). Thirty years' experience in the field of radiography. *Journal of the American Dental Association*, 13(6), 693–711.

Kordzadeh, N., & Warren, J. (2013). Toward a typology of health 2.0 collaboration platforms and websites. *Health and Technology*, 3, 37–50. https://doi.org/10.1007/s12553-013-0043

Laxminarayan, S., & Istepanian, R.S. (2000). UNWIRED E-MED: the next generation of wireless and internet telemedicine systems. *IEEE Transaction on Information Technology and Biomedicine*, 4(3), 189–193.

McCabe, J. S. (2008). Defining Health 3.0 and 4.0. *Health Management Rx*. http://healthmgmtrx.blogspot.com/2008/04/defining-health-30-and-40.html

Mechael, P., & Sloninsky, D. (2008). Towards the development of an mHealth strategy: a literature review. *The Millennium Villages Project*. http://www.who.int/goe/mobile_health/mHealthReview_Aug09.pdf

Ministerstwo Zdrowia, & Narodowy Fundusz Zdrowia. (2020). Raport z badania satysfakcji pacjentów korzystających z teleporad u lekarza podstawowej opieki zdrowotnej w okresie epidemii COVID-19. https://www.nfz.gov.pl/download/gfx/nfz/pl/defaultaktualnosci/370/7788/1/raport_-_teleporady_u_lekarza_poz.pdf

Mitchell, J., & John Mitchell & Associates. (1999). *From Telehealth to e-Health: The Unstoppable Rise of e-Health*. Canberra, Australia: National Office for the Information Technology.

Musser, J., & O'Reilly, T. (2006). Web 2.0. Principles and best practices. http://www.oreilly.com/catalog/web2report/chapter/web20_report_excerpt pdf.

Nash, D. B. (2008). Health 3.0. *Pharmacy and Therapeutics*, 33(2), 69–75.

Norman, C.D., & Skinner, H.A. (2006). eHEALS: the eHealth literacy scale. *Journal of Medical Internet Research*, 8(4), e27. https://doi.org/10.2196/jmir.8.4.e27

Nykänen, P. (2006). E-health systems: their use and vision of the future. In T.A.M. Spil & R.W. Schuring (Eds.), *E-health Systems Diffusion and Use. The Innovation, the User and the Use IT Model* (pp. 281–293). Hershey, London, Melbourne, Singapore: Idea Group Publishing.

O'Reilly, T. (2005). What is Web 2.0. Design patterns and business models for the next generation of software. *O'Reilly*. https://www.oreilly.com/pub/a//web2/archive/what-is-web-20.html

Odone, A., Buttigieg, S., Ricciardi, W., Azzopardi-Muscat, N., & Staines, A. (2019). Public health digitalization in Europe. *European Journal of Public Health*, 29 (Supplement_3), 28–35. https://doi.org/doi.org/10.1093/eurpub/ckz161

Pagliari, C., Sloan, D., Gregor, P., Sullivan, F., Detmer, D., Kahan, J.P., Oortwijn, W., & MacGillivray, S. (2005). What is eHealth (4): a scoping exercise to map the field. *Journal of Medical Internet Research*, 7(1), e9. https://doi.org/10.2196/jmir.7.1.e9

Ruotsalainen, P., Nykanen, P., Doupi, P., Cheshire, P., Pohionen, H., & Kinnunen, J. (2003). The state of eHealth in Europe (Rep. No D1). *Stakes, Helsinki: MEDITRAV-project, EUIST, 11490.*

Siau, K., & Shen, K. (2003). Mobile communications and mobile services. *International Journal of Mobile Communications*, 1, 3–14.

Sosa-Iudicissa, M., Wootton, R., & Ferrer-Roca, O. (1998). History of telemedicine. In O. Ferrer-Roca & M. Sosa-Iudicissa (Eds.), *Handbook of Telemedicine* (pp. 1–17). Amsterdam, Berlin, Oxford, Tokyo, Washington, DC: IOS-Press.

Thuemmler, C., & Bai, C. (2017). Health 4.0: application of industry 4.0 design principles in future asthma management. In *Health 4.0: How Virtualization and Big Data Are Revolutionizing Healthcare* (pp. 23–37). Springer International Publishing. https://doi.org/10.1007/978-3-319-47617-9_2

Van De Belt, T.H., Engelen, L.J.L.P.G., Berben, S.A.A., & Schoonhoven, L. (2010). Definition of Health 2.0 and Medicine 2.0: a systematic review. *Journal of Medical Internet Research*, 12(2), e18. https://doi.org/10.2196/jmir.1350

Van Der Vaart, R., & Drossaert, C. (2017). Development of the digital health literacy instrument: measuring a broad spectrum of Health 1.0 and Health 2.0 skills. *Journal of Medical Internet Research*, 19(1), e27. https://doi.org/10.2196/jmir.6709

World Health Organization. (2005). WHA58.28. In *58 World Health Assembly*. World Health Organization.

Wittson, C., & Benschotter, R. (1972). Two-way television: helping the medical center reach out. *American Journal of Psychiatry*, 129, 625–627. https://doi.org/10.1176/ajp.129.5.62

Wolf, B., & Scholze, C. (2017). Medicine 4.0. The role of electronics, information technology and microsystems in modern medicine. *Current Directions in Biomedical Engineering*, 3(2), 183–186. https://doi.org/10.1515/cdbme-2017-0038

Wootton, R. (2006). Realtime telemedicine. In R. Wootton, J. Craig, & V. Patterson (Eds.), *Introduction to Telemedicine* (2nd Edition). London: CRC Press.

Wright, D. (1998). The International Telecommunication Union's report on Telemedicine and Developing Countries. *Journal of Telemedicine and Telecare*, 4 (Supplement_1), 75–79. https://doi.org/10.1258/1357633981931560

3 Technologies enhancing Health 4.0

Mariusz Duplaga and Szczepan Jakubowski

Introduction

Health 4.0 is a new concept that has arisen from the introduction of the strategies and technologies shaping the Fourth Industrial Revolution, which, by considering the previous phases of industrial developments, is called Industry 4.0 (Thuemmler, 2017). In this chapter, the term Health 4.0 will be used in relation to the benefits expected from applying the concepts and technologies of Industry 4.0 to medicine, healthcare, and public health. Although some authors may disagree, the distinction between Health 4.0 and Healthcare 4.0 is not clearly defined in the literature. However, it would appear that all attempts to define Health 4.0, which do not refer to the stages of industrial development, come together to the use of Industry 4.0's critical technologies (Karboub et al., 2019). According to Aceto et al. (2020), the developments attributed to Industry 4.0 arise mainly from the advances in cyber-physical systems (CPS), which can integrate computing, communication, and control systems. These advances are dependent on the pillar technologies for Industry 4.0, which include the Internet of Things (IoT), cloud and fog computing (CFC), and Big Data (BD) analytics (Aceto et al., 2020). It appears that Health 4.0 is inheriting most of the technological advances applicable to Industry 4.0, but their importance for health-related domains may vary and will depend on the specific areas of application.

Initially, this chapter presents the key technologies shaping Industry 4.0, which are relevant for Health 4.0., and then addresses the other domains of technological progress shaping the Health 4.0 environment. The use of specific technologies in the context of the 4P model for medicine and health services emphasising participatory, predictive, preventive, and personalised strategies will be discussed (Hood et al., 2004). Their importance for achieving the right care at the right time and the right place will also be emphasised.

Cyber-physical systems

The term CPS refers to integrations of computation and physical processes. Embedded computers and networks can monitor and control the physical

DOI: 10.4324/9781003144403-3

processes, usually with feedback loops where the physical processes affect computations and vice versa (Lee, 2008). In practical terms, CPS links the virtual cybernetic world with the world of physical reality (Lhotska, 2020).

Health CPS (HCPS) is a specific type of CPS that facilitates intelligent and consistent communication between medical devices and computing units (Jain et al., 2021). Haque et al. proposed a taxonomy of HCPSs based on key elements, including the application, architecture, sensing, data management, computation, communication, security and control/actuation of the system (Haque et al., 2014). Following this taxonomy, they indicated the major HCPS applications, the so called "notable applications" ranged from electronic medical records, through applications supporting daily living, enabling the monitoring of medical status to solutions for controlling the intake of medication (Haque et al., 2014). It is believed that HCPSs based on the use of cloud computing (CC) and BD analytics will provide efficient tools for addressing the challenges of heterogeneous healthcare data collected from multiple sources (Zhang et al., 2015). The data generated by devices and sensors integrated into HCPS could be analysed by machine learning (ML) methods to provide personalised therapies for patients. The infrastructure of HCPSs, essential for Health 4.0, also enables the long-term monitoring of patients at various stages of the disease and care processes, adding to the continuity of care (Sarangi et al., 2021).

The pillar technologies

Internet of Things

The IoT means "a set of smart things or objects addressed according to a unique addressing scheme and connected to the Internet through a unified framework like cloud computing" (Zainab et al., 2015). The architecture of the IoT consists of three component parts: information items, e.g. sensing or control items; an independent network; and the intelligent applications to enable control, data exchange, and data processing (Zainab et al., 2015). The IoT may be perceived as a huge network of not only interconnected things encompassing various devices, machines, but also people who can communicate with each other (Lakhwani et al., 2020). The value of the IoT for Health 4.0 relies on having the ability to connect and integrate various types of devices and items used in healthcare, including biosensors, artificial organs, smart devices, and smart drugs. The IoT facilitates interactions between smart devices to obtain information about a user and the surrounding environment, which may be critical for making health-related decisions (Santos et al., 2016). It is expected that continuing developments of the IoT will lead to advanced virtualisation of physical processes to enhance the services available in the healthcare system and provide several levels of care and support the concept of personalised medicine (Estrela et al., 2018).

Taking into consideration the variety of the technologies and processes involved, Trappey et al. (2017) identified four functional layers of the IoT:

- The perception layer – consisting of sensors and actuator devices allowing physical objects to perceive
- The transmission layer – the layer responsible for the transmission of the information collected by sensors to the upper layer
- The computation layer – in this layer, data are received, processed, decisions taken, and delivered to the application layer
- The application layer – the most advanced layer in which the information collected, processed, and transmitted from the lower layers is used. It is formed by consumers and business categories of applications allowing for the delivery of services also related to health

Several types of IoT specific for the healthcare and medicine sectors can be found in the literature. In general, the application of IoT technology in the health-related domain is called the Internet of Health Things (IoHT). This usually means the combination of mobile applications, wearables, and other specialised devices, with applications to facilitate the delivery of health services (Terry, 2016). The term Wearable Internet of Things (WIoT) is frequently applied to telemonitoring solutions employing sensors integrated into wearable devices to control physiological parameters and daily activities of people (Hiremath et al., 2014). Medical and lifestyle interventions are probably two of the most promising fields which can benefit from the significant progress being made in the WIoT. The Internet of mobile-health Things (m-IoT) relies on a low-power personal connectivity model, which enables data transfer at any time to create a global network of mobile participating entities (Istepanian et al., 2011). Finally, the Internet of Medical Things (IoMT) focuses on the use of mobile devices that function as personal hubs for the data transmitted from medical implants and wearable devices (Terry, 2016). Such an approach anticipates educational information and instructions from health provider being transmitted to patients via mobile devices in an attempt to improve their compliance with the treatment modes (Estrela et al., 2018). The Internet of Nano Things (IoNT) stems from embedding nanomachines in the environment and combining the main areas of nanomedicine, e.g. drug delivery systems or diagnostic tools, with the IoT technologies (Omanović-Mikličanin et al., 2015).

The main devices relevant to the IoHT include mobile and wearable devices with integrated biosensors. Mobile devices, smartphones, or tablets have evolved from tools used primarily for communication to become advanced multifunctional devices supporting many other activities than telephone communication. The part of the e-health domain based on the use of mobile devices for monitoring, informing, and educating patients in an attempt to improve their health is called mobile health or m-health (Silva et al., 2015). Mobile devices carried by people can be considered as personals hubs to deliver personalised medical services (Terry, 2016). For many users, mobile devices have become the main source of information about their health (Krebs & Duncan, 2015). There is a variety of mobile applications to support patients who want to manage their health, for health professionals to give access to electronic medical records, or to receive support for decisions made about their patients (O'Neill & Brady, 2012). Advances in artificial intelligence (AI) promise significant progress in the development of tools for personal health assistance based on modelling of the users' lifestyle, who will use mobile devices to support those who wish to control their nutritional behaviour, undertake physical activities, or remember their medication (Watters, 2018).

Wearables are defined as devices with electronic components embedded in items worn by the user or located directly on the user's body which, because of their small size, can be accessed and operated seamlessly in daily activities (Perera et al., 2015). The primary health-related function of such a device is to track the user's health status based on signals registered by the embedded sensors. Data acquired from the user may be transmitted through wireless connections to platforms dedicated to the provision of personalised, real-time goal-oriented feedback (Hiremath et al., 2014). The various categories of wearables are described in Chapter 4.

For the transmission of data registered by sensors to other devices and then to the monitoring centre, a reliable IoT connection network is essential (Corak et al., 2018). Depending on the connected devices, various forms of communications, technologies, protocols, and infrastructures should be used to facilitate access to the IoT and the sharing of data (Souri et al., 2019). Four main IoT connectivity solutions depending on the range, power consumption, and data rate have been identified (Alsen et al., 2017). Unlicensed connectivity solutions, e.g. Wi-Fi, Bluetooth, Zigbee, or Z-Wave, are not exclusively licenced to a particular company, and they can be used to access any IoT device, but the possible data range can differ significantly. Low-power wide-area (LPWA) connectivity provides a signal range of at least 500 m from the gateway device to the end point. Devices using LPWA can operate for years, provided that they do not collect and analyse data more frequently than once per hour. Cellular connectivity provides wide bandwidth, with average data transmission rates above 100 MBps for 5G technologies and a possible range of more than 10 km, but its use is characterised by high power consumption and high costs. Extraterrestrial connectivity is based on microwave technologies, with satellite communication being one of the best-known examples. These connections are characterised by low-to-medium bandwidth, high range, and high costs (Alsen et al., 2017).

Cloud and fog computing

The National Institute of Standards and Technology (NIST) of the US Department of Commerce described CC as a system "enabling ubiquitous, convenient, on-demand network access to a shared pool of configurable computing resources (e.g., networks, servers, storage, applications and services) that can be rapidly provisioned and released with minimal management effort or service provider interaction" (Mell & Grance, 2011). CC may be perceived as a cluster of services, including access to hardware, software, and data, enabling the user to execute their own applications. Such a model for accessing information technology (IT) infrastructure increases and simplifies the operations because the user, e.g. healthcare institution, only pays for the actual use of the resources (Sultan, 2014). It must be remembered that in many cases, legal requirements specific to the healthcare sector preclude the use of common cloud services, so it is necessary for special cloud-based infrastructure to be developed (Gia et al., 2015).

A variant of CC is fog computing (FC), in which services are moved to a network, also called an edge network, close to the users' devices (Yousefpour et al., 2019). FC is characterised by the partial use of the users' devices, such as those belonging to a medical facility. Distributing the system capacity between the end users' devices and the traditional centres results in several benefits, including short latency of data transfer, rapid response, local security, improved scalability, and enhanced performance of the total system (Vaquero & Rodero-Merino, 2014). The use of FC results in improved timing of service delivery and reduced costs compared to the use of CC (Kumari et al., 2018). CC can exploit the potential of IoT for processing and integrating data from mobile and smart devices and sensors (Aceto et al., 2020). The use of CC and FC advances the processing of large amounts of medical data and the provision of the required services anywhere and anytime in line with the requirements of the Health 4.0 concept (Botta et al., 2016).

Big data analytics and artificial intelligence

Initially, the term "Big Data" (BD) was applied to describe the enormous data sets that were very difficult to process and store using the currently available computing facilities. BD may include information that is structured, semi-structured, or unstructured. In addition, the relationships existing between the data may be very complex considering its syntactic, semantic, social, cultural, economic, or organisational context (Benke & Benke, 2018). Currently, the term "BD analytics" is used frequently to address the technology designed to rapidly process and analyse large amounts of miscellaneous data (Gantz & Reinsel, 2011). Significant progress in BD analytics is associated with the development of efficient methods of AI, the growth of social media generating large data sets, and the rapid reduction of the cost of processors, which consequently give easier access to high computing power (Benke & Benke, 2018).

Typical attributes of BD are described as the "Five Vs" (Kalbandi & Anuradha, 2015):

1 Volume – the volume of data sets, which is constantly growing
2 Velocity – data capture and analysis need to be very rapid because of limited time

3 Variety – the data in the available collections ranges from primary unstructured to secondary partially or fully processed
4 Veracity – according to its provenance, management, and processing, data has varying degrees of trustworthiness
5 Value – the key task related to BD analytics is to extract value from vast amounts of data

The healthcare sector generates huge amounts of heterogeneous data. The application of BD analytics to the data may bring substantial benefits to enhance diagnosis and the selection of effective personalised therapy. For example, the strategies used in precision medicine, which rely on DNA profiling and the development of personalised treatment, are dependent on the efficient handling of vast amounts of data (Rubin, 2016).

AI is a generic term for a machine, or a process, that responds to environmental stimuli or new data and modifies its operation in order to maximise its performance index (Benke & Benke, 2018). Learning process is an inherent element of AI models and encompasses an interactive procedure of training on data with adjustments of the applied parameters to achieve the lowest possible difference between the predictions produced by the model and the experimental data. Currently, AI is perceived as a key approach for the handling of BD, particularly that generated in medicine and healthcare (Mesko 2017). It opens the possibility of moving from a level of descriptive processing of medical data to the level of predictive analysis, especially with technologies such as ML and deep learning (DL) (Lewis et al., 2019). Ioppolo et al. (2020) emphasised that in Health 4.0, AI will be used to achieve flexibility and the personalisation of high-quality therapies for patients. Applying AI to very large data sets brings the promise of achieving the paradigms of patient-centred and precision medicine (Mesko, 2017).

Further advances in AI, applied for diagnosis and seeking the optimum modes of therapy, are supported by the potential of the IoT to integrate data flowing from multiple sensors and other sources (Benke & Benke, 2018). Processing data generated from the IoT and their integration with that obtained from medical diagnostic procedures and healthcare is beyond the capability of health professionals, and it seems inevitable that AI will be used for this purpose.

ML may be understood as "a program that learns to automatically perform a task or make a decision based on data, rather than having the behaviour explicitly programmed" (Beam & Kohane, 2018). Thus, the main aim of ML is to discover patterns in the data that would allow for tracing and the prediction of trends and schemes. ML is already used to create analytical models enabling the extraction of features that can be applied to medical diagnosis, selecting the optimum therapy, or conducting epidemic surveillance on large data sets accumulated by healthcare entities (Wong & Bressler, 2016). The most common ML scenarios are supervised and unsupervised learning

(Mohri et al., 2018). In supervised learning, a learning algorithm receives a set of training data, which consist of labelled examples, and then makes predictions for unseen points. In unsupervised learning, only unlabelled training data are provided, and then predictions are made for all unseen points. Other ML scenarios include semi-supervised learning, transductive inference, online, reinforcement, and active learning (Mohri et al., 2018). It seems that supervised learning, rather than unsupervised learning, is better for clinical applications as it enables the optimum therapy or the probability of contracting an infectious disease to be predicted (Chen et al., 2017).

Unsupervised learning is used when the priority is to find the patterns in data sets without prior knowledge. In the health context, it may be feasible for grouping patients with similar characteristics into clusters, e.g. to distinguish various phenotypes of a disease (Kwon et al., 2014; Miotto et al., 2016). There are expectations that ML will be used to automatically classify patients according to the feasibility of diagnostic procedures or therapeutic methods (Jha & Topol, 2016).

In the case of complex data sets, a DL approach can be applied. DL is a subtype of representation learning which aims to describe complex data representations using simpler hierarchised structures defined from a set of specific features (Montagnon et al., 2020). DL is a subset of ML that is able to obtain multilevel representations from raw input data without the need for time-consuming, manual features labelling (Cui et al., 2020). Such an approach finds extensive use in medical image analysis but can also be applied for analysing structured and unstructured data in other healthcare areas, e.g. to process aggregated electronic health record data, to capture the internal structure of data sets generated by high-throughput biological methods, or to analyse data generated by sensors embedded in wearables and smartphones (Miotto et al., 2018).

Other technologies shaping the Health 4.0 environment

Blockchain technology

Blockchain technology owes its popularity to the development of cryptocurrencies such as Bitcoin or Ethereum. Blockchains are models for storing and sharing data in a distributed, transparent, permanent manner. The innovation related to blockchain technology lies in the omission of intermediaries and the decentralisation of the transaction checking process (Mistry et al., 2020). Modern healthcare systems using the technologies incorporated into the Health 4.0 concept are characterised by high complexity and operational costs. It is believed that improvements to the flow, storage, and use of data from electronic medical records will lead to considerable savings. The use of blockchain infrastructure in healthcare systems would considerably simplify the authentication procedures (Tanwar et al., 2020). According to Tanwar et al. (2020), a broader introduction of blockchain solutions to the healthcare sector will lead to increased interoperability of medical databases and optimisation of access to patients' data.

It appears that blockchain technology has the potential to address a number of challenges facing the healthcare sector, such as authentication, the integrity of medical systems, sharing of medical records, interoperability, IoT security, and protection of edge (patient-owned) devices (McGhin et al., 2019).

Robotic systems

Robots were first used in surgery for performing guided brain tumour biopsies in the 1980s (Troccaz, 2013). Robotic systems were then developed for transurethral resection of prostate glands (Puma 560) and for orthopaedic surgery (ROBODOC). In the early 2000s, the Da Vinci system was introduced and is still in use. The main motivation for using robotic surgical systems has been the desire to reduce the invasiveness of procedures. In the last decade, small robots dedicated to specific indications have been developed. Today various robotic systems are utilised in many areas of medicine and healthcare other than surgery.

Kyrarini et al. (2021) distinguished several categories of non-surgical robots:

- Care robots – used for delivery or assisting people in patient care
- Hospital robots – include robotic nursing assistants helping to perform non-critical tasks, robots helping in transportation, and laboratory robots designed to support medical staff in tasks such as loading and unloading centrifuges or sorting test tubes
- Assistive robots – introduced to support people with disabilities for performing everyday tasks
- Rehabilitation robots – aiding humans with physical impairments during the rehabilitation
- Walking assisting robots – supporting people with impaired walking ability.

Many of the functionalities described above are integrated into socially assistive humanoid robots, which are considered as a promising technology for meeting the health and social needs of an ageing population (Papadopoulos et al., 2020).

The use of robots became particularly important during the COVID-19 pandemic. Common tasks performed by robots include the disinfection of hospital and outdoor spaces and the delivery of medication and supplies to the patient care areas. The exposure of the medical staff to contagious agents can be reduced by using wheeled telepresence robots to facilitate virtual face-to-face patient assessment or even performing diagnostic testing (Tavakoli et al., 2020).

Virtual reality and augmented reality

In 1992, Steuer (1992) proposed that "virtual reality" (VR) should be defined without a reference to specific hardware systems as "a real or simulated environment in which a perceiver experiences telepresence". Augmented reality (AR) is a technique that enables additional information about the real world to be shown by overlaying virtual elements (Kaplan et al., 2020). The techniques on the continuum between reality and VR ("virtuality continuum"), including AR, are called mixed reality (Milgram & Kishino, 1994). It seems that the renewed interest in these techniques is associated with the progress in graphic processing units, tracking technologies, and display technologies (Sutherland et al., 2019). Both VR and AR have been explored for educational purposes in medicine, e.g. for motor skill training (Joda et al., 2019) and areas of medical application, including medical image diagnosis, surgical planning, and navigation (Sutherland et al., 2019). Interventions based on VR and AR are also used in therapeutic interventions, e.g. for pain relief, therapy of eating disorders, phobias, or post-traumatic stress disorder, and for cognitive and motor rehabilitation (Sutherland et al., 2019).

3D printing

The concept of precision medicine means moving from common therapeutic strategies used for all patients to therapies that are adjusted to the characteristics of the individual patient. Progress in the field of three-dimensional printing (3DP; or additive manufacturing) enables the implementation of precision medicine by providing patient-specific implants, the controlled delivery of pharmaceutical agents, or even patient-specific in vitro models for drug screening (Prendergast & Burdick, 2020).

3DP employs various printing techniques and a variety of construction materials, e.g. plastic or thermoplastic materials, solutions, photopolymers, and powders (Jamróz et al., 2018). In the pharmaceutical industry, it is used for the development of patient-centred dosage forms based on structure design (Jamróz et al., 2018). Bioprinting, a subcategory of 3DP, can be used to print structures with viable cells, biomaterials, or biological materials (Murphy & Atala, 2014). The aim of bioprinting is to deliver products that can replace autologous or allogeneic tissue implants. It may also lead to the avoidance of tests on animals during research on the disease pathology or the development of pharmaceutical agents (Kačarević et al., 2018).

The real-life use of 3DP depends on the area of application. In dentistry, it appears that 3DP is almost routinely used to produce high-precision personalised prostheses or models (Liaw & Guvendiren, 2017). 3D printed models are useful to enable a better understanding of anatomical conditions to be obtained before surgical procedures are carried out. They have the advantage over 3D virtual models by providing tactile feedback to surgeons (Pugliese et al., 2018). The next aim for 3DP in surgery is the broader use of personalised instrumentations and implants (Kumar et al., 2020). According to Spencer and Kay Watts (2020), the most common applications of 3DP in medicine include the development of 3D models for use in radiation therapy and medical dosimetry and surgery planning. Customised 3D printed implants have a growing role in prosthetics. Finally, 3D printed models are used ever more widely for medical and patient education (Spencer & Kay Watts, 2020).

Conclusions

The key technologies contributing to the Fourth Industrial Revolution include CPS and three pillar technologies of Industry 4.0, the IoT, CC, and BD. However, the concept of Health 4.0 cannot be limited to these technologies. It is not only the matter of new technology but also the processes implemented for the delivery of products and services. Depending on the area of healthcare, medicine, or public health, specific solutions can be indicated. To show the versatility of innovative health-related domain, also robotic solutions bringing closer the integration of cyber- and physical systems, advanced visualisation techniques with the potential of further enhancement of health services as well as 3DP providing a new quality of medication delivery or the development of biostructures are discussed.

References

Aceto, G., Persico, V., & Pescapé, A. (2020). Industry 4.0 and health: Internet of Things, Big Data, and cloud computing for Healthcare 4.0. *Journal of Industrial Information Integration, 18*, 100129. https://doi.org/10.1016/j.jii.2020.100129

Alsen, D., Patel, M., & Shangkuan, J. (2017). *The Future of Connectivity: Enabling the Internet of Things*. McKinsey & Company. Available online at https://www.mckinsey.com/featured-insights/internet-ofthings/our-insights/the-future-of-connectivity-enabling-the-internet-ofthings.

Beam, A. L., & Kohane, I. S. (2018). Big data and machine learning in health care. *JAMA – Journal of the American Medical Association, 319*(13), 1317–1318. https://doi.org/10.1001/jama.2017.18391

Benke, K., & Benke, G. (2018). Artificial intelligence and big data in public health. *International Journal of Environmental Research and Public Health, 15*(12), 2796. https://doi.org/10.3390/ijerph15122796

Botta, A., de Donato, W., Persico, V., & Pescapé, A. (2016). Integration of cloud computing and Internet of Things: A survey. *Future Generation Computer Systems, 56*, 684–700. https://doi.org/10.1016/j.future.2015.09.021

Chen, M., Hao, Y., Hwang, K., Wang, L., & Wang, L. (2017). Disease prediction by machine learning over big data from healthcare communities. *IEEE Access, 5*, 8869–8879. https://doi.org/10.1109/ACCESS.2017.2694446

Corak, B. H., Okay, F. Y., Guzel, M., Murt, S., & Özdemir, S. (2018). Comparative analysis of IoT communication protocols. *2018 International Symposium on Networks, Computers and Communications (ISNCC)*. https://doi.org/10.1109/ISNCC.2018.8530963

Cui, S., Tseng, H.-H., Pakela, J., Haken, R. K. T., & Naqa, I. E. (2020). Introduction to machine and deep learning for medical physicists. *Medical Physics*, 47(5), e127–e147. https://doi.org/10.1002/mp.14140

Estrela, V. V., Monteiro, A. C. B., França, R. P., Iano, Y., Khelassi, A., & Razmjooy, N. (2018). Health 4.0: Applications, management, technologies and review. *Medical Technologies Journal, 2*(4), 262–276. https://doi.org/10.26415/2572-004X-vol2iss4p262-276

Gantz, J., & Reinsel, D. (2011). Extracting value from chaos. *IDC's Digital Universe Study, Sponsored by EMC*, 12, 1–12.

Gia, T. N., Jiang, M., Rahmani, A., Westerlund, T., Liljeberg, P., & Tenhunen, H. (2015). Fog computing in healthcare Internet of Things: A case study on ECG feature extraction. *2015 IEEE International Conference on Computer and Information Technology; Ubiquitous Computing and Communications; Dependable, Autonomic and Secure Computing; Pervasive Intelligence and Computing*, 356–363. https://doi.org/10.1109/CIT/IUCC/DASC/PICOM.2015.51

Haque, S. A., Aziz, S. M., & Rahman, M. (2014). Review of Cyber-Physical System in Healthcare. *International Journal of Distributed Sensor Networks, 10*(4), 217415. https://doi.org/10.1155/2014/217415

Hiremath, S., Yang, G., & Mankodiya, K. (2014). Wearable Internet of Things: Concept, architectural components and promises for person-centered healthcare. *2014 4th International Conference on Wireless Mobile Communication and Healthcare – Transforming Healthcare Through Innovations in Mobile and Wireless Technologies (MOBIHEALTH)*, 304–307. https://doi.org/10.1109/MOBIHEALTH.2014.7015971

Hood, L., Heath, J. R., Phelps, M. E., & Lin, B. (2004). Systems biology and new technologies enable predictive and preventative medicine. *Science, 306*(5696), 640–643. https://doi.org/10.1126/science.1104635

Ioppolo, G., Vazquez, F., Hennerici, M. G., & Andrès, E. (2020). Medicine 4.0: New technologies as tools for a Society 5.0. *Journal of Clinical Medicine, 9*(7). https://doi.org/10.3390/jcm9072198

Istepanian, R. S. H., Hu, S., Philip, N. Y., & Sungoor, A. (2011). The potential of Internet of m-health Things "m-IoT" for non-invasive glucose level sensing. *2011 Annual International Conference of the IEEE Engineering in Medicine and Biology Society*, 5264–5266. https://doi.org/10.1109/IEMBS.2011.6091302

Jain, R., Gupta, M., Nayyar, A., & Sharma, N. (2021). Adoption of fog computing in Healthcare 4.0. In S. Tanwar (Ed.), *Fog Computing for Healthcare 4.0 Environments: Technical, Societal, and Future Implications* (pp. 3–36). Springer International Publishing. https://doi.org/10.1007/978-3-030-46197-3_1

Jamróz, W., Szafraniec, J., Kurek, M., & Jachowicz, R. (2018). 3D printing in pharmaceutical and medical applications – Recent achievements and challenges. *Pharmaceutical Research, 35*(9), 176. https://doi.org/10.1007/s11095-018-2454-x

Jha, S., & Topol, E. J. (2016). Adapting to artificial intelligence: Radiologists and pathologists as information specialists. *JAMA, 316*(22), 2353–2354. https://doi.org/10.1001/jama.2016.17438

Joda, T., Gallucci, G. O., Wismeijer, D., & Zitzmann, N. U. (2019). Augmented and virtual reality in dental medicine: A systematic review. *Computers in Biology and Medicine, 108*, 93–100. https://doi.org/10.1016/j.compbiomed.2019.03.012

Kačarević, Ž. P., Rider, P. M., Alkildani, S., Retnasingh, S., Smeets, R., Jung, O., Ivanišević, Z., & Barbeck, M. (2018). An introduction to 3D bioprinting: Possibilities, challenges and future aspects. *Materials, 11*(11), 2199. https://doi.org/10.3390/ma11112199

Kalbandi, I., & Anuradha, J. (2015). A brief introduction on big data 5Vs characteristics and Hadoop technology. *Procedia Computer Science, 48*, 319–324. https://doi.org/10.1016/j.procs.2015.04.188

Kaplan, A. D., Cruit, J., Endsley, M., Beers, S. M., Sawyer, B. D., & Hancock, P. A. (2020). The effects of virtual reality, augmented reality, and mixed reality as training enhancement methods: A meta-analysis. *Human Factors*. https://doi.org/10.1177/0018720820904229

Karboub, K., Tabaa, M., Dandache, A., Dellagi, S., & Moutaouakkil, F. (2019, December 20). Toward Health 4.0: Challenges and Opportunities. *The 8th International Conference on Innovation and New Trends in Information Technology*. Tangier, Morocco.

Krebs, P., & Duncan, D. T. (2015). Health app use among US mobile phone owners: A national survey. *JMIR MHealth and UHealth*, *3*(4). Scopus.https://doi.org/10.2196/mhealth.4924

Kumar, P., Vatsya, P., Rajnish, R. K., Hooda, A., & Dhillon, M. S. (2020). Application of 3D printing in hip and knee arthroplasty: A narrative review. *Indian Journal of Orthopaedics*. https://doi.org/10.1007/s43465-020-00263-8

Kumari, A., Tanwar, S., Tyagi, S., & Kumar, N. (2018). Fog computing for Healthcare 4.0 environment: Opportunities and challenges. *Computers & Electrical Engineering*, *72*, 1–13. https://doi.org/10.1016/j.compeleceng.2018.08.015

Kwon, Y., Kang, K., & Bae, C. (2014). Unsupervised learning for human activity recognition using smartphone sensors. *Expert Systems with Applications*, *41*(14), 6067–6074. Scopus. https://doi.org/10.1016/j.eswa.2014.04.037

Kyrarini, M., Lygerakis, F., Rajavenkatanarayanan, A., Sevastopoulos, C., Nambiappan, H. R., Chaitanya, K. K., Babu, A. R., Mathew, J., & Makedon, F. (2021). A survey of robots in healthcare. *Technologies*, *9*(1), 8. https://doi.org/10.3390/technologies9010008

Lakhwani, K., Gianey, H. K., Wireko, J. K., & Hiran, K. K. (2020). *Internet of Things (IoT): Principles, Paradigms and Applications of IoT.* Bpb Publications. https://vbn.aau.dk/en/publications/internet-of-things-iot-principles-paradigms-and-applications-of-i

Lee, E. A. (2008). Cyber physical systems: Design challenges. *11th IEEE International Symposium on Object and Component-Oriented Real-Time Distributed Computing (ISORC)*, 363–369. https://doi.org/10.1109/ISORC.2008.25

Lewis, S. J., Gandomkar, Z., & Brennan, P. C. (2019). Artificial intelligence in medical imaging practice: Looking to the future. *Journal of Medical Radiation Sciences*, *66*(4), 292–295. https://doi.org/10.1002/jmrs.369

Lhotska, L. (2020). Application of Industry 4.0 concept to health care. *Studies in Health Technology and Informatics*, *273*, 23–37. https://doi.org/10.3233/SHTI200613

Liaw, C.-Y., & Guvendiren, M. (2017). Current and emerging applications of 3D printing in medicine. *Biofabrication*, *9*(2), 024102. https://doi.org/10.1088/1758-5090/aa7279

McGhin, T., Choo, K.-K. R., Liu, C. Z., & He, D. (2019). Blockchain in healthcare applications: Research challenges and opportunities. *Journal of Network and Computer Applications*, *135*, 62–75. https://doi.org/10.1016/j.jnca.2019.02.027

Mell, P., & Grance, T. (2011). *The NIST Definition of Cloud Computing* (NIST Special Publication (SP) 800-145). National Institute of Standards and Technology. https://doi.org/10.6028/NIST.SP.800-145

Mesko, B. (2017). The role of artificial intelligence in precision medicine. *Expert Review of Precision Medicine and Drug Development*, *2*(5), 239–241. https://doi.org/10.1080/23808993.2017.1380516

Milgram, P., & Kishino, F. (1994). A taxonomy of mixed reality visual displays. *IEICE Transactions on Information and Systems*, *77*, 1321–1329. https://www.semanticscholar.org/paper/A-Taxonomy-of-Mixed-Reality-Visual-Displays-Milgram-Kishino/f78a31be8874eda176a5244c645289be9f1d4317

Miotto, R., Li, L., & Dudley, J. T. (2016). Deep learning to predict patient future diseases from the electronic health records. *Lecture Notes in Computer Science (Including Subseries Lecture Notes in Artificial Intelligence and Lecture Notes in Bioinformatics)*, *9626*, 768–774. Scopus. https://doi.org/10.1007/978-3-319-30671-1_66

Miotto, R., Wang, F., Wang, S., Jiang, X., & Dudley, J. T. (2018). Deep learning for healthcare: Review, opportunities and challenges. *Briefings in Bioinformatics*, *19*(6), 1236–1246. https://doi.org/10.1093/bib/bbx044

Mistry, I., Tanwar, S., Tyagi, S., & Kumar, N. (2020). Blockchain for 5G-enabled IoT for industrial automation: A systematic review, solutions, and challenges. *Mechanical Systems and Signal Processing*, *135*, 106382. https://doi.org/10.1016/j.ymssp.2019.106382

Mohri, M., Rostamizadeh, A., & Talwalkar, A. (2018). *Foundations of Machine Learning* (2nd edition). MIT Press.

Montagnon, E., Cerny, M., Cadrin-Chênevert, A., Hamilton V., Derennes, T., Ilinca, A., Vandenbroucke-Menu, F., Turcotte, S., Kadoury, S., & Tang, A. (2020). Deep learning workflow in radiology: A primer. *Insights into Imaging*, *11*. https://doi.org/10.1186/s13244-019-0832-5

Murphy, S. V., & Atala, A. (2014). 3D bioprinting of tissues and organs. *Nature Biotechnology*, *32*(8), 773–785. https://doi.org/10.1038/nbt.2958

Omanović-Mikličanin, E., Maksimović, M., & Vujović, V. (2015). The future of healthcare: Nanomedicine and Internet of Nano Things. *Folia Medica Facultatis Medicinae Universitatis Saraeviensis*, *50*(1), Article 1. http://www.foliamedica.mf.unsa.ba/index.php/FM/article/view/33

O'Neill, S., & Brady, R. R. W. (2012). Colorectal smartphone apps: Opportunities and risks. *Colorectal Disease: The Official Journal of the Association of Coloproctology of Great Britain and Ireland*, *14*(9), e530–534. https://doi.org/10.1111/j.1463-1318.2012.03088.x

Papadopoulos, I., Koulouglioti, C., Lazzarino, R., & Ali, S. (2020). Enablers and barriers to the implementation of socially assistive humanoid robots in health and social care: A systematic review. *BMJ Open*, *10*(1), e033096. https://doi.org/10.1136/bmjopen-2019-033096

Perera, C., Liu, C. H., & Jayawardena, S. (2015). The emerging Internet of Things marketplace from an industrial perspective: A survey. *IEEE Transactions on Emerging Topics in Computing*, *3*(4), 585–598. https://doi.org/10.1109/TETC.2015.2390034

Prendergast, M. E., & Burdick, J. A. (2020). Recent advances in enabling technologies in 3D printing for precision medicine. *Advanced Materials*, *32*(13), 1902516. https://doi.org/10.1002/adma.201902516

Pugliese, L., Marconi, S., Negrello, E., Mauri, V., Peri, A., Gallo, V., Auricchio, F., & Pietrabissa, A. (2018). The clinical use of 3D printing in surgery. *Updates in Surgery*, *70*(3), 381–388. https://doi.org/10.1007/s13304-018-0586-5

Rubin, R. (2016). A precision medicine approach to clinical trials. *JAMA*, *316*(19), 1953–1955. https://doi.org/10.1001/jama.2016.12137

Santos, J., Rodrigues, J. J. P. C., Silva, B. M. C., Casal, J., Saleem, K., & Denisov, V. (2016). An IoT-based mobile gateway for intelligent personal assistants on mobile health environments. *Journal of Network and Computer Applications*, *71*, 194–204. https://doi.org/10.1016/j.jnca.2016.03.014

Sarangi, A. K., Mohapatra, A. G., Mishra, T. C., & Keswani, B. (2021). Healthcare 4.0: A voyage of fog computing with IOT, cloud computing, big data, and machine learning. In S. Tanwar (Ed.), *Fog Computing for Healthcare 4.0 Environments: Technical, Societal, and Future Implications* (pp. 177–210). Springer International Publishing. https://doi.org/10.1007/978-3-030-46197-3_8

Silva, B. M., Rodrigues, J. J., de la Torre Díez, I., López-Coronado, M., & Saleem, K. (2015). Mobile-health: A review of current state in 2015. *Journal of biomedical informatics*, 56, 265–272.

Souri, A., Hussien, A., Hoseyninezhad, M., & Norouzi, M. (2019). A systematic review of IoT communication strategies for an efficient smart environment. *Transactions on Emerging Telecommunications Technologies, e3736*(n/a), 1–19. https://doi.org/10.1002/ett.3736

Spencer, S. R., & Kay Watts, L. (2020). Three-dimensional printing in medical and allied health practice: A literature review. *Journal of Medical Imaging and Radiation Sciences, 51*(3), 489–500. https://doi.org/10.1016/j.jmir.2020.06.003

Steuer, J. (1992). Defining virtual reality: Dimensions determining telepresence. *Journal of Communication, 42*(4), 73–93. https://doi.org/10.1111/j.1460-2466.1992.tb00812.x

Sultan, N. (2014). Making use of cloud computing for healthcare provision: Opportunities and challenges. *International Journal of Information Management, 34*(2), 177–184. https://doi.org/10.1016/j.ijinfomgt.2013.12.011

Sutherland, J., Belec, J., Sheikh, A., Chepelev, L., Althobaity, W., Chow, B. J. W., Mitsouras, D., Christensen, A., Rybicki, F. J., & La Russa, D. J. (2019). Applying modern virtual and augmented reality technologies to medical images and models. *Journal of Digital Imaging, 32*(1), 38–53. https://doi.org/10.1007/s10278-018-0122-7

Tanwar, S., Parekh, K., & Evans, R. (2020). Blockchain-based electronic healthcare record system for Healthcare 4.0 applications. *Journal of Information Security and Applications, 50*, 102407. https://doi.org/10.1016/j.jisa.2019.102407

Tavakoli, M., Carriere, J., & Torabi, A. (2020). Robotics, smart wearable technologies, and autonomous intelligent systems for healthcare during the COVID-19 pandemic: An analysis of the state of the art and future vision. *Advanced Intelligent Systems, 2*(7), 2000071. https://doi.org/10.1002/aisy.202000071

Terry, N. P. (2016). Will the Internet of Things transform healthcare. *Vanderbilt Journal of Entertainment & Technology Law, 19*, 327. http://dx.doi.org/10.2139/ssrn.2760447

Thuemmler, C. (2017). The case for Health 4.0. In C. Thuemmler & C. Bai (Eds.), *Health 4.0: How Virtualization and Big Data Are Revolutionizing Healthcare* (pp. 1–22). Springer International Publishing. https://doi.org/10.1007/978-3-319-47617-9_1

Trappey, A. J. C., Trappey, C. V., Hareesh Govindarajan, U., Chuang, A. C., & Sun, J. J. (2017). A review of essential standards and patent landscapes for the Internet of Things: A key enabler for Industry 4.0. *Advanced Engineering Informatics, 33*, 208–229. https://doi.org/10.1016/j.aei.2016.11.007

Troccaz, J. (Ed.). (2013). *Medical Robotics* (1st edition). London: John Wiley & Sons.

Vaquero, L. M., & Rodero-Merino, L. (2014). Finding your way in the fog: Towards a comprehensive definition of fog computing. *ACM SIGCOMM Computer Communication Review, 44*(5), 27–32. https://doi.org/10.1145/2677046.2677052

Watters, S. (2018). *Powered by AI: Technology, Digital Health, and a New Era of Care.* Medium. https://medium.com/gene-global/powered-by-ai-technology-digital-health-and-a-new-era-of-care-a55e34cfd118

Wong, T. Y., & Bressler, N. M. (2016). Artificial intelligence with deep learning technology looks into diabetic retinopathy screening. *JAMA, 316*(22), 2366–2367. https://doi.org/10.1001/jama.2016.17563

Yousefpour, A., Fung, C., Nguyen, T., Kadiyala, K., Jalali, F., Niakanlahiji, A., Kong, J., & Jue, J. P. (2019). All one needs to know about fog computing and related edge computing paradigms: A complete survey. *Journal of Systems Architecture, 98*, 289–330. https://doi.org/10.1016/j.sysarc.2019.02.009

Zainab, H., Hesham, A., & Mahmoud, M. (2015). Internet of Things (IoT): Definitions, challenges and recent research directions. *International Journal of Computer Applications*, *128*(1), 37–47. https://doi.org/10.5120/ijca2015906430

Zhang, Y., Qiu, M., Tsai, C., Hassan, M. M., & Alamri, A. (2015). Health-CPS: Healthcare cyber-physical system assisted by cloud and big data. *IEEE Systems Journal*, *11*(1), 88–95. https://doi.org/10.1109/JSYST.2015.2460747

4 The landscape of Health 4.0

Areas of application

Mariusz Duplaga

Introduction

The key technologies incorporated in Health 4.0 have been presented in Chapter 3. Their inclusion was dictated by their importance for the development of Health 4.0 and their relationship with the Fourth Industrial Revolution. The technologies perceived as key components of Industry 4.0 have been addressed, and those more specific for healthcare were included.

In this chapter, the advances related to the Health 4.0 concept are presented for areas of medicine and public health, selected arbitrarily by the author, after considering their significance for healthcare applications to overcome medical or public health problems. In addition, the perceptions of healthcare stakeholders, patients, and medical professionals are addressed. The range of technology-based solutions related to the Health 4.0 domain is too wide to be adequately considered in one chapter, and other authors could discuss other applications and systems for this context.

The decision to take the perspective of medical or health problems to present the potential of Health 4.0 is because specific components of Industry 4.0 are relevant, such as the Internet of Things (IoT), Big Data (BD) analytics, artificial intelligence (AI), or cyber-physical systems (CPS), in various sectors of medicine and public health. For example, AI is being used for diagnosis based on medical imaging or next-generation sequencing and for the discovery of patterns in the course of chronic diseases and decision-making. IoT offers fascinating opportunities for long-term monitoring of patients with chronic conditions, the realisation of the concept of ambient assisted living (AAL), as well as providing support for a healthy lifestyle in the general population.

4P medicine

The concept of "P4 medicine" assumes that medicine should be predictive, preventive, personalised, and participatory. This concept was introduced by Hood et al. (2004) in the early 2000s following developments in the field of systems medicine. Systems medicine is understood to be "the application of

DOI: 10.4324/9781003144403-4

system biology to the challenge of human disease" (Flores et al., 2013). Flores et al. (2013) emphasised that P4 medicine emerged as a result of progress in three domains: systems biology and systems medicine; consumer-driven healthcare; and the social network and digital revolution.

According to Hood (2003), biology should be perceived as an informational science because computer science, mathematics, and statistics are essential tools for modern biology. The realisation of the important role of information technologies for discoveries in biology and medicine was triggered by the achievements of the Human Genome Project announced in the early 2000s (International Human Genome Sequencing Consortium, 2001).

One of the main concepts of the 4P model is personalised medicine. Schleidgen et al. (2013) recognised that personalised medicine had been vaguely defined for a long time, but the need for holistic care and treatment targeted at stratified subgroups had been frequently addressed. Based on the findings of an extensive systematic review, these authors proposed the following definition: "personalised medicine seeks to improve stratification and timing of health care by utilising biological information and biomarkers on the level of molecular disease pathways, genetics, proteomics as well as metabolomics" (Schleidgen et al., 2013).

The environment of Health 4.0, with its key concepts and technologies, is well suited for the implementation of the 4P model of medicine. The advances attributed to Health 4.0 include the increasing use of AI algorithms for disease prediction and the personalised approach based on the analysis of BD obtained from next-generation sequencing (NGS) and medical imaging modalities as well as other types of data collected in electronic health records and during large clinical trials.

Oncology is frequently indicated as a field in which both the BD approach and the use of AI may be particularly useful (Dlamini et al., 2020). AI and computational methods facilitate the time-effective extraction of relevant information from NGS data sets (Baro et al., 2015). The use of AI enhances diagnosis in various modalities of medical imaging, from X-ray and ultrasounds scanning, through computed tomography, magnetic resonance imaging, and positron emission tomography to digital pathology (Dlamini et al., 2020). Recent reports indicate that AI may be a real-time supporting tool for the enhanced detection of neoplastic lesions during endoscopy (Mori et al., 2021; Wu et al., 2021).

AI is used for the automated analysis of medical imaging data, including data processing, automated detection, disease stratification, and the optimisation of prescribed therapy (Dlamini et al., 2020). One of the most widely known medical AI-based solutions used for decision support in oncological treatment is IBM's "Watson for Oncology" (Garcia & Uzbelger, 2020). A systematic review prepared by Huang et al. (2019) showed that AI based on machine learning (ML) had been already applied in the diagnosis and prognosis of many types of tumours.

Bi et al. (2019) identified three categories of image-based clinical tasks in which AI tools may be used: the detection of abnormalities; the characterisation of a suspected lesion by defining its shape, volume, histopathologic diagnosis, the stage of a disease, and its molecular profile; and the determination of prognosis or response to treatment. The authors commented that most studies evaluating AI applications in oncology had not been extensively validated for reproducibility or generalisation. However, their review showed that efforts to employ AI technology for clinical use are increasing (Bi et al., 2019).

In other fields of medicine, the application of AI is increasingly common. In cardiology, one of the first applications of AI was the early detection of atrial fibrillation. In 2014, the US Food and Drug Administration approved a mobile application for electrocardiogram (ECG) monitoring in which a multicentre study showed it was effective in detecting atrial fibrillation (Halcox et al., 2017). Other examples of AI-based solutions in cardiology include applications for predicting the risk of cardiovascular disease (Jamthikar et al., 2019), readmissions (Mortazavi et al., 2016), mortality related to heart failure (Adler et al., 2020), and the early detection of aortic aneurysms (Li et al., 2018). In addition, there are numerous examples of AI being used to support point-of-care ultrasonography (POCUS) (Seetharam et al., 2019). Recently, a mobile application for using AI to improve the diagnostic ability of heart auscultation was proposed (Guven et al., 2021). There are many other examples of AI being applied in other medical fields. In respiratory medicine, AI was applied for the analysis of pulmonary function tests (Delclaux, 2019), in diabetology for predicting changes in the level of blood glucose (Lawton et al., 2018) and in neurology for detecting the likelihood of seizures occurring in epileptic patients (Regalia et al., 2019).

It must be recognised that, despite many promising reports on the possibility of applying AI to process and interpretation of data obtained from patients, the validation and replication of individual studies is a challenge. Additionally, there are reservations about the quality of the studies on the use of AI in a clinical context (Briganti & Le Moine, 2020).

Remote monitoring

Demographic changes and the epidemiological transformation in the 20th century resulted in higher life expectancy but also increased prevalence of long-term diseases. Currently, one of the greatest challenges for healthcare systems is the provision of care to patients with chronic conditions. These patients require regular interactions with their healthcare providers and, in cases of disease exacerbation, may require admission to a hospital. The successful management of a patient's chronic disease relies on the long-term monitoring of its severity, adherence to the prescribed treatment, and efficient communication with the healthcare providers. The critical measures which should be monitored when following the course of chronic disease are defined by national and international guidelines. For example, blood glucose is assessed in patients with diabetes, peak expiratory flow in those with chronic pulmonary disorders associated with airway obstruction, and blood pressure and body weight for those with congestive heart failure. The involvement of patients in the monitoring and treatment of the disease is an essential requirement for ensuring adequate care.

The challenges resulting from chronic conditions may be partially addressed with the tools available in the e-health environment. Remote monitoring is one of the key technologies for enhancing the quality of care of those with chronic conditions. Health-related remote monitoring can be defined as the transmission of the data of a patient remaining outside the healthcare facility to provide data about their status, the course, and any exacerbation of the disease. Remote monitoring in healthcare relies on registering the signals and measures that reflect the patient's status and wellbeing and then their transmission to the centre acting as the patient's care provider. The presence of a monitoring centre that receives transmitted data enables the loop to be closed and provide feedback to the patient concerning their status and the effectiveness of the therapy. An important feature of remote monitoring is its integration with electronic health records (Gandrup et al., 2020).

Remote monitoring is usually applied to patients outside the healthcare facilities who require special attention and support. Depending on the type of chronic disease, the long-term monitoring may require the registration and transmission of subjective symptoms experienced by the patient, e.g. dyspnoea or mood changes, or the measurements of parameters using dedicated devices, e.g. blood glucose assessed with a glucometer or the heart rate with an ECG monitor to the monitoring centre. Data transmitted to the monitoring centre may be registered by patients when they self-assess the severity of subjective symptoms or make measurements with specific devices, e.g. glucometers, blood pressure metres, or peak expiratory flow metres.

Patients suffering from chronic diseases are probably the largest group of potential users of remote monitoring systems. Apart from following the course of chronic conditions, remote monitoring may be used on patients discharged from the hospital to ensure better control during their convalescence. It may provide important information on the patient's status while being transported to a medical centre in an emergency. In addition, the technology may be applied to deliver care to post-surgery patients, pregnant women, neonates, elderly persons, and those with disabilities.

Considerable progress has been made in remote monitoring by the use of wearables embedded with sensors and wireless communication. The introduction of wearable devices equipped with wireless sensors has enabled the automated registration of physiological signals and patient-free transmission to the monitoring centre. The progress in implantable devices has resulted in solutions enabling monitoring of the functioning of such devices. Therefore, the definition of remote monitoring proposed by the Heart Rhythm Society, regarding the use of cardiovascular implantable electronic devices, was extended to "the automated transmission of data based on a pre-alert related to device functionality, clinical events and the clinical conditions of patients" (Slotwiner et al., 2015).

It appears that the use of wearable devices could bring new opportunities for real-life implementation of the postulates of the 4P model of medicine (Lin, 2019). Wearable devices evolved from accessories worn by the patients, through sensors integrated with clothing and body attachments, to epidermal sensors or even body inserts. Currently, the next stages of the development of remote monitoring stem from the use of flexible and stretchable materials offering an efficient interface with the patient's skin and silicon-based electronics for processing and transmission of the data registered by sensors (Khan et al., 2016).

Guk et al. (2019) identified four categories of wearable devices: portable, attachable, implantable, and ingestible. The portable category includes devices worn on the wrist (watches, bracelets), on the head (spectacles, helmets), clothing, various types of smart jewellery, belts, and chest straps. Wearable skin patches used for monitoring cardiovascular signal, body fluids, such as sweat, and body temperature are examples of attachable devices. Contact lenses used to monitor glucose and lactate levels in tear fluid belong in this category. Implantable devices were introduced in 1958 when the first cardiac pacemakers were used to treat arrhythmias. They were followed by implantable cardiovascular defibrillators (ICDs) for patients at risk of fatal arrhythmia and implantable deep brain stimulators for patients suffering from Parkinson's disease. Skin or mucosa electronic tattoos (e-tattoos) to monitor the physical and chemical parameters of sweat or salivary excretion are also classified as implantable wearables. Smart pills, enabling monitoring of the time at which medication is taken, and precise assessment of adherence to therapy are examples of ingestible devices. In addition, ingestible pills with sensors may be used for monitoring selected parameters in the gastrointestinal tract, e.g. the level of enzymes or microbial content (Guk et al., 2019).

It should be appreciated that in the IoT environment, wearable devices may not be the only source of information about patients' status (Kadhim et al., 2020). The data coming from sensors monitoring the environment in which patients live, or their everyday activities registered by cameras or sensors located in the accommodation or integrated with furniture, can be used for remote monitoring. Depending on the type of sensors, remote monitoring systems can be divided into contact-based or contactless systems. Image and radar signal analysis are mainly used in the latter category (Malasinghe et al., 2019).

The main motivation behind the introduction of remote monitoring is associated with the attempt to provide continuous monitoring of patients in their real-life conditions and the early detection of disease or its exacerbation. It is expected that remote monitoring may reduce the need for visits to emergency departments, hospitalisation, mortality, and costs related to the overuse of health services (Malasinghe et al., 2019). There is growing evidence for the clinical and non-clinical benefits that can be obtained by remote monitoring. The review by Hong & Lee (2019) showed that remote monitoring was more efficient than standard methods of care by reducing emergency room visits and hospitalisation rates in patients with chronic obstructive pulmonary disease (COPD). The effect was more marked for patients with severe disease than for those with moderate disease. According to the review by Salehi et al. (2020), remote monitoring of patients with Type 2 diabetes leads to a significantly greater reduction of their glycolysed haemoglobin level, indicating better disease control compared to the usual standard of care. The use of telehealth and m-health interventions resulted in improved quality of life, medication adherence, medication monitoring, and lower disease activity for patients with inflammatory bowel disease (Davis et al., 2020). Interactive smartphone apps and remote monitoring solutions are interventions leading to a higher quality of life in patients with bronchial asthma (Snoswell et al., 2020). Jang et al. (2020) reported that remote monitoring achieved with a wearable device was associated with significantly higher detection rates of atrial arrhythmia. In turn, Ding et al. (2020) found that remote monitoring for medication support, based on m-health applications, is associated with an improvement in all-cause mortality and reduced hospitalisation. A recent systematic review assessing the effects of digital alerting systems combined with remote monitoring showed that they might reduce hospitalisations and the length of hospital stay for some cohorts of patients (Iqbal et al., 2021).

However, the benefits from the use of remote monitoring are not always clinically feasible. A systematic review performed by Choi et al. (2020) showed that remote home blood pressure monitoring was associated with a decrease of systolic and diastolic blood pressure in comparison to normal care, but the benefit was so minor that it did not have a clinically significant effect against the onset of cardiovascular events. In some areas, additional requirements are needed to obtain clinically valid benefits. For example, the application of telemonitoring in the care provided to COPD patients may lead to reduced exacerbation rates, but only if the intervention lasts longer than 6 months or the pulmonary function is monitored (Sul et al., 2020).

Ambient assisted living

AAL technologies involve information and communication technologies (ICT), stand-alone assistive devices, and smart home technologies, which enable individuals to remain active for longer, to remain socially connected and to live independently in old age (Blackman et al., 2016). Although the concept of AAL builds on the benefits resulting from the use of monitoring technologies, it goes much further. It explores different types of technologies that can be used to provide support for an older person wishing to live independently. AAL is also inherently associated with assistive technologies, which are often dependent on advanced technological products. In general, AAL solutions encompass services, products, and concepts to improve the quality of life, the wellbeing, and safety of the elderly or those with disabilities. Apart from health, AAL applications also target safety, independence, mobility, and social inclusion. According to Yusif et al. (2016), the major problems of the elderly that can be tackled with AAL include (1) limitations in the activities of daily life, (2) the risk of falling, (3) chronic diseases, (4) dementia, (5) depressive disorders, (6) the social divide, (7) poor management of medication, and (8) decreased wellbeing.

Nilsson et al. (2021) distinguished nine categories of interventions that can be delivered by AAL technologies: (1) exercise to improve physical fitness; (2) activities for social engagement, comfort, or wellbeing; (3) support for daily needs and activities; (4) monitoring symptoms to enable self-care; (5) education to support self-efficacy and social inclusion; (6) training and maintenance of cognitive ability; (7) supervision for increased safety; (8) exercise to regain physical functions; and (9) receiving therapy from a remote source. Depending on the category of intervention, various specific AAL technologies can be employed. For example, interventions aimed at maintaining social engagement, comfort, and wellbeing could entail the use of robotic pets, social robots, tablets for apps or videos, videoconferences, virtual reality technologies, and even light therapy (Nilsson et al., 2021).

The development of the AAL domain is dependent on key Industry 4.0 technologies such as IoT, AI, and wearables. According to Manoj & Thyagaraju (2018), AAL may be treated as the result of the synergy arising from the use of sensor technologies, IoT, AI, and ML, and context awareness. The IoT originated from innovative concepts of ubiquitous communication, pervasive computing, and ambient intelligence (Dohr et al., 2010). It is based on smart devices, which are able to communicate with each other and build networks (The Information Society Technologies Advisory Group [ISTAG], 2009). The concept of the ambient intelligence characteristic for IoT is also essential for AAL. To ensure that the living environment of older persons is safe and supportive, especially their home, it must become "intelligent". IoT is able to provide all the features that are expected from the ambient assisted environment, being connected, context-sensitive, personal, adaptive, and anticipative (Dohr et al., 2010).

According to Byrne et al. (2018), AAL systems can be divided into four primary categories: smart homes, intelligent life assistants, wearables, and robotics. Based on these primary functions, the AAL system can be further categorised. Smart homes offer the functions of health monitoring, telepresence, assistance in the activities of daily life, assistance for physical mobility, social inclusion, and health provision. Wearables have been discussed in the subchapter on remote monitoring. In the context of AAL systems, their most popular applications include, in addition to health monitoring, fall detection and the monitoring of the activities of daily life. Intelligent life assistants include tools for preventing wandering, electronic home control systems, and fall detection systems. A system ensuring robotic assistance encompasses intelligent aids for physical movement, robots used for health assistance, and for providing service and companionship (Byrne et al., 2018).

Robotic surgery

The use of robots in medicine has lagged behind many other fields. The first robotic systems for surgical operations were introduced when robots were already commonly used in industry and for exploring extreme environments. Significant use of robotic surgery was preceded by the concept of minimally invasive surgery (MIS), giving advantages as less invasiveness meant shorter hospital stays, quicker return to normal activity, reduced levels of pain, and lower risks of infection (Lanfranco et al., 2004). However, MIS has limitations related to the absence of haptic feedback, compromised hand-eye coordination, restricted degrees of movement, and the augmented transmission of the surgeon's physiological tremors caused by rigid instruments. One of the key motivations for the introduction of robots to surgery was to increase the surgeon's capabilities beyond what could be offered by traditional laparoscopy (Lanfranco et al., 2004).

The first robotic solutions for surgery were developed in the 1980s and early 1990s (Lane, 2018). The first robots were used for neurosurgical biopsies (PUMA 560), transurethral resection of the prostate (PROBOT), and hip replacement surgeries (ROBODOC). In the following decade, several solutions were approved by regulatory bodies and then commercialised, e.g. AESOP – a voice-activated robotic endoscope (Computer Motion, Santa Barbara, California, USA), the Da Vinci Surgical System (Intuitive Surgical, Sunnyvale, California, USA), the Zeus System (Computer Motion, Goleta, California, USA). After the merger of the companies that developed the Da Vinci and Zeus systems in the early 2000s, there has been a lasting monopoly in the surgical robotics market, with Da Vinci solutions being the main products available for surgeons. Robotic systems aspiring for the market can be divided into three categories: MIS robotic systems, e.g. the Telelap ALF-X (TransEntrix Inc., Morrisville, USA) or the Versius (CMR Surgical, UK); single port surgery and the natural orifice transluminal endoscopic surgery (NOTES) robotic systems, e.g. SPORT (Titan Medical, Chapel Hill, North Carolina, USA); and finally, novel non-minimally invasive robotic systems, e.g. the Avicenna Roboflex (ELMED, Turkey) or Medical Microinstruments (Medical Microinstruments, Italy) (Brodie & Vasdev, 2018).

The remote control of surgical robots enables them to be used in telesurgery. The main limitation to their application is the latency of data transmission, which increases with distance. However, in 2001, the so-called Operation Lindbergh showed that telesurgery could work at transatlantic distances if a high-speed fibreoptic connection is available (Marescaux et al., 2001; Rayman et al., 2006). In 2007, the next barrier for telesurgery was overcome when a portable robotic device was used during a flight on a NASA C-9 aircraft (Doarn et al., 2009).

Currently, the scope of procedures that can be performed with surgical robots is compelling. The variants of robotic surgery ensuring minimum invasiveness, which are raising the interest of surgeons, include NOTES, laparoendoscopic single-site surgery, or even "microbots" offering a completely new surgical approach (Khandalavala et al., 2020). In addition, the concept of cybernetic surgery, combining robotics with real-time image guidance, is now being operationalised. For these applications, medical images, obtained by computed tomography or magnetic resonance imaging, are used to generate a virtual reality 3D environment providing the possibility of navigating through the patient's anatomy (Nicolau et al., 2011).

The three main areas of AI application in surgery are preoperative planning, intraoperative guidance, and support for surgical robotics (Zhou et al., 2020). For surgical robotics, the application of AI for instrument segmentation and tracking or tracing the interaction between surgical tools and the environment may result in developments in autonomous systems. It should be realised that with the assistance of AI, human-robot interaction allows the robotic surgical systems to be controlled by the surgeons' gaze, head movement, speech/voice, and hand gestures.

Taking account of the advances in BD analytics, AI, and cloud computing (CC), automated robotic surgery is the next major target in the development in the surgical field. Currently available programmable robotic systems are already used for oncological radiosurgery, joint replacement, and spine surgery (Bhandari et al., 2020). It is anticipated that the operation of the next generation of intelligent and autonomous robots will be based on deep learning models to enable the recognition of organs and the automatic performance of tasks or under the supervision of a surgeon (Bhandari et al., 2020). The development of these systems will require large amounts of annotated data obtained from many potential sources, including intraoperative sensors, video data, and data from monitoring devices during anaesthesia (Chand et al., 2018). According to Bhandari et al. (2020), the availability of relevant data to facilitate surgical scene segmentation, depth map reconstruction, surgical skill evaluation, and surgical simulation and planning is an essential prerequisite for developing autonomous surgical robots (Bhandari et al., 2020). First experiences with autonomous surgical robots seem to be promising. The study performed by Shademan et al. (2016) showed that the quality of intestinal anastomosis performed by supervised autonomous robots (Smart Tissue Autonomous Robot [STAR]) was higher on some metrics than the use of robotic-assisted surgery, a laparoscopic approach, and manual surgery. According to Connor et al. (2020), preclinical and clinical evidence supports the use of autonomous robotic urological surgery. However, it should be stressed that the level of autonomy applied in robotic surgery may differ significantly, from robot assistance, through task autonomy and conditional autonomy, to high and full autonomy.

Public health and epidemic surveillance

The World Health Organisation has distinguished the core and essential enabling public health operations (EPHOs). The first group encompasses operations related to surveillance of the population's health and wellbeing, monitoring and responding to health hazards and emergencies, and actions focused on service delivery: health promotion, health protection, and disease prevention. The enabling operations include activities related to governance, the public health workforce, funding, communication, and research.

Both the core and enabling EPHOs may benefit from achievements in Health 4.0. Analogous to precision medicine, included in the 4P model, some authors have started to use the term "precision public health" to identify a new field, driven by technological advances, leading to a more precise characterisation of individuals and population groups (Baynam et al., 2017). The growth of this field benefits from progress in the BD and AI technologies used to provide risk assessment and interventions adjusted to the needs of specific and homogenous subpopulations (Dolley, 2018).

According to Mooney & Pejaver (2018), there are at least five main categories of big sets of public health data:

- Measures of participant biology, e.g. genomic data sets
- Measures of participants context, e.g. geospatial data
- Data collected in electronic medical records
- Participant's measurements obtained automatically as a result of personal monitoring, e.g. from global positioning systems (GPS) or health bands
- Measures compiled from electronic environments, including records of search terms, social media postings, or cell phone records (named after Mooney & Pejavar as "effluent data")

The potential of using the BD sets belonging to the last category will now be explored. The use of data types falling into the first four categories was discussed to a limited extent in the sections addressing 4P medicine and remote monitoring.

In 2009, Eysenbach proposed the term "infodemiology" for the field researching the determinants and the distribution of information in electronic environments, particularly on the Internet, in relation to the aims of public health. Later, other authors have proposed the term "digital epidemiology" to be applied in a similar context (Salathé et al., 2012). Infodemiology is based on the assumption that information and communication patterns on the Internet may reflect the health trends in the population. Therefore, the occurrence of information on WWW pages, in social media, posts in discussion fora, blogs and microblogs, as well as the search activities using search engines, may be useful sources of data. The sources of information on the Internet, which are analysed in infodemiology, can be divided into two categories; the first associated with the demand side (what is searched for on the Internet) and the second related to the supply side (what is published on the Internet) (Eysenbach, 2009). Continuous supply and demand for electronic information enable the implementation of infoveillance mechanisms based on the analysis of an unstructured free text. The importance of BD analytics and AI, especially ML, for progress in infodemiology has been confirmed by many authors (Bragazzi et al., 2020; Dolley, 2018; Mooney & Pejaver, 2018).

Typical examples of infodemiology studies include an analysis of searches in search engines in order to identify outbreaks of infectious diseases (Yang et al., 2017), monitoring the health status of microblog users (syndromic surveillance) (Edo-Osagie et al., 2020; Samaras et al., 2019), discovering and assessing the gaps in access to health-related information (Sharma & Kaur, 2017), and identification and monitoring of online content important for public health, e.g. websites maintained by antivaccination movements (Donzelli et al., 2018). A significant association between web searches and influenza morbidity for many countries has been reported (Cook et al., 2011; Nguyen-Tran et al., 2020; Yuan et al., 2013). The importance of infoveillance was also confirmed for other infectious diseases: dengue (Espina & Estuar, 2017), plague (Bragazzi & Mahroum, 2019), Zika (Gianfredi et al., 2018), Ebola (Gianfredi et al., 2018), and recently for COVID-19 (Higgins et al., 2020; Mavragani, 2020b).

A scoping review published in 2020 by Mavragani revealed that, in recent years, the number of published papers on infodemiology had increased considerably. The most popular sources of information researched up to 2018 were Twitter (45%), Google (24.6%), websites and platforms (13.9%), blogs and forums (10.1%), Facebook (8.9%), and other search engines (5.6%) (Mavragani, 2020a). According to Barros et al. (2020), the most popular areas for infoveillance studies were infectious diseases (66.7%), chronic diseases (10.5%), and multiple diseases (8.6%).

Conclusions

Healthcare systems undergo a deep transformation resulting from the accelerating penetration of technologies forming the Industry 4.0 revolution. This process is uneven, and various areas of medicine and public health benefit to a varying degree from specific technologies. It should also be underlined that, although the expectations are high, the full, real-life implementation of many applications qualifying as Health 4.0 is still to come. On the other hand, the provision of high-quality care based on the paradigm of 4P medicine cannot be fulfilled without such technologies as IoT, cloud computing (CC), BD analytics, and AI. Currently, health professionals are overburdened with the data flowing from various sources, and their efficient handling is hardly possible without decision support tools employing ML algorithms. Common prevalence of chronic medical conditions requiring repetitive interactions from the healthcare system urges for solutions allowing for monitoring patient status and providing feedback about therapy. Ageing societies seek the solution supporting seniors in satisfactory independent life enriched with social interactions. Health 4.0 technologies bring the opportunity of forming smart environments providing such support and assuring the safety of elderly people and persons with disabilities.

References

Adler, E. D., Voors, A. A., Klein, L., Macheret, F., Braun, O. O., Urey, M. A., Zhu, W., Sama, I., Tadel, M., Campagnari, C., Greenberg, B., & Yagil, A. (2020). Improving risk prediction in heart failure using machine learning. *European Journal of Heart Failure*, 22(1), 139–147. https://doi.org/10.1002/ejhf.1628

Baro, E., Degoul, S., Beuscart, R., & Chazard, E. (2015). Toward a literature-driven definition of Big Data in healthcare. *BioMed Research International*, 2015, 639021. https://doi.org/10.1155/2015/639021

Barros, J. M., Duggan, J., & Rebholz-Schuhmann, D. (2020). The application of internet-based sources for public health surveillance (infoveillance): Systematic review. *Journal of Medical Internet Research*, 22 (3), e13680. https://doi.org/10.2196/13680

Baynam, G., Bauskis, A., Pachter, N., Schofield, L., Verhoef, H., Palmer, R. L., Kung, S., Helmholz, P., Ridout, M., Walker, C. E., Hawkins, A., Goldblatt, J., Weeramanthri, T. S., Dawkins, H. J. S., & Molster, C. M. (2017). 3-dimensional facial analysis—Facing precision public health. *Frontiers in Public Health*, 5, 31. https://doi.org/10.3389/fpubh.2017.00031

Bhandari, M., Zeffiro, T., & Reddiboina, M. (2020). Artificial intelligence and robotic surgery. *Current Opinion in Urology*, 30(1), 48–54. https://doi.org/10.1097/MOU.0000000000000692

Bi, W. L., Hosny, A., Schabath, M. B., Giger, M. L., Birkbak, N. J., Mehrtash, A., Allison, T., Arnaout, O., Abbosh, C., Dunn, I. F., Mak, R. H., Tamimi, R. M., Tempany, C. M., Swanton, C., Hoffmann, U., Schwartz, L. H., Gillies, R. J., Huang, R. Y., & Aerts, H. J. W. L. (2019). Artificial intelligence in cancer imaging: Clinical challenges and applications. *CA: A Cancer Journal for Clinicians*, 69(2), caac.21552. https://doi.org/10.3322/caac.21552

Blackman, S., Matlo, C., Bobrovitskiy, C., Waldoch, A., Fang M. L., Jackson, P., Mihailidis, A., Nygård, L., Astell, A., & Sixsmith, A. (2016). Ambient assisted living technologies for aging well: A scoping review. *Journal of Intelligent Systems*, 25(1), 55–69. https://doi.org/10.1515/jisys-2014-0136

Bragazzi, N. L., Dai, H., Damiani, G., Behzadifar, M., Martini, M., & Wu, J. (2020). How Big Data and artificial intelligence can help better manage the COVID-19 pandemic. *International Journal of Environmental Research and Public Health*, 17(9), 3176. https://doi.org/10.3390/ijerph17093176

Bragazzi, N. L., & Mahroum, N. (2019). Google trends predicts present and future plague cases during the plague outbreak in Madagascar: Infodemiological study. *JMIR Public Health and Surveillance*, 5(1), e13142. https://doi.org/10.2196/13142

Briganti, G., & Le Moine, O. (2020). Artificial intelligence in medicine: Today and tomorrow. *Frontiers in Medicine*, 7, 27. https://doi.org/10.3389/fmed.2020.00027

Brodie, A., & Vasdev, N. (2018). The future of robotic surgery. *The Annals of The Royal College of Surgeons of England*, 100(Supplement 7), 4–13. https://doi.org/10.1308/rcsann.supp2.4

Byrne, C. A., Collier, R., & O'Hare, G. M. P. (2018). A review and classification of assisted living systems. *Information*, 9(7), 182. https://doi.org/10.3390/info9070182

Chand, M., Ramachandran, N., Stoyanov, D., & Lovat, L. (2018). Robotics, artificial intelligence and distributed ledgers in surgery: Data is key! *Techniques in Coloproctology*, 2(9), 645–648. Springer-Verlag Italia s.r.l. https://doi.org/10.1007/s10151-018-1847-5

Choi, W. S., Choi, J. H., Oh, J., Shin, I.-S., & Yang, J.-S. (2020). Effects of remote monitoring of blood pressure in management of urban hypertensive patients: A systematic review and meta-analysis. *Telemedicine and E-Health*, 26(6), 744–759. https://doi.org/10.1089/tmj.2019.0028

Connor, M. J., Dasgupta, P., Ahmed, H. U., & Raza, A. (2020). Autonomous surgery in the era of robotic urology: Friend or foe of the future surgeon? *Nature Reviews Urology*, 17(11), 643–649. https://doi.org/10.1038/s41585-020-0375-z

Cook, S., Conrad, C., Fowlkes, A. L., & Mohebbi, M. H. (2011). Assessing Google Flu trends performance in the United States during the 2009 influenza virus A (H1N1) pandemic. *PLoS ONE*, 6(8), e23610. https://doi.org/10.1371/journal.pone.0023610

Davis, S. P., Ross, M. S. H., Adatorwovor, R., & Wei, H. (2020). Telehealth and mobile health interventions in adults with inflammatory bowel disease: A mixed-methods systematic review. *Research in Nursing & Health*, 44, 155–172. https://doi.org/10.1002/nur.22091

Delclaux, C. (2019). No need for pulmonologists to interpret pulmonary function tests. *European Respiratory Journal*, 54, 1900829. https://doi.org/10.1183/13993003.00829-2019

Ding, H., Chen, S. H., Edwards, I., Jayasena, R., Doecke, J., Layland, J., Yang, I. A., & Maiorana, A. (2020). Effects of different telemonitoring strategies on chronic heart failure care: Systematic review and subgroup meta-analysis. *Journal of Medical Internet Research*, 22(11), e20032. https://doi.org/10.2196/20032

Dlamini, Z., Francies, F. Z., Hull, R., & Marima, R. (2020). Artificial intelligence (AI) and Big Data in cancer and precision oncology. *Computational and Structural Biotechnology Journal*, 18, 2300–2311. https://doi.org/10.1016/j.csbj.2020.08.019

Doarn, C. R., Anvari, M., Low, T., & Broderick, T. J. (2009). Evaluation of teleoperated surgical robots in an enclosed undersea environment. *Telemedicine and E-Health*, 15(4), 325–335. https://doi.org/10.1089/tmj.2008.0123

Dohr, A., Modre-Osprian, R., Drobics, M., Hayn, D., & Schreier, G. (2010). The Internet of Things for Ambient Assisted Living. *ITNG2010 – 7th International Conference on Information Technology: New Generations*, 804–809. https://doi.org/10.1109/ITNG.2010.104

Dolley, S. (2018). Big Data's role in precision public health. *Frontiers in Public Health*, 6, 68. https://doi.org/10.3389/fpubh.2018.00068

Donzelli, G., Palomba, G., Federigi, I., Aquino, F., Cioni, L., Verani, M., Carducci, A., & Lopalco, P. (2018). Misinformation on vaccination: A quantitative analysis of YouTube videos. *Human Vaccines & Immunotherapeutics*, 14(7), 1654–1659. https://doi.org/10.1080/21645515.2018.1454572

Edo-Osagie, O., De La Iglesia, B., Lake, I., & Edeghere, O. (2020). A scoping review of the use of Twitter for public health research. *Computers in Biology and Medicine*, 122, 103770. https://doi.org/10.1016/j.compbiomed.2020.103770

Espina, K., & Estuar, M. R. J. E. (2017). Infodemiology for syndromic surveillance of dengue and typhoid fever in the Philippines. *Procedia Computer Science*, 121, 554–561. https://doi.org/10.1016/j.procs.2017.11.073

Eysenbach, G. (2009). Infodemiology and infoveillance: Framework for an emerging set of public health informatics methods to analyze search, communication and publication behavior on the Internet. *Journal of Medical Internet Research*, 11.1, e11. https://doi.org/10.2196/jmir.1157

Flores, M., Glusman, G., Brogaard, K., Price, N. D., & Hood, L. (2013). P4 medicine: How systems medicine will transform the healthcare sector and society. *Personalized Medicine*, 10 (6), 565–576). https://doi.org/10.2217/pme.13.57

Gandrup, J., Ali, S. M., McBeth, J., van der Veer, S. N., & Dixon, W. G. (2020). Remote symptom monitoring integrated into electronic health records: A systematic review. *Journal of the American Medical Informatics Association*, 27(11), 1752–1763. https://doi.org/10.1093/jamia/ocaa177

Garcia, C., & Uzbelger, G. (2020). Artificial intelligence to help the practitioner choose the right treatment: Watson for Oncology. In B. Nordlinger, C. Villani, & D. Rus (Eds.), *Healthcare and Artificial Intelligence* (pp. 81–83). Springer. https://doi.org/doi.org/10.1007/978-3-030-32161-1_11

Gianfredi, V., Bragazzi, N. L., Nucci, D., Martini, M., Rosselli, R., Minelli, L., & Moretti, M. (2018). Harnessing Big Data for communicable tropical and subtropical disorders: Implications from a systematic review of the literature. *Frontiers in Public Health*, 6, 90. https://doi.org/10.3389/fpubh.2018.00090

Guk, K., Han, G., Lim, J., Jeong, K., Kang, T., Lim, E.-K., & Jung, J. (2019). Evolution of wearable devices with real-time disease monitoring for personalized healthcare. *Nanomaterials*, 9(6), 813. https://doi.org/10.3390/nano9060813

Guven, M., Hardalac, F., Ozisik, K., & Tuna, F. (2021). Heart diseases diagnose via artificial intelligence-powered mobile application. *Preprints*, 2021010291. https://doi.org/10.20944/preprints202101.0291.v1

Halcox, J. P. J., Wareham, K., Cardew, A., Gilmore, M., Barry, J. P., Phillips, C., & Gravenor, M. B. (2017). Assessment of remote heart rhythm sampling using the AliveCor heart monitor to screen for atrial fibrillation the REHEARSE-AF study. *Circulation*, 136(19), 1784–1794. https://doi.org/10.1161/CIRCULATIONAHA.117.030583

Higgins, T. S., Wu, A. W., Sharma, D., Illing, E. A., Rubel, K., Ting, J. Y., & Alliance, S. F. (2020). Correlations of online search engine trends with coronavirus disease (COVID-19) incidence: Infodemiology study. *JMIR Public Health and Surveillance*, 6(2), e19702. https://doi.org/10.2196/19702

Hong, Y., & Lee, S. H. (2019). Effectiveness of tele-monitoring by patient severity and intervention type in chronic obstructive pulmonary disease patients: A systematic review and meta-analysis. *International Journal of Nursing Studies*, 92, 1–15. https://doi.org/10.1016/j.ijnurstu.2018.12.006

Hood, L. (2003). Systems biology: Integrating technology, biology, and computation. *Mechanisms of Ageing and Development*, 124(1), 9–16. https://doi.org/10.1016/S0047-6374(02)00164-1

Hood, L., Heath, J. R., Phelps, M. E., & Lin, B. (2004). Systems biology and new technologies enable predictive and preventative medicine. *Science*, 306 (5696), 640–643. https://doi.org/10.1126/science.1104635

Huang, S., Yang, J., Fong, S., & Zhao, Q. (2019). Artificial intelligence in cancer diagnosis and prognosis: Opportunities and challenges. *Cancer Letters*, 471, 61–61. https://doi.org/10.1016/j.canlet.2019.12.007

International Human Genome Sequencing Consortium. (2001). Initial sequencing and analysis of the human genome. *Nature*, 409, 860–921.

Iqbal, F. M., Lam, K., Joshi, M., Khan, S., Ashrafian, H., & Darzi, A. (2021). Clinical outcomes of digital sensor alerting systems in remote monitoring: A systematic review and meta-analysis. *NPJ Digital Medicine*, 4 (1), 1–12. https://doi.org/10.1038/s41746-020-00378-0

Jamthikar, A., Gupta, D., Khanna, N. N., Saba, L., Araki, T., Viskovic, K., Suri, H. S., Gupta, A., Mavrogeni, S., Turk, M., Laird, J. R., Pareek, G., Miner, M., Sfikakis, P. P., Protogerou, A., Kitas, G. D., Viswanathan, V., Nicolaides, A., Bhatt, D. L., & Suri, J. S. (2019). A low-cost machine learning-based cardiovascular/stroke risk assessment system: Integration of conventional factors with image phenotypes. *Cardiovascular Diagnosis and Therapy*, 9(5), 420–430. https://doi.org/10.21037/cdt.2019.09.03

Jang, J.-P., Lin, H.-T., Chen, Y.-J., Hsieh, M.-H., & Huang, Y.-C. (2020). Role of remote monitoring in detection of atrial arrhythmia, stroke reduction, and use of anticoagulation therapy – A systematic review and meta-analysis. *Circulation Journal*, 84, 1922–1930. https://www.jstage.jst.go.jp/article/circj/84/11/84_CJ-20-0633/_pdf

Kadhim, K., Alsahlany, A., Wadi, S., & Kadhum, H. (2020). An overview of patient's health status monitoring system based on Internet of Things (IoT). *Wireless Personal Communications*, 114, 2235–2262. https://link.springer.com/content/pdf/10.1007/s11277-020-07474-0.pdf

Khan, Y., Ostfeld, A. E., Lochner, C. M., Pierre, A., & Arias, A. C. (2016). Monitoring of vital signs with flexible and wearable medical devices. *Advanced Materials*, 28(22), 4373–4395. https://doi.org/10.1002/adma.201504366

Khandalavala, K., Shimon, T., Flores, L., Armijo, P. R., & Oleynikov, D. (2020). Emerging surgical robotic technology: A progression toward microbots. *Annals of Laparoscopic and Endoscopic Surgery*, 5, 3. https://doi.org/10.21037/ales.2019.10.02

Lane, T. (2018). A short history of robotic surgery. *Annals of the Royal College of Surgeons of England*, 100, 5–7. https://doi.org/10.1308/rcsann.supp1.5

Lanfranco, A. R., Castellanos, A. E., Desai, J. P., & Meyers, W. C. (2004). Robotic surgery: A current perspective. *Annals of Surgery*, 239(1), 14–21. https://doi.org/10.1097/01.sla.0000103020.19595.7d

Lawton, J., Blackburn, M., Allen, J., Campbell, F., Elleri, D., Leelarathna, L., Rankin, D., Tauschmann, M., Thabit, H., & Hovorka, R. (2018). Patients' and caregivers' experiences of using continuous glucose monitoring to support diabetes self-management: Qualitative study. *BMC Endocrine Disorders*, 18(1), 1–10. https://doi.org/10.1186/s12902-018-0239-1

Li, J., Pan, C., Zhang, S., Spin, J. M., Deng, A., Leung, L. L. K., Dalman, R. L., Tsao, P. S., & Snyder, M. (2018). Decoding the genomics of abdominal aortic aneurysm. *Cell*, 174(6), 1361–1372.e10. https://doi.org/10.1016/j.cell.2018.07.021

Lin, B. (2019). Wearable smart devices for P4 medicine in heart disease: Ready for medical cyber-physical systems? *OMICS: A Journal of Integrative Biology*, 23(5), 291–292. https://doi.org/10.1089/omi.2019.0059

Malasinghe, L. P., Ramzan, N., & Dahal, K. (2019). Remote patient monitoring: A comprehensive study. *Journal of Ambient Intelligence and Humanized Computing*, 10(1), 57–76. https://doi.org/10.1007/s12652-017-0598-x

Manoj, T., & Thyagaraju, G. (2018). Active and assisted living: A comprehensive review of enabling technologies and scenarios. *International Journal of Advanced Research in Computer Science*, 9(1), 461–471. https://doi.org/10.26483/ijarcs.v9i1.5284

Marescaux, J., Leroy, J., Gagner, M., Rubino, F., Mutter, D., Vix, M., Butner, S. E., & Smith, M. K. (2001). Transatlantic robot-assisted telesurgery. *Nature*, 413(6854), 379–380. https://doi.org/10.1038/35096636

Mavragani, A. (2020a). Infodemiology and infoveillance: Scoping review. *Journal of Medical Internet Research*, 22(4), e16206. https://doi.org/10.2196/16206

Mavragani, A. (2020b). Tracking COVID-19 in Europe: Infodemiology approach. *JMIR Public Health and Surveillance*, 6(2), e18941. https://doi.org/10.2196/18941

Mooney, S. J., & Pejaver, V. (2018). Big Data in public health: Terminology, machine learning, and privacy. *Annual Review of Public Health*, 39, 95–112. https://doi.org/10.1146/annurev-publhealth-040617-014208

Mori, Y., Neumann, H., Misawa, M., Kudo, S., & Bretthauer, M. (2021). Artificial intelligence in colonoscopy – Now on the market. What's next? *Journal of Gastroenterology and Hepatology*, 36, 7–11. https://doi.org/10.1111/jgh.15339

Mortazavi, B. J., Downing, N. S., Bucholz, E. M., Dharmarajan, K., Manhapra, A., Li, S. X., Negahban, S. N., & Krumholz, H. M. (2016). Analysis of machine learning techniques for heart failure readmissions. *Circulation: Cardiovascular Quality and Outcomes*, 9(6), 629–640. https://doi.org/10.1161/CIRCOUTCOMES.116.003039

Nguyen-Tran, M.-D., Nguyen-Tran, N.-V., Phuc, N. N. Do, Tran, H. L. T., Zayan, A. H., Abdelrahman, A. S., Vu, T. T., Nguyen, K. A. L., Nguyen, T. T., Vo, Y. N. Le, Minh, N., Chu, N., Tran, Q. T. H., Pham, M. H., Vu, H. N., & Huy, N. T. (2020). A systematic review of the correlation between web-based query and outbreak of emerging infectious diseases and meta-analysis of influenza-like illnesses. *Research Square Preprints*. https://doi.org/10.21203/RS.3.RS-66084/V1

Nicolau, S., Soler, L., Mutter, D., & Marescaux, J. (2011). Augmented reality in laparoscopic surgical oncology. *Surgical Oncology*, 20 (3), 189–201. https://doi.org/10.1016/j.suronc.2011.07.002

Nilsson, M. Y., Andersson, S., Magnusson, L., & Hanson, E. (2021). Ambient assisted living technology-mediated interventions for older people and their informal carers in the context of healthy ageing: A scoping review. *Health Science Reports*, 4(1), e225. https://doi.org/10.1002/hsr2.225

Rayman, R., Croome, K., Galbraith, N., McClure, R., Morady, R., Peterson, S., Smith, S., Subotic, V., Van Wynsberghe, A., & Primak, S. (2006). Long-distance robotic telesurgery: A feasibility study for care in remote environments. *International Journal of Medical Robotics and Computer Assisted Surgery*, 2(3), 216–224. https://doi.org/10.1002/rcs.99

Regalia, G., Onorati, F., Lai, M., Caborni, C., & Picard, R. W. (2019). Multimodal wrist-worn devices for seizure detection and advancing research: Focus on the Empatica wristbands. *Epilepsy Research* (Elsevier B.V.), 153, 79–82. https://doi.org/10.1016/j.eplepsyres.2019.02.007

Salathé, M., Bengtsson, L., Bodnar, T. J., Brewer, D. D., Brownstein, J. S., Buckee, C., Campbell, E. M., Cattuto, C., Khandelwal, S., Mabry, P. L., & Vespignani, A. (2012). Digital epidemiology. *PLoS Computational Biology*, 8(7), e1002616. https://doi.org/10.1371/journal.pcbi.1002616

Salehi, S., Olyaeemanesh, A., Mobinizadeh, M., Nasli-Esfahani, E , & Riazi, H. (2020). Assessment of remote patient monitoring (RPM) systems for patients with type 2 diabetes: A systematic review and meta-analysis. *Journal of Diabetes and Metabolic Disorders*, 19(1), 115–127. https://doi.org/10.1007/s40200-019-00482-3

Samaras, L., García-Barriocanal, E., & Sicilia, M. A. (2019). Syndromic surveillance using web data: A systematic review. *Innovation in Health Informatics*, 39–77. https://doi.org/10.1016/B978-0-12-819043-2.00002-2

Schleidgen, S., Klingler, C., Bertram, T., Rogowski, W. H., & Marckmann, G. (2013). What is personalized medicine: Sharpening a vague term based on a systematic literature review. *BMC Medical Ethics*, 14(1), 55. https://doi.org/10.1186/1472-6939-14-55

Seetharam, K., Kagiyama, N., & Sengupta, P. P. (2019). Application of mobile health, telemedicine and artificial intelligence to echocardiography. *Echo Research and Practice*, 6(2), R41–R52. https://doi.org/10.1530/ERP-18-0081

Shademan, A., Decker, R. S., Opfermann, J. D., Leonard, S., Krieger, A., & Kim, P. C. W. (2016). Supervised autonomous robotic soft tissue surgery. *Science Translational Medicine*, 8(337), 337ra64–337ra64. https://doi.org/10.1126/scitranslmed.aad9398

Sharma, P., & Kaur, P. D. (2017). Effectiveness of web-based social sensing in health information dissemination – A review. *Telematics and Informatics*, 34 (1), 194–219. https://doi.org/10.1016/j.tele.2016.04.012

Slotwiner, D., Varma, N., Akar, J. G., Annas, G., Beardsall, M., Fogel, R. I., Galizio, N. O., Glotzer, T. V., Leahy, R. A., Love, C. J., McLean, R. C., Mittal, S., Morichelli, L., Patton, K. K., Raitt, M. H., Pietro Ricci, R., Rickard, J., Schoenfeld, M. H., Serwer, G. A., Shea, J., Varosy, P., Verma, A. & Yu, C. M. (2015). HRS expert consensus statement on remote interrogation and monitoring for cardiovascular implantable electronic devices. *Heart Rhythm*, 12(7), e69–e100. https://doi.org/10.1016/j.hrthm.2015.05.008

Snoswell, C. L., Rahja, M., & Lalor, A. F. (2020). A systematic review and meta-analysis of change in health-related quality of life for interactive telehealth interventions for patients with asthma. *Value in Health*, 24(2), 291–302. https://doi.org/10.1016/j.jval.2020.09.006

Sul, A. R., Lyu, D. H., & Park, D. A. (2020). Effectiveness of telemonitoring versus usual care for chronic obstructive pulmonary disease: A systematic review and meta-analysis. *Journal of Telemedicine and Telecare*, 26(4), 189–199. https://doi.org/10.1177/1357633X18811757

The Information Society Technologies Advisory Group [ISTAG]. (2009). Revising Europe's ICT Strategy. ISTAG's Report on Revising Europe's ICT Strategy, final version, February 2009. https://ec.europa.eu/eurostat/cros/system/files/16_Revising%20Europes%20ICT-strategy.pdf

Wu, A. D., Begoray, D. L., MacDonald, M., Wharf Higgins, J., Frankish, J., Kwan, B., Fung, W., & Rootman, I. (2021). Developing and evaluating a relevant and feasible instrument for measuring health literacy of Canadian high school students. *Health Promotion International*, 25(4), 444–452. https://doi.org/10.1093/heapro/daq032

Yang, S., Kou, S. C., Lu, F., Brownstein, J. S., Brooke, N., & Santillana, M. (2017). Advances in using Internet searches to track dengue. *PLOS Computational Biology*, 13(7), e1005607. https://doi.org/10.1371/journal.pcbi.1005607

Yuan, Q., Nsoesie, E. O., Lv, B., Peng, G., Chunara, R., & Brownstein, J. S. (2013). Monitoring influenza epidemics in China with search query from Baidu. *PLoS ONE*, 8(5), e64323. https://doi.org/10.1371/journal.pone.0064323

Yusif, S., Soar, J., & Hafeez-Baig, A. (2016). Older people, assistive technologies, and the barriers to adoption: A systematic review. *International Journal of Medical Informatics*, 94, 112–116. https://doi.org/10.1016/j.ijmedinf.2016.07.004

Zhou, X. Y., Guo, Y., Shen, M., & Yang, G. Z. (2020). Application of artificial intelligence in surgery. *Frontiers of Medicine*, 14(4), 417–430. https://doi.org/10.1007/s11684-020-0770-0

5 Patient empowerment in Health 4.0

Mariusz Duplaga

Introduction

Patient empowerment is seen as one of the key concepts for the modern approach to the delivery of healthcare services. In this chapter, the origin and the definition of patient empowerment are described. The importance of patient empowerment in the context of interactions between patients and healthcare systems and healthcare providers is discussed. Subsequently, the possible impact of Health 4.0 on the aims and benefits related to patient empowerment is discussed. The importance of technological tools being used to support patient empowerment is signalled, and specific solutions are presented. Finally, the role of Internet tools, personal health records (PHR), remote monitoring, electronic patient-physician communication, and participation in online patient communities are described.

The concept of patient empowerment

The concept of patient empowerment was formulated in the early 2000s (Aujoulat et al., 2007; Funnell & Anderson, 2004). It originated from the empowerment theory proposed by Zimmerman (2000). It should be emphasised that the term empowerment is used not only in relation to health but also in other areas, such as business, politics, and education. Empowerment may be regarded as the description of a process or an outcome (Schulz et al., 1995). Johnston Roberts (1999) pointed out that definitions of empowerment may be formulated at different levels – individual, organisational, and community.

In healthcare, empowerment is the outcome by which a patient has "the knowledge, skills, attitudes, and self-awareness necessary to influence their own behaviour, and that of others … to improve the quality of their lives" (Funnell & Anderson, 2004). This understanding of patient empowerment corresponds with the psychological or micro-level definition of empowerment (Johnston Roberts, 1999). Johnston Roberts (1999) also suggested that patients can become empowered either by participating in health education programmes or by interactions with physicians. According to the definition

DOI: 10.4324/9781003144403-5

endorsed by the World Health Organization (WHO), patient empowerment is the process "through which people gain greater control over the decisions and actions affecting their health" (Nutbeam & Kickbusch, 1998).

Angelmar and Berman (2007) distinguished four fundamental components of the process of patient empowerment: (1) the patient understanding his/her role; (2) patients acquiring sufficient knowledge to be able to engage with their healthcare provider; (3) patient skills; and (4) the presence of a facilitating environment. According to Nutbeam, patient empowerment is the ultimate goal of health literacy. Crondahl and Karlsson (2016) believed that a critical level of health literacy is required for the patient to achieve empowerment. However, they also indicated that the mechanisms associating health literacy with patient empowerment were not fully apparent (Crondahl & Karlsson, 2016). Furthermore, health literacy does not automatically lead to empowerment.

Bravo et al. (2015) developed a comprehensive conceptual model of patient empowerment. In their model, the key components of patient empowerment include the underpinning ethos, moderators, interventions, indicators, and outcomes. Three levels were identified for the underpinning ethos: the patient, the healthcare provider, and the level of the healthcare system. Patient level ethos addresses the patient's rights, responsibilities, and opportunities associated with autonomy, self-determination, and power in the interactions with healthcare providers, who are responsible for respecting the patient's autonomy and acting as a partner with the patient. Finally, the level of the healthcare system in the model developed by Bravo et al. should enable patients with chronic diseases to develop the skills necessary for the self-managing of their conditions. Empowering interventions can be developed on the level of the healthcare provider and focused on the individual or the level of the healthcare system with the focus on groups of patients. Individual interventions, other than patient-centred training, include shared decision-making, motivational interviewing, counselling, health coaching, and signposting to the support services (Bravo et al., 2015). Training programmes for clinicians or patients are types of intervention on the level of the healthcare system. There are two types of moderators, those that can be handled by providers, e.g. personal characteristics, or by the local environment, e.g. the political context.

Two types of indicators of patient empowerment were identified: patient capacities; state and resources, e.g. self-efficacy, knowledge, skills, health literacy, and behaviours, such as participating in shared decision-making, managing one's own health, and empowering themselves by joining support groups or using the Internet to acquire or share health information. In the model, there are two types of outcomes: these associated with patients, e.g. adaptation to chronic disease, quality of life, or independence, and clinical outcomes, e.g. measures of health status.

The review prepared by Pekonen et al. (2019) showed that there is still no consensus on the understanding of patient empowerment. Key terms or dimensions in the current definitions include the patient's capacity, power, knowledge, activities and behaviours, shared decision-making, and self-management of illness. Furthermore, there are several related terms used in literature, including enablement, engagement, activation, or personal control (Pekonen et al., 2019; Risling et al., 2017).

Many tools to address various constructs are used for assessing patient empowerment. A systematic review carried out by Barr et al. (2015) revealed that the measures related to four domains could be identified: patients' states, experiences, and capacities; patients' actions and behaviours; patient self-determination within the healthcare relationship; and the development of patient skills. The available measurement tools may be categorised as generic, e.g. the Patient Empowerment Scale (Faulkner, 2001), the Treatment-Related Empowerment Scale (Webb et al., 2001), or the Health Care Empowerment Inventory (Johnson et al., 2012), or as condition- or speciality-specific, e.g. the Empowerment Questionnaire for Inpatients (mental health patients) (Lopez et al., 2010), the Diabetes Empowerment Scale (diabetes patients) (Funnell & Anderson, 2004), or the Patient Empowerment Scale – version for cancer patients (Bulsara et al., 2006).

Patient empowerment is a necessary requirement for the efficient delivery of care to patients, especially those with chronic conditions. Anderson and Funnell (2010) formulated the fundamental principles of empowerment in the context of diabetes care. These authors pointed out that diabetic patients themselves provide a major part of their health, care, and wellbeing, principally as a result of self-management and their actions in daily life. Healthcare professionals are unable to control the patient's everyday self-care decisions, so their main responsibility is to empower patients with the ability to make self-management decisions. This perception is obviously not restricted to patients with diabetes. McAllister et al. (2012) posed the question, should patient empowerment be considered as a measurable patient-reported outcome for chronic conditions?

Patient empowerment and Health 4.0

There are several descriptions of the stages of medicine and healthcare development from Medicine 1.0 to Medicine 4.0. Those proposed by Wolf and Scholze (2017) were characterised by the changing capacities of physicians and healthcare systems when responding to health challenges. In their view, Medicine 4.0 was shaped by the use of advanced ICTs and electronic and microstructural technologies leading to an efficient level of innovative therapeutic modalities.

Sharma et al. described the evolution of healthcare from Stage 1.0 to 4.0 by considering the relationship between patient and healthcare and the strategy of responding to health challenges. Healthcare 1.0 corresponded to paternalistic care, 2.0 to reactive care, 3.0 to proactive care engaging the patient, and 4.0 is identified as predictive and personalised care, benefiting from the use of Industry 4.0's key technologies including Internet of Things (IoT), remote monitoring, wearables, wireless body area networks, decision support systems, and a smart healthcare ecosystem (Sharma et al., 2019). Such a perception of the evolution of healthcare refers to the attributes of medicine postulated by Hood et al., who in the early 2000s proposed a 4P model (Hood et al., 2004) in which medicine should be predictive, preventive, personalised, and participatory.

In the various perspectives of the evolution in medicine and healthcare, the fourth stage that materialises now, or should in the near future, depends strongly on the developments in ICTs. It appears that the new perception of patients' (and citizens') role in the healthcare processes and their relationship with health providers will benefit from advances in technology and ensures both personalised and participatory care. The recognition of the Health 4.0, or Healthcare 4.0, phase in the evolution of health services has added new dimensions to the concept of patient empowerment. According to Shelke (2020), the Internet of Medical Things (IoMT) will lead to considerable progress in the areas of critical importance for patient empowerment, such as remote diagnosis and communication, treatment planning, follow-up after surgical procedures, electronic health records and preventive healthcare, and patient education. Blockchain-based patient care applications are interesting, and Durnerva et al. (2020) indicated that it provides tangible benefits that ensure data privacy and security of health data, facilitates interoperability of heterogeneous health IT systems, and improves the quality of healthcare outcomes. The use of blockchain technology in patient care applications should lead to improved patient empowerment and engagement.

Modelling the impact of ICT on patient empowerment

Many authors postulated that technology usage might enhance patient empowerment. Karni et al. (2020) developed a comprehensive framework, the 'ICT for Patient Empowerment Model (ICT4PEM)', focussing on ICT-based interventions to target patient empowerment. They based their framework on a simplified and modified version of the patient empowerment model proposed earlier by Bravo et al. (2015), emphasising the relationship between the attributes of patient empowerment, such as control, coping psychologically, self-efficacy, understanding, legitimacy or support, and outcomes of empowerment. The latter includes patient-specific outcomes, e.g. health-related quality of life, clinical outcomes, and healthcare system effects. The ICT4PEM anticipates that, in a project focused on the development of specific interventions, decisions should be made on the attributes they are to be addressed and what effects are anticipated from using ICT (Karni et al., 2020). The interventional strategies foreseen within ICT4PEM encompass education, feedback, and monitoring, which are also included in the Behavioural Interventional Technology (BIT) model proposed by Mohr et al. (2014). Karni et al. (2020) added communication, analysis, and engagement as strategies. The last corresponds with aim 'setting and motivation' in the BIT model. In a specific intervention, the proportion and use of these strategies will vary depending on the attributes addressed and the outcomes of patient empowerment (Karni et al., 2020).

Skinstad and Farshchian (2016) tried mapping ICT concepts to the dimensions of patient empowerment. They envisaged that the choice and responsibility, based on shared decision-making and self-determination, may be accomplished by communication, action planning, and co-design. The development of skills enabling self-efficacy and management may be achieved by ICT-based actions for monitoring, logging, feedback, and prompting, with education as an empowerment dimension being achieved by providing information understandable by the patient.

Technologies empowering patients

In a review on the impact of web-based interventions on patient empowerment, Samoocha et al. (2010) identified the interventions as being all interactive web applications accessed on the Internet or an intranet. They excluded those having no aspects of health education or intentions to change health-related behaviour and only assessed those exerting positive effects on patient empowerment when measured with the appropriate scales. However, they admitted that the effects, although significant, were relatively low, and it was uncertain if they had clinical relevance.

In 2015, a literature review by Calvillo et al. (2015) postulated that other than the development of health literacy and self-care mechanisms, remote access to health services is a critical feature for patient empowerment. They stated that, although there are many promising technologies, like games, virtual worlds, or telemonitoring, web services are most commonly used to empower patients. According to their analysis, the use of technological tools to educate patients, enabling them to make informed decisions, to increase their participation and compliance in the treatment of disease, and to reduce anxiety is the best way of achieving patient empowerment. Improved access and reduced complexity of daily tasks obtained with enhanced patient-doctor communication, online access to administrative tasks, and the use of other telemedicine services is another approach. One should also consider self-care achieved by having access to relevant health information and reliable advice. Finally, Calvillo et al. (2015) indicated that developing patients as providers of support and advice to their peers should be regarded as a feature of patient empowerment.

The analysis of web-based applications supporting patient empowerment and physical activity by cancer survivors showed that the common components included education, self-monitoring, feedback or tailored information, self-management training, personal exercise programmes, and communications with providers or other patients (Kuijpers et al., 2013).

Groen et al. (2015) reviewed the technologies that can be used to empower cancer survivors and identified five requirements: (1) providing educational services, e.g. an electronic survivorship care plan; (2) patient-to-patient services; (3) electronic patient-reported outcome services; (4) multicomponent services; and (5) portal services. The impacts of these in the context of patient empowerment were mainly based on knowledge enhancement and, to a limited extent, enhancing autonomy and skills. Educational services relied mainly on the interactive Internet or offline systems to enhance patients' knowledge about their disease or treatment. The electronic survivorship care plan, as for other chronic diseases, is an individual overview of one's disease, treatment, and the possible side effects. Patient-to-patient services included online support groups and bulletin boards where patients could share their experiences and share advice about disease-related issues. Patient-reported outcomes are an essential part of long-term follow-up but not only for cancer survivors. The use of electronic tools to obtain patient feedback may be more efficient than the traditional collection of patient-reported outcomes, as it facilitates integration with electronic health records. Patient portals offer access to electronic health records and, in a more advanced version, additional services, such as personalised educational programmes, e-consultation with healthcare providers, maintaining diaries, and ordering medication.

Many implemented services rely on multiple enlisted features. The Comprehensive Health Enhancement Support System (CHESS) has been frequently cited as a multicomponent e-health system developed to support women with breast cancer (Owens & Robbins, 1996). The integrated patient empowerment platform for patients with cancer developed within the iManageCancer project is a more recent example (Kondylakis et al., 2020). The tools in this platform include a personal health system, serious games, psycho-emotional monitoring, and decision support functions. Through the Intelligent Personal Health Record, patients can gain access to applications recording and visualising specific patient information, e.g. medication or laboratory results, to health management applications handling appointments or medical documents, to intelligent applications providing recommendations, and finally, to applications enabling the monitoring of patient's psycho-emotional status using online questionnaires (Kondylakis et al., 2020).

Personal health records

The potential of PHR to empowering patients was discussed by Ball et al. in 2007. They indicated that access to their PHR might support patients in the management of chronic conditions, participation in decision-making, and adhering to therapy (Ball et al., 2007). According to Alhomod & Alzahrani (2019), mobile PHR may provide additional benefits when compared with traditional PHR, such as access to data at the point of care, serving as a vault for data storage of the results of diagnostic procedures, reports on interventions, and prescribed medication.

Irizarry et al. (2015) analysed patient portals, understood to be electronic PHR linked to institutional electronic health records with patient engagement. They used the definition of patient engagement proposed by the US Agency for Healthcare Research and Quality (Rockville et al., 2012). This states that patient engagement is "the involvement in their own care by individuals (and others they designate to engage on their behalf), with the goal of making competent, well-informed decisions about their health and health care and take action to support those decisions". This understanding closely corresponds with many features in definitions of patient empowerment. The authors' analysis revealed that patients' interest and the ability to use patient portals depend strongly on sociodemographic characteristics, including age, ethnicity, education, health literacy, and health status. Other factors associated with patients' attitudes include the portal's usability and its endorsement by the healthcare provider.

Risling et al. (2017) assessed how patient empowerment is evaluated in association with e-health technology, mainly understood as patient portals. The use of e-health interventions was frequently hypothesised as having an impact on patient empowerment. The increase of self-efficacy and providing the tools for self-management were the main supportive features. The review of Risling et al. (2017) indicated that the use of patient portals was associated with improved self-reported levels of engagement or activity and enhanced knowledge. Furthermore, in various studied groups, portal use was positively associated with better health outcomes. However, it seems that the benefits attributed to the use of patient portals were rather small. Similar findings were earlier reported by Ammenwerth et al. (2005), who commented that there was no clear evidence of substantial and consistent positive effects of patient portals on patient empowerment and health-related outcomes.

Remote monitoring

Remote monitoring is an important component of technology-supported care for chronic diseases, and many studies report on the successful implementation of remote monitoring systems for specific medical conditions. Kuo et al. (2018) reported that Internet-based self-management interventions implemented for patients with metabolic disorders lead to improved body weight, exercise habits, and laboratory measures, in addition to greater empowerment and a better quality of life. McGloin et al. (2020) reported the empowering effect of remote monitoring for patients with type 2 diabetes transitioning to insulin therapy. Sleurs et al. (2019) found that many mobile applications are available for the management of chronic respiratory diseases offering an option of remote monitoring. However, few provided options, such as personalized feedback, to support patient empowerment.

Jaana et al. (2019) reported ambiguous effects from the use of telemonitoring systems by seniors with chronic heart failure. In a longitudinal study of 6 months' duration, they carried out an assessment of self-care, patient empowerment, and adoption factors. Although the study confirmed patients' confidence in their ability to evaluate symptoms and address them, their ability to be involved in the decision-making process related to their disease had significantly decreased by the end of the study period (Jaana et al., 2019).

The positive impact of real-time data monitoring on patient empowerment was reported for patients with ulcerative colitis (Walsh et al., 2019). The possibility of web-based patient-reported outcomes having the potential to improve patient-centred care and communications between healthcare professionals and patients for those with multiple sclerosis has been reported by Engelhard et al. (2017). The benefits of remote monitoring integrated with electronic health record were analysed by Gandrup et al. (2020), and patient empowerment was an anticipated benefit.

The review of Vo et al. (2019) addressing patients' perceptions of m-health applications revealed that the main benefits included enhanced patient empowerment and the engagement of patients in their own care. However, they indicated many reservations about the trustworthiness, appropriateness, personalisation, and accessibility of m-health applications.

Electronic patient-physician communication

There are many tools facilitating electronic patient-physician communications. According to Voruganti et al. (2017), solutions providing text-based asynchronous communication for patients with diabetes or chronic respiratory conditions prevail. Fewer tools supporting web-based communication were found for patients with cardiovascular diseases. The proposed use of web-based solutions for text exchange by patients suffering from chronic conditions is expected to support self-management.

Furthermore, patient empowerment was indicated as one of the key outcomes of online interactions between healthcare professionals and patients (Shang et al., 2019). The availability of such interactions changed the paradigm existing in offline communication to the role of a healthcare professional primarily moving towards a patient-centred pattern. According to the review of Shang et al. (2019), a set of empowerment outcomes, such as the higher acceptance of the disease and an increased capacity for self-management, results from the provision of online health services. It was also observed that such online interactions positively influenced the health behaviours of patients and improved their treatment adherence, e.g. keeping to pharmacotherapy regimens.

Participating in online patient communities

The use of online health-related resources and communities is perceived as being supplementary to the services provided by healthcare systems. Smailhodzic et al. (2016) showed that the use of social media by patients influences their communication between patients and healthcare professionals, leading to more equal relations, improved interactions and increased changes of physicians.

These results comply, at least partially, with the expected indicators of patient empowerment. The authors identified seven effects on patients caused by the use of social media. Apart from positive impacts, such as improved self-management and control or better psychological wellbeing, diminished subjective wellbeing, addiction to social media, loss of privacy, and being targeted for promotion were also reported.

Johansson et al. (2020) carried out a systematic review assessing the role of online communities as a driver for patient empowerment, which appears to support the claim that participation in online communities frequently acts as a complementary resource to traditional healthcare. According to the authors, the communities help patients to maximise the benefit of their consultations with healthcare professionals because they have a better understanding of the whole care trajectory. Patients participating in online communities were more engaged and participated more actively in the patient-provider relationship. Additionally, patients received support for coping with the emotional burdens related to the course of their disease. The authors commented that participation in online communities supported patient empowerment as a process and an outcome (Johansson et al., 2020). The team proposed a hierarchical framework of the levels of patient empowerment from the stages of being a motivated patient through a self-caring patient, a producing patient, and finally, a patient activist. In their framework, greater involvement, by assisting other patients and participating in collective actions to change policies, was related to higher levels of patient empowerment (Johansson et al., 2020).

Conclusions

It seems that patient empowerment is one of the critical concepts for modern healthcare. It can be understood as a process or as a state in which a patient is a partner for a physician in making decisions about their own health and interacting efficiently with the healthcare system. It is frequently emphasised that the process of patient empowerment was accelerated by the ability to access health-related resources on the Internet. However, patient empowerment benefits not only from the content provided in electronic media but also from many other ICT tools and platforms developed in a health context. A quick review of the literature discussed above shows that probably web-based resources have been most frequently pointed out as technologies supporting patient empowerment. However, many other solutions, e.g. electronic health records or tools for remote monitoring, are now a reality of the delivery of healthcare services. The potential for support of patient empowerment with technological tools is further enhanced with the rise of Health 4.0. Although the common use of IoT, cloud computing (CC), or Big Data (BD) analytics is still to come, the potential of Health 4.0 in the realisation of postulates behind the concept of patient empowerment is enormous.

References

Alhomod, A., & Alzahrani, S. (2019). Patient empowerment via mobile personal health records and mobile health applications: A review of the current use. *Portland International Conference on Management of Engineering and Technology (PICMET)*, 1–4.

Ammenwerth, E., Hoerbst, A., Lannig, S., Mueller, G., Siebert, U., & Schnell-Inderst, P. (2005). Effects of Adult Patient Portals on Patient Empowerment and Health-Related Outcomes: A Systematic Review. In L. Ohon-Machado & B. Seroussi (Eds.), *MEDINFO 2019: Health and Wellbeing e-Networks for All* (pp. 1106–1110). International Medical Informatics Association (IMIA) and IOS Press. https://doi.org/10.1267/NUKL05040119

Anderson, R. M., & Funnell, M. M. (2010). Patient empowerment: Myths and misconceptions. *Patient Education and Counseling*, 79(3), 277–282. https://doi.org/10.1016/j.pec.2009.07.025

Angelmar, R., & Berman, P. C. (2007). Patient Empowerment and Efficient Health Outcomes. In *Financing Sustainable Healthcare in Europe: New Approaches for New Outcomes* (pp. 139–160). Luxembourg: Luxembourg's Ministry of Health, Sitra and Pfizer, Inc. https://media.sitra.fi/2017/02/28141943/The_Cox_Report-2.pdf

Aujoulat, I., D'Hoore, W., & Deccache, A. (2007). Patient empowerment in theory and practice: Polysemy or cacophony? *Patient Education and Counseling*, 66(1), 13–20. https://doi.org/10.1016/j.pec.2006.09.008

Ball, M. J., Smith, C., & Bakalar, R. S. (2007). Personal health records: Empowering consumers. *Journal of Healthcare Information Management*, 21(1), 77. http://rdcms-himss.s3.amazonaws.com/files/production/public/HIMSSorg/Content/files/phr_empowering_cons.pdf

Barr, P. J., Scholl, I., Bravo, P., Faber, M. J., Elwyn, G., & McAllister, M. (2015). Assessment of patient empowerment – A systematic review of measures. *PLoS ONE*, 10(5), e0126553. https://doi.org/10.1371/journal.pone.0126553

Bravo, P., Edwards, A., Barr, P. J., Scholl, I., Elwyn, G., & McAllister, M. (2015). Conceptualising patient empowerment: A mixed methods study. *BMC Health Services Research*, 15(1), 252. https://doi.org/10.1186/s12913-015-0907-z

Bulsara, C., Styles, I., Ward, A. M., & Bulsara, M. (2006). The psychometrics of developing the patient empowerment scale. *Journal of Psychosocial Oncology*, 24(2), 1–16. https://doi.org/10.1300/J077v24n02_01

Calvillo, J., Román, I., & Roa, L. M. (2015). How technology is empowering patients? A literature review. *Health Expectations*, 18(5), 643–652. https://doi.org/10.1111/hex.12089

Crondahl, K., & Karlsson, L. E. (2016). The nexus between health literacy and empowerment: A scoping review. *SAGE Open*, 1–7. https://journals.sagepub.com/doi/pdf/10.1177/2158244016646410

Durneva, P., Cousins, K., & Chen, M. (2020). The current state of research, challenges, and future research directions of blockchain technology in patient care: Systematic review. *Journal of Medical Internet Research*, 22(7), e18619.

Engelhard, M. M., Patek, S. D., Sheridan, K., Lach, J. C., & Goldman, M. D. (2017). Remotely engaged: Lessons from remote monitoring in multiple sclerosis. *International Journal of Medical Informatics*, 100, 26–31. https://doi.org/10.1016/j.ijmedinf.2017.01.006

Faulkner, M. (2001). A measure of patient empowerment in hospital environments catering for older people. *Journal of Advanced Nursing*, 34(5), 676–686. https://doi.org/10.1046/j.1365-2648.2001.01797.x

Funnell, M. M., & Anderson, R. M. (2004). Empowerment and self-management of diabetes. *Clinical Diabetes*, 22(3), 123–127. https://doi.org/10.2337/diaclin.22.3.123

Gandrup, J., Ali, S. M., McBeth, J., van der Veer, S. N., & Dixon, W. G. (2020). Remote symptom monitoring integrated into electronic health records: A systematic review. *Journal of the American Medical Informatics Association*, 27(11), 1752–1763. https://doi.org/10.1093/jamia/ocaa177

Groen, W. G., Kuijpers, W., Oldenburg, H. S. A., Wouters, M. W. J. M., Aaronson, N. K., & Van Harten, W. H. (2015). Empowerment of cancer survivors through information technology: An integrative review. *Journal of Medical Internet Research*, 17(11), e270. https://doi.org/10.2196/jmir.4818

Hood, L., Heath, J. R., Phelps, M. E., & Lin, B. (2004). Systems biology and new technologies enable predictive and preventative medicine. *Science*, 306(5696), 640–643. https://doi.org/10.1126/science.1104635

Irizarry, T., De Vito Dabbs, A., & Curran, C. R. (2015). Patient portals and patient engagement: A state of the science review. *Journal of Medical Internet Research*, 17(6), e148. https://doi.org/10.2196/jmir.4255

Jaana, M., Sherrard, H., & Paré, G. (2019). A prospective evaluation of telemonitoring use by seniors with chronic heart failure: Adoption, self-care, and empowerment. *Health Informatics Journal*, 25(4), 1800–1814. https://doi.org/10.1177/1460458218799458

Johansson, V., Sigridur Islind, A., Lindroth, T., Angenete, E., & Gellerstedt, M. (2020). Online communities as a driver for patient empowerment: A systematic review (preprint). *Journal of Medical Internet Research*, 23(2), e19910. https://doi.org/10.2196/19910

Johnson, M. O., Rose, C. D., Dilworth, S. E., & Neilands, T. B. (2012). Advances in the conceptualization and measurement of health care empowerment: Development and validation of the health care empowerment inventory. *PLoS ONE*, 7(9), e45692. https://doi.org/10.1371/journal.pone.0045692

Johnston Roberts, K. (1999). Patient empowerment in the United States: A critical commentary. *Health Expectations*, 2(2), 82–92. https://doi.org/10.1046/j.1369-6513.1999.00048.x

Karni, L., Dalal, K., Memedi, M., Kalra, D., & Klein, G. O. (2020). Information and communications technology-based interventions targeting patient empowerment: Framework development. *Journal of Medical Internet Research*, 22(8), e17459. https://doi.org/10.2196/17459

Kondylakis, H., Bucur, A., Crico, C., Dong, F., Graf, N., Hoffman, S., Koumakis, L., Manenti, A., Marias, K., Mazzocco, K., Pravettoni, G., Renzi, C., Schera, F., Triberti, S., Tsiknakis, M., & Kiefer, S. (2020). Patient empowerment for cancer patients through a novel ICT infrastructure. *Journal of Biomedical Informatics*, 101, 103342. https://doi.org/10.1016/j.jbi.2019.103342

Kuijpers, W., Groen, W. G., Aaronson, N. K., & Van Harten, W. H. (2013). A systematic review of web-based interventions for patient empowerment and physical activity in chronic diseases: Relevance for cancer survivors. *Journal of Medical Internet Research*, 15(2), e37. https://doi.org/10.2196/jmir.2281

Kuo, C.-C., Su, Y.-J., & Lin, C.-C. (2018). A systematic review and meta-analysis: Effectiveness of internet empowerment-based self-management interventions on adults with metabolic diseases. *Journal of Advanced Nursing*, 74(8), 1787–1802. https://doi.org/10.1111/jan.13574

Lopez, J. E., Orrell, M., Morgan, L., & Warner, J. (2010). Empowerment in older psychiatric inpatients: Development of the empowerment questionnaire for inpatients (EQuIP). *American Journal of Geriatric Psychiatry*, 18(1), 21–32. https://doi.org/10.1097/JGP.0b013e3181b2090b

McAllister, M., Dunn, G., Payne, K., Davies, L., & Todd, C. (2012). Patient empowerment: The need to consider it as a measurable patient-reported outcome for chronic conditions. *BMC Health Services Research*, 12(1), 1–8. https://doi.org/10.1186/1472-6963-12-157

McGloin, H., O'Connell, D., Glacken, M., Sharry, P. M., Healy, D., Winters-O'Donnell, L., Crerand, K., Gavaghan, A., & Doherty, L. (2020). Patient empowerment using electronic telemonitoring with telephone support in the transition to insulin therapy in adults with type 2 diabetes: Observational, pre-post, mixed methods study. *Journal of Medical Internet Research*, 22(5), e16161. https://doi.org/10.2196/16161

Mohr, D. C., Schueller, S. M., Montague, E., Burns, M. N., & Rashidi, P. (2014). The behavioral intervention technology model: An integrated conceptual and technological framework for ehealth and mhealth interventions. *Journal of Medical Internet Research*, 16(6), e146. https://doi.org/10.2196/jmir.3077

Nutbeam, D., & Kickbusch, I. (1998). Health promotion glossary. *Health Promotion International*, 13(4), 349–364. https://doi.org/10.1093/heapro/13.4.349

Owens, B., & Robbins, K. (1996). CHESS: Comprehensive health enhancement support system for women with breast cancer. *Plastic Surgery Nursing*, 16(3), 172–175.

Pekonen, A., Eloranta, S., Stolt, M., Virolainen, P., & Leino-Kilpi, H. (2019). Measuring patient empowerment – A systematic review. *Patient Education and Counseling*, 103, 777–787. https://doi.org/10.1016/j.pec.2019.10.019

Risling, T., Martinez, J., Young, J., & Thorp-Froslie, N. (2017). Evaluating patient empowerment in association with ehealth technology: Scoping review. *Journal of Medical Internet Research*, 19(9), e329. https://doi.org/10.2196/jmir.7809

Rockville, M., Maurer, M., Dardess, P., Carman, K., Frazier, K., & Smeeding, L. (2012). Guide to Patient and Family Engagement: Environmental Scan Report. http://www.ahrq.gov/research/findings/final-reports/ptfamilyscan/ptfamilyscan.pdf

Samoocha, D., Bruinvels, D. J., Elbers, N. A., Anema, J. R., & van der Beek, A. J. (2010). Effectiveness of web-based interventions on patient empowerment: a systematic review and meta-analysis. *Journal of Medical Internet Research*, 12(2), e23. https://doi.org/10.2196/jmir.1286

Schulz, A. J., Israel, B. A., Zimmerman, M. A., & Checkoway, B. N. (1995). Empowerment as a multi-level construct: Perceived control at the individual, organizational and community levels. *Health Education Research*, 10(3), 309–327. https://doi.org/10.1093/her/10.3.309

Shang, L., Zuo, M., Ma, D., & Yu, Q. (2019). The antecedents and consequences of health care professional-patient online interactions: Systematic review. *Journal of Medical Internet Research*, 21(9), e13940. https://doi.org/10.2196/13940

Sharma, D., Singh Aujla, G., & Bajaj, R. (2019). Evolution from ancient medication to human-centered Healthcare 4.0: A review on health care recommender systems. *International Journal of Communication Systems*, e4058. https://doi.org/10.1002/dac.4058

Shelke, Y. (2020). IoMT and Healthcare Delivery in Chronic Diseases. In T. A. Rashid, C. Chakraborty, & K. Fraser (Eds.), *Advanced in Telemedicine for Health Monitoring. Technologies, Design and Applications*. (pp. 239–258).

Skinstad, T., & Farshchian, B. (2016). Empowerment or concealed compliance? A review of literature on mobile ICT solutions for patient empowerment. *Proceedings of the 9th ACM International Conference on Pervasive Technologies Related to Assistive Environments*, 29-June-2016, 1–4. https://doi.org/10.1145/2910674.2910710

Sleurs, K., Seys, S. F., Bousquet, J., Fokkens, W. J., Gorris, S., Pugin, B., & Hellings, P. W. (2019). Mobile health tools for the management of chronic respiratory diseases. *Allergy*, 74(7), 1292–1306. https://doi.org/10.1111/all.13720

Smailhodzic, E., Hooijsma, W., Boonstra, A., & Langley, D. J. (2016). Social media use in healthcare: A systematic review of effects on patients and on their relationship with healthcare professionals. *BMC Health Services Research*, 16(1), 442. https://doi.org/10.1186/s12913-016-1691-0

Vo, V., Auroy, L., & Sarradon-Eck, A. (2019). Patients' perceptions of mhealth apps: Meta-ethnographic review of qualitative studies. *JMIR mHealth and uHealth*, 7(7), e13817. https://doi.org/10.2196/13817

Voruganti, T., Grunfeld, E., Makuwaza, T., & Bender, J. L. (2017). Web-based tools for text-based patient-provider communication in chronic conditions: Scoping review. *Journal of Medical Internet Research*, 19(10), e366. https://doi.org/10.2196/jmir.7987

Walsh, A., Matini, L., Hinds, C., Sexton, V., Brain, O., Keshav, S., Geddes, J., Goodwin, G., Collins, G., Travis, S., & Peters, M. (2019). Real-time data monitoring for ulcerative colitis: Patient perception and qualitative analysis. *Intestinal Research*, 17(3), 365–374. https://doi.org/10.5217/ir.2018.00173

Webb, D. G., Horne, R., & Pinching, A. J. (2001). Treatment-related empowerment: Preliminary evaluation of a new measure in patients with advanced HIV disease. *International Journal of STD and AIDS*, 12(2), 103–107. https://doi.org/10.1258/0956462011916875

Wolf, B., & Scholze, C. (2017). Medicine 4.0. The role of electronics, information technology and microsystems in modern medicine. *Current Directions in Biomedical Engineering*, 3(2), 183–186. https://doi.org/10.1515/cdbme-2017-0038

Zimmerman, M. A. (2000). Empowerment Theory. In *Handbook of Community Psychology* (pp. 43–63). Springer US. https://doi.org/10.1007/978-1-4615-4193-6_2

6 People with disabilities in the information society

Mariusz Duplaga

Introduction

The main aim of this chapter is to review the benefits and threats to persons with disabilities (PWD), which can be related to the use of the Internet. Initially, the changes in the perception of disability that have occurred in recent decades, from being perceived as an individual's misfortune to it being a challenge for society, are discussed, and the main models of disability are presented. The potential of information and communication technologies (ICT) for the support of PWD and the progress made in assistive technologies (AT), driven by ICT developments, shortly described. Finally, the narrative review of studies focusing on the benefits associated with Internet use by PWD, published from the late 1990s, is carried out. The risks originating from the use of the Internet by PWD are also addressed.

Disability – Not an individual misfortune but a challenge for society

The understanding of disability has evolved during recent decades. Before the 1970s, public opinion associated disability with an individual's misfortune. As a result of advocacy and actions undertaken by the organisations of people with disability, it started to be seen as a consequence of the interactions occurring between a person and society (The Union of the Physically Impaired Against Segregation & The Disability Alliance [UPIAS], 1975). The definition of disability proposed by UPIAS stated that it is "the disadvantage or restriction of activity caused by a contemporary social organisation which takes no or little account of people who have physical impairments and thus excludes them from participation in the mainstream of social activity" (UPIAS, 1975). The World Health Organization (WHO) accepted the concept and states on its website that it is a complex phenomenon reflecting the interaction between the features of a person's body and society in which he or she lives (World Health Organization, n.d.). The disability may be associated with a state of impairment, limitation of an activity, or restriction to participation (World Health Organization, n.d.). These concepts were included

DOI: 10.4324/9781003144403-6

in the latest editions of the International Classification of Functioning, Disability and Health (ICF) (World Health Organization, 2013).

There are many models of disability resulting from various perspectives. Historically, disability was associated with sin and shame and, as a result, induced a feeling of guilt (the moral or religious model). Treating the disability as an individual's misfortune was the basis for a charity or tragedy model (Swain & French, 2000). The more recent medical model is based on the assumption that most disabilities are related to medical conditions, and therefore, PWD should remain under the care of medical professionals (Brisenden, 1986). The medical model may be also perceived as a specific case of an individual model of disability (Oliver, 2013). The rehabilitation model is another variant. Currently, the social model of disability is commonly accepted (Lang, 2007). It shifts the emphasis from the functional limitations of the person with the impairment to obstacles resulting from the disabling environment, culture, and society (Barnes & Mercer, 2010). The opportunities provided to PWD by ICT and the growth of the information society (IS) comply with the postulates of reducing the barriers existing in society (Guo et al., 2005). Unfortunately, this potential has not yet been fully exploited.

Unfulfilled expectations from digital inclusion

The broad introduction of ICT has resulted in dramatic advances in AT, usually defined as "any product or service designed to enable independence for disabled and older people" (Abbott, 2007). The introduction of sophisticated solutions falling into the category of augmented and alternative communication devices (AACD) (Baxter et al., 2012) or computer-based speech recognition and synthesis (Lancioni et al., 2013) may be considered as convincing examples. The use of computerised devices to support PWD suffering sensory impairments is another example. The broad integration of ICT with AT has also resulted in advanced tools supporting learning or professional activities.

The rapid growth of the Internet was accompanied by expectations of a considerable positive impact on the quality of life of PWD. From the outset, the Internet and web-based applications were perceived as a game changer for the strategies of support offered to PWD who suffer from social isolation or are limited in their interactions with family members and their peers (Anderson et al., 1995; D'Alessandro et al., 1996; Mike, 1996). It was also stressed that access to the resources available on the Internet might help PWD achieve independent living (Ritchie & Blanck, 2003). The opportunity to search conveniently for information about disability, medical conditions, preserving health, or rehabilitation services was perceived as being of considerable benefit for PWD. The quick adoption of computer-mediated forms of communication (email, bulletin boards, Internet support groups) to conduct advocacy and participate in giving and receiving peer support was reported in the early 1990s (Fullmer & Walls, 1994). Finn emphasised that the benefits for PWD from online groups are related to the accessibility of computer networks combined with self-help (Finn, 1999). He undertook a qualitative analysis of messages from an online self-help group for PWD, showing that it provides many of the processes used in face-to-face self-help and mutual aid groups. Among them, mutual problem-solving, information sharing, expression of feelings, catharsis and mutual support, and empathy were the most frequently identified.

Today, it seems obvious that the Internet may have a profound impact on the health knowledge of PWD and the services and care opportunities available to them. Apart from the access to information, it also provides the opportunity to join online communities, to receive and forward news of advocacy, to purchase goods online, or to be involved in remote vocational activities (Chadwick & Wesson, 2016; Shin, 2019). For PWD who experience limited mobility, Internet access may be their only opportunity to engage in activities that would otherwise be unavailable.

The growth of the IS and the diversity of ICT have brought great promises for PWD. Unfortunately, to date, these expectations have been only partially fulfilled. PWD still experience a significant digital divide. Therefore, the term disability digital divide (DDD) was formulated and is used throughout the literature (Dobransky & Hargittai, 2006; Vicente & López, 2010).

DDD is related to the fact that the disability does not only cause activity limitations and restrictions to participation, but it is often associated with social and economic deprivation, which prevents or limits access to innovative technologies. It should be remembered that the prevalence of disabilities increases with age, and the elderly usually exhibit a lower readiness to adopt new technologies. The use of online services by PWD may be further hampered by the designer's practices who tend to produce interfaces more suited to younger users without impairments but are not appropriate for older people or PWD suffering from various forms of motor or sensory limitations (Bitterman & Shalev, 2004; Davies et al., 2010; Wong et al., 2009).

Although the Web Accessibility Initiative Guidelines (WAIG) have been available for some time (Web Accessibility Initiative [WAI], n.d.), there are many websites that do not follow these guidelines, and their content may be very difficult for PWD to access, especially those with sensory impairments (Laurin et al., 2014; Oliveira & Eler, 2017; Sik-Lanyi & Orbán-Mihálykó, 2019).

Secondary, socioeconomic circumstances seem to prevail as a barrier to the use of the Internet rather than the limitations related to disability. According to the report of Lenhart et al. from the Pew Internet & American Life Project, published in 2003, nearly 20% of PWD asserted that their use of the Internet is difficult because of their limitations (Lenhart et al., 2003). However, the report from the same project published in 2011 revealed that the disability itself was the reason for non-use of the Internet by only 3% of respondents (Fox, 2011).

Lissitsa & Madar (2018) underlined that disability intersects with low rates of Internet adoption and being a member of an underprivileged group.

Vicente & López (2010) found that the lower use of the Internet by PWD in Europe was related to the simple fact that they could not afford it. When compared to the same income groups in the general population, PWD were still unable to meet the costs of Internet access because of the additional finance needed to purchase the adaptive technology required to access the technology. Furthermore, after adjusting for socioeconomic factors, PWD were more likely to be intimidated by the technology. According to Vicente & López (2010), technical accessibility barriers are the main reason for the situation.

The use of the Internet by PWD also depends on the degree of the disability, and it decreases considerably for those with the most severe forms (Choi & Dinitto, 2013; Duplaga, 2017; Duplaga & Szulc, 2019). Finally, it seems also that, although there are many initiatives to increase the access and use of the Internet by the general population, the information needs of PWD are addressed less frequently, even though they comprise about 15% of the total population (World Health Organization, 2011).

The gap in Internet access between PWD and the general population has been reported frequently. The studies emerging from the late 1990s reported a significant difference between the access and use of the Internet by PWD and other citizens in various populations (Duplaga, 2017; Duplaga & Szulc, 2019; Fox, 2011; Kaye, 2000; Office of Communications [Ofcom], 2013; US Department of Commerce, 2000; Vicente & López, 2010). In 2000, the US Department of Commerce reported a decrease in the digital divide between the rich and poor but a persisting gap between PWD and the general population (US Department of Commerce, 2000). The Pew Internet Survey carried out 10 years later indicated a difference of about 25% (Fox, 2011). The analysis of the 2010 European eUser Survey results revealed that the rates of Internet use by PWD were only 50% of that for the general population (Vicente & López, 2010). Similar differences were found for the United Kingdom (Ofcom, 2013), Israel (Lissitsa & Madar, 2018), and more recently for Poland (Duplaga & Szulc, 2019).

Benefits from internet use

The introduction of innovative ICT-based solutions for health care and rehabilitation resulted in unquestionable benefits to patients, health professionals, and health care providers. Improved access to services, the ability to provide care and support in a home environment, the effect of enhanced shared care, maintaining the continuity of care, and in many cases, higher cost-effectiveness of services were most frequently cited in this context (Alvandi, 2017; Farabi et al., 2019). The progress resulting from ICT has also changed the area of AT dedicated to the support of PWD.

However, the applications falling into the categories of telemedicine or AT are usually designed to respond to the needs of well-defined groups of PWD, and their positive impact is embedded in the development process. Less is known about the net effect of digital inclusion for PWD. The number of papers reporting evidence of PWD benefitting from the use of the Internet is unexpectedly low in contrast to prolific statements indicating the potential of the Internet and related technologies for improving the life of PWD. In his 2011 review, Cheatham (2012) identified only six studies that assessed the potential benefits to wellbeing associated with the use of the Internet. Only in three of these studies was Internet use associated with the improvement of wellbeing measures.

The effects resulting from access and use of the Internet by PWD have not been systematically examined. To date, the studies reporting the effects have been mainly based on the observations of relatively small groups of PWD, usually groups with specific types of impairment. Comparisons between users and non-user have been rare. Furthermore, in the available studies, diversified types of outcomes reflecting wellbeing, mental health, or health behaviour have been used. Below, a selection of the studies reporting the positive influence of Internet use by PWD is presented with reference to the year of publication.

Grimaldi and Gette (1999) examined the role of the Internet on the level of perceived independence by people with physical disabilities. The survey demonstrated that the number of Internet services used by the respondent was associated with their perceived level of independence. In the study published in 2003, Bradley and Poppen (2003) reported the results of an assessment of the effects of the Computer for Homebound and Isolated Persons Program, which focused on the development of the online community for homebound persons, including PWD. A follow-up survey 1 year later revealed that participants reported a significant increase in their level of satisfaction from their increased contact with others. Seymour and Lupton (2004) suggested that communications based on the Internet enable PWD to escape the binary distinction of those with and without disabilities typical for the real-world interactions. Later, other authors pointed out that PWD may avoid the stigma of disability in online interactions; however, the repercussions of disguising one's real self on the Internet may be complex (Jaeger et al., 2013). The attitudes and behaviours related to IT among persons with psychiatric disabilities were studied by Cook et al. (2005). The survey revealed that there was a statistically significant relationship between the frequency of Internet use and the self-assessed degree of self-determination.

Houlihan et al. (2003) published a study on the impact of Internet access on a group of 23 people in the United States with spinal cord injury. A qualitative assessment revealed that the main benefit of Internet use by the study participants was their improved quality of life. The same team continued the research on the relationship between Internet use and health-related quality of life (HRQoL) for persons with spinal cord injuries using a quantitative approach (Drainoni et al., 2004). Their analysis revealed that there was a significant relationship between the frequency of Internet use and HRQoL indicators, including self-perceived health status, state of health compared with the situation 1 year earlier, and the scores for occupation and social integration.

Guo et al. (2005) observed that Internet use led to an increased frequency and quality of social interaction. Furthermore, based on the survey involving 122 from 25 provinces in China, they also concluded that the Internet reduced existing societal barriers to the physical and social environment of PWD. According to the report of a Consumer Expert Group published in the United Kingdom in 2009, although PWD highlighted the problem of lower accessibility to online services in comparison to their offline alternatives, they appreciated the increased independence that they gained from using the Internet (Consumer Expert Group, 2009). Smedema and McKenzie (2010) studied the relationship between Internet use and perceived social support by persons with visual impairments or blindness. The results of their analysis were not unequivocal. The frequency and type of Internet use were not significantly associated with the perception of social support by PWD with visual impairments. However, there was a positive association between the use of online chat and social support with wellbeing.

Erhag et al. (2019) analysed the data from 1136 people aged 70 years old participating in the Swedish Gothenburg H70 Birth Cohort Study from 2014 to 2016. They found that after controlling for health factors, hearing and visual impairments, and social contacts, the use of the Internet was still associated with a higher self-rated quality of health. However, the explanatory power of Internet use was relatively low but significant in comparison to the health factors.

The analysis of the data from the 2015 edition of The Social Diagnosis, a large-scale national study undertaken in Poland, showed that the use of the Internet was associated with outcomes related to wellbeing, mental health, and health behaviours (Duplaga & Szulc, 2019). In the 2015 wave of the Social Diagnosis study, 11,740 households and 26,308 individuals participated, from which the data of 2,529 PWD were extracted. Of these, only about 32.9% were Internet users. The multivariate analysis, after adjusting for key sociodemographic variables and the severity of a disability, revealed that Internet users were nearly twice as likely to self-assess their life as happy, and they were 40% less prone to experience loneliness. Furthermore, they reported suicidal thoughts and searching for psychological help only half as often. Finally, they more frequently engaged themselves in some form of physical activity and less frequently smoked cigarettes and consumed alcohol excessively.

The use of social media by various groups of PWD has been a subject of interest for many researchers. The effects of an intervention relying on learning to use social media by young people with communication disabilities in two rural Australian towns were analysed by Raghavendra et al. (2015). Interviews with the eight participants indicated that the intervention resulted in an increased feeling of social connections both by the participants and their parents, resulting in an improved frequency and nature of communication and, finally, improved speech intelligibility and literacy. Positive experiences associated with the use of Twitter by five persons using AACD were reported by Hemsley et al. (2015). They concluded that Twitter could play an important role for conversation and provide a forum for people with communication disabilities, enabling them to exchange ideas and participate socially in online communities. Caton and Chapman (2016) published a systematic review of studies examining the use of social media by people with intellectual disability. The review was based on a thematic analysis of 10 primary studies published between 2000 and June 2014. According to the review, some people with intellectual disabilities confirmed that the use of social media provided them with positive experiences, including friendship, the development of social identity, enhanced self-esteem, and enjoyment.

Finally, Lee and Cho (2019) reported the results of a study exploring the association between the use of social media and wellbeing in people with physical disabilities. Their study involved a survey of 91 users of social network sites and online communities and interviews with a focus group of 15 participants. The quantitative assessment based on hierarchical regression analysis revealed that both the intensity of the use of social network sites and online communities were predictors of instrumental, informational, and appraisal support, but not of emotional support. The greater intensity of using both types of online resources was associated with lower levels of depression.

The risks associated with internet use

The use of the Internet by PWD was not always associated with clear benefits. Some authors were afraid that PWD might be endangered by the Internet paradox described in the late 1990s by Kraut et al. (1998) in the general population. Kraut et al. (1998) reported that higher Internet use was associated with decreased levels of communication with family members and the participants' social circles and with an increase in depression and loneliness. Although the observations from the general population cannot be easily transferred to the population of PWD, some authors feared that Internet use might lead to undesirable effects for such people. It also seems that following the expectations of the progress resulting from the growth of IS in the QoL of PWD, few researchers studied the potential risks related to Internet use.

In the previous section, the studies reporting the positive impact of Internet use by persons with spinal cord injury were described. Miller (2008) also studied this group of PWD for perceived social support associated with the use of the Internet. She observed that for the group of 137 persons with spinal cord injury, unexpectedly, the use of the Internet was not associated with a perception of social support. Furthermore, Internet use showed a significant negative association with the overall sense of wellbeing. As for specific types of online activity, it appeared that online gaming was negatively associated with the sense of wellbeing. Finally, searching for information about disability was negatively associated with psychological and financial wellbeing and also with perceived social support.

A later study focused on students with physical disabilities reported that they experienced restricted participation in computer-based educational activities compared to students from the general population (Lidström et al., 2012). The difference persisted for students with disabilities whether or not they used computer-based AT devices. According to the authors, this situation could be remedied by having an individual plan for each student, which would ensure the appropriate diagnosis of the student's needs in terms of computer-based AT devices, their inclusion in education, and full utilisation of the students' digital skills.

Macdonald and Clayton (2013) analysed the impact of digital technologies on improving the life chances of PWD from deprived neighbourhoods in the northeast of England. They found no evidence that digital or AT had any impact on reducing the social exclusion for PWD. Interestingly, the authors concluded that these technologies could even result in new forms of disabling barriers concerning the digital divide.

The study by Caton and Chapman (2016), cited earlier, demonstrated that although there were potential benefits in using social media for people with intellectual difficulties, they encountered barriers that limited their successful use. These barriers included concerns about safeguarding, the difficulties caused by limited literacy and communication skills, cyber language, and cyber etiquette. In turn, Jenaro et al. observed in a group of 216 young adults with intellectual disabilities that they tended to explcit the more social and recreational features of the Internet and mobile phones more than the educational functions (Jenaro et al., 2018) and used these features more often than their peer group without disabilities. Teachers also indicated the potential risks for persons with intellectual disabilities arising from the use of the Internet. The survey carried out by Chiner et al.(2019) on 582 pre-service and in-service teachers revealed that they see more risks than benefits associated with the use of the Internet by students with intellectual disabilities. According to the respondents, the Internet was not safe enough for such students.

Recently, Borgström et al. (2019) carried out a review using a thematic analysis of papers reporting the use of social media by young people with intellectual disabilities. The risks addressed in the papers included cyberbullying (Buijs et al., 2017), barriers to sexual knowledge (Jahoda & Pownall, 2014), the discrepancy in the views of the Internet among young people with intellectual disabilities and adults (Löfgren-Mårtenson, 2008), and the limited capability to evaluate recommendations made on Internet forums (Salmerón et al., 2016).

Conclusions

The innovations which have been observed in the ICT domain in the recent decades have resulted in significant progress in solutions enabling efficient support for PWD. There is no doubt that computer-based AT, telecare, and telehealth platforms, as well as assisted ambient living technologies, may enhance the lives of PWD having specific forms of impairment and activity limitations.

From the outset, the Internet has been perceived as a major technology that could improve QoL and increase life opportunities for PWD. Unfortunately, this positive potential collides with the reality of the digital divide commonly observed for PWD for whom the consequences of disability go far beyond activity limitations. In the longer perspective, they lead to economic and social deprivation, which in turn precludes or limits their access to innovative technologies, including the Internet and the adaptative solutions to exploit it. In addition, although considerable efforts have been made to increase the use of the Internet by the general population, the problem of limited use of the Internet by PWD has not been addressed systematically.

As for the general population, many positive outcomes were anticipated, but there are also risks related to the use of the Internet. Although the phenomenon of the DDD has been frequently researched, the impact of Internet use among PWD has not been comprehensively assessed. Frequently, it was studied for small groups of PWD with specific disabilities, e.g. on persons who suffered spinal cord injury or among those with intellectual disabilities. Only a few studies have focused on the net effects of Internet use in the whole population of PWD. However, they do seem to confirm the positive influence of Internet use concerning wellbeing, mental health, and even the promotion of favourable health behaviours. The observations made on PWD with specific forms of disabilities allow for a targeted diagnosis of their needs regarding web-based services. The analysis of the repercussions of Internet use in the broader population of PWD may provide arguments for the development of strategies supporting their digital inclusion.

References

Abbott, C. (2007). Defining assistive technologies – a discussion. *Journal of Assistive Technologies*, 1(1), 6–9. https://doi.org/10.1108/17549450200700002

Alvandi, M. (2017). Telemedicine and its role in revolutionizing healthcare delivery. *The American Journal of Accountable Care*, 5(1), e1–e5. https://www.ajmc.com/journals/ajac/2017/2017-vol5-n1/telemedicine-and-its-role-in-revolutionizing-healthcare-delivery

Anderson, R. H., Bikson, T. K., Law, S. A., & Mitchell, B. M. (1995). *Universal access to e-mail: Feasibility and societal implications*. Santa Monica: Rand Corp Center for Information Revolution Analyses.

Barnes, C., & Mercer, G. (2010). Competing models and approaches. In C. Barnes & G. Mercer (Eds.), *Exploring disability* (2nd ed., pp. 14–42). Polity Press.

Baxter, S., Enderby, P., Judge, S., & Evans, P. (2012). Barriers and facilitators to use of high technology augmentative and alternative communication devices: A systematic review and qualitative synthesis. *International Journal of Language & Communication Disorders*, 47(2), 115–129. https://doi.org/10.1111/j.1460-6984.2011.00090.x

Bitterman, N., & Shalev, I. (2004). The silver surfer: Making the internet usable for seniors. *Ergonomics in Design*, 12(1), 24–28. https://doi.org/10.1177/106480460401200107

Borgström, Å., Daneback, K., & Molin, M. (2019). Young people with intellectual disabilities and social media: A literature review and thematic analysis. *Scandinavian Journal of Disability Research*, 21(1), 129–140. https://doi.org/10.16993/sjdr.549

Bradley, N., & Poppen, W. (2003). Assistive technology, computers and internet may decrease sense of isolation for homebound elderly and disabled persons. *Technology and Disability*, 15(1), 19–25. https://doi.org/10.3233/tad-2003-15104

Brisenden, S. (1986). Independent living and the medical model of disability. *Journal of Disability, Handicap & Society*, 1(2), 173–178. https://doi.org/10.1080/02674648666780171

Buijs, P. C. M., Boot, E., Shugar, A., Fung, W. L. A., & Bassett, A. S. (2017). Internet safety issues for adolescents and adults with intellectual disabilities. *Journal of Applied Research in Intellectual Disabilities*, 30(2), 416–418. https://doi.org/10.1111/jar.12250

Caton, S., & Chapman, M. (2016). The use of social media and people with intellectual disability: A systematic review and thematic analysis. *Journal of Intellectual and Developmental Disability*, 41(2), 125–139. https://doi.org/10.3109/13668250.2016.1153052

Chadwick, D., & Wesson, C. (2016). Digital inclusion and disability. In *Applied cyberpsychology* (pp. 1–23). UK: Palgrave Macmillan. https://doi.org/10.1057/9781137517036_1

Cheatham, L. P. (2012). Effects of Internet use on well-being among adults with physical disabilities: A review. *Disability and Rehabilitation: Assistive Technology*, 7(3), 181–188. https://doi.org/10.3109/17483107.2011.625071

Chiner, E., Gómez-Puerta, M., & Mengual-Andrés, S. (2019). Opportunities and hazards of the internet for students with intellectual disabilities: The views of pre-service and in-service teachers. *International Journal of Disability*, 1–16. https://doi.org/10.1080/1034912X.2019.1696950

Choi, N. G., & Dinitto, D. M. (2013). The digital divide among low-income homebound older adults: Internet use patterns, ehealth literacy, and attitudes toward computer/internet use. *Journal of Medical Internet Research*, 15(5), e93. https://doi.org/10.2196/jmir.2645

Consumer Expert Group. (2009). Consumer Expert Group Report into the Use of the Internet by Disabled People: Barriers and Solutions. (Issue October). http://www.dundeecity.gov.uk/dundeecity/uploaded_publications/publication_1679.pdf

Cook, J., Fitzgibbon, G., Batteiger, D., Grey, D., Caras, S., Dansky, H., & Priester, F. (2005). Information technology attitudes and behaviors among individuals with psychiatric disabilities who use the Internet: Results of a web-based survey. *Disability Studies Quarterly*, 25(2). https://dsq-sds.org/article/view/549/726

D'Alessandro, M. P., Galvin, J. R., D'Alessandro, D. M., Erkonen, W. E., Curry, D. S., & Choi, T. A. (1996). The Iowa Health Book: creating, organizing and distributing a digital medical library of multimedia consumer health information on the internet to improve rural health. *Proceedings of the Third Forum on Research and Technology Advances in Digital Libraries*, 28–34.

Davies, T. C., Chau, T., Fehlings, D. L., Ameratunga, S., & Stott, N. S. (2010). Youth with cerebral palsy with differing upper limb abilities: How do they access computers? *Archives of Physical Medicine and Rehabilitation*, 91(12), 1952–1956. https://doi.org/10.1016/j.apmr.2010.08.013

Dobransky, K., & Hargittai, E. (2006). The disability divide in internet access and use. *Information, Communication & Society*, 9(3), 313–334. https://doi.org/10.1080/13691180600751298

Drainoni, M. L., Houlihan, B., Williams, S., Vedrani, M., Esch, D., Lee-Hood, E., & Weiner, C. (2004). Patterns of internet use by persons with spinal cord injuries and relationship to health-related quality of life. *Archives of Physical Medicine and Rehabilitation*, 85(11), 1872–1879. https://doi.org/10.1016/j.apmr.2004.07.350

Duplaga, M. (2017). Digital divide among people with disabilities: Analysis of data from a nationwide study for determinants of Internet use and activities performed online. *PLoS ONE*, 12(6). https://doi.org/10.1371/journal.pone.0179825

Duplaga, M., & Szulc, K. (2019). The association of internet use with wellbeing, mental health and health behaviours of persons with disabilities. *International Journal of Environmental Research and Public Health*, 16(18), 3252. https://doi.org/10.3390/ijerph16183252

Erhag, F. H., Ahlner, F., Rydberg Sterner, T., Skoog, I., & Bergström, A. (2019). Internet use and self-rated health among Swedish 70-year-olds: A cross-sectional study. *BMC Geriatrics*, 19(1), 1–8. https://doi.org/10.1186/s12877-019-1392-8

Farabi, H., Rezapour, A., Jahangiri, R., Jafari, A., Rashki Kemmak, A., & Nikjoo, S. (2019). Economic evaluation of the utilization of telemedicine for patients with cardiovascular disease: a systematic review. *Heart Failure Reviews*, 25(6), 1063–1075. https://doi.org/10.1007/s10741-019-09864-4

Finn, J. (1999). An exploration of helping processes in an online self-help group focusing on issues of disability. *Health & Social Work*, 24 (3), 220–231. https://academic.oup.com/hsw/article-abstract/24/3/220/667525

Fox, S. (2011). Americans Living with Disability and Their Technology Profile. http://www.pewinternet.org/~/media//Files/Reports/2011/PIP_Disability.pdf

Fullmer, S., & Walls, R. (1994). Interests and participation on disability-related computer bulletin boards. *Journal of Rehabilitation*, 60(1), 24–30. http://search.proquest.com/openview/3c8eae1a832882d2318cf8c4723ae84b/1?pq-origsite=gscholar&cbl=1819158

Grimaldi, C., & Goette, T. (1999). The Internet and the independence of individuals with disabilities. *Internet Research*, 9(4), 272–280. https://doi.org/10.1108/10662249910286743

Guo, B., Bricout, J. C., & Huang, J. (2005). A common open space or a digital divide? A social model perspective on the online disability community in China. *Disability and Society*, 20(1), 49–66. https://doi.org/10.1080/0968759042000283638

Hemsley, B., Dann, S., Palmer, S., Allan, M., & Balandin, S. (2015). "We definitely need an audience": Experiences of Twitter, Twitter networks and tweet content in adults with severe communication disabilities who use augmentative and alternative communication (AAC). *Disability and Rehabilitation*, 37(17), 1531–1542. https://doi.org/10.3109/09638288.2015.1045990

Houlihan, B. V., Drainoni, M., Warner, G., Nesathurai, S., & Wierbicky, J. (2003). The impact of Internet access for people with spinal cord injuries. *Disability and Rehabilitation*, 25, 422–431.

Jaeger, L., Kroenung, J., & Kupetz, A. (2013). Me vs. cyber-me analyzing the effects of perceived stigma of physically disabled people on the disguise of the real self in virtual environments. *Proceedings of the 34th International Conference on Information Systems*. https://aisel.aisnet.org/icis2013/proceedings/ConferenceTheme/2/

Jahoda, A., & Pownall, J. (2014). Sexual understanding, sources of information and social networks; the reports of young people with intellectual disabilities and their non-disabled peers. *Journal of Intellectual Disability Research*, 58(5), 430–441. https://doi.org/10.1111/jir.12040

Jenaro, C., Flores, N., Cruz, M., Pérez, M. C., Vega, V., & Torres, V. A. (2018). Internet and cell phone usage patterns among young adults with intellectual disabilities. *Journal of Applied Research in Intellectual Disabilities*, 31(2), 259–272. https://doi.org/10.1111/jar.12388

Kaye, H. (2000). *Computer and internet use among people with disabilities, National Institute on Disability and Rehabilitation Research*. San Francisco, CA: US Department of Education.

Kraut, R., Patterson, M., Lundmark, V., Kiesler, S., Mukopadhyay, T., & Scherlis, W. (1998). Internet paradox: A social technology that reduces social involvement and psychological well-being? *American Psychologist*, 53(9), 1017–1031. https://doi.org/10.1037/0003-066X.53.9.1017

Lancioni, G., Sigafoos, J., O'Reilly, M., & Singh, N. (2013). *Speech-generating devices for communication and social development*. New York: Springer Science+Business Media.

Lang, R. (2007). *The development and critique of the social model of disability*. London: Leonard Cheshire Disability and Inclusive Development Centre. https://www.ucl.ac.uk/epidemiology-health-care/sites/iehc/files/wp-3.pdf

Laurin, S., Cederbom, A., Martinez-Usero, J., Kubitschke, L., Wynne, R., & Cullen, K. (2014). Measures to Improve Accessibility of Public Websites in Europe. http://universaldesign.ie/Web-Content-/Measures-to-improve-accessibility-of-public-websites-in-Europe.pdf

Lee, H. E., & Cho, J. (2019). Social media use and well-being in people with physical disabilities: Influence of SNS and online community uses on social support, depression, and psychological disposition. *Health Communication*, 34(9), 1043–1052. https://doi.org/10.1080/10410236.2018.1455138

Lenhart, A., Horrigna, J., Rainie, L., Allen, K., Boyce, A., Madden, M., & O'Grady, E. (2003). The Ever-Shifting Internet Population: A New Look at Internet Access and the Digital Divide. https://www.pewresearch.org/internet/wp-content/uploads/sites/9/media/Files/Reports/2003/PIP_Shifting_Net_Pop_Report.pdf.pdf

Lidström, H., Granlund, M., & Hemmingsson, H. (2012). Use of ICT in school: A comparison between students with and without physical disabilities. *European Journal of Special Needs Education*, 27(1), 21–34. https://doi.org/10.1080/08856257.2011.613601

Lissitsa, S., & Madar, G. (2018). Do disabilities impede the use of information and communication technologies? Findings of a repeated cross-sectional study – 2003–2015. *Israel Journal of Health Policy Research*, 7(1), 66–83. https://doi.org/10.1186/s13584-018-0260-x

Löfgren-Mårtenson, L. (2008). Love in cyberspace: Swedish young people with intellectual disabilities and the Internet1. *Scandinavian Journal of Disability Research*, 10(2), 125–138. https://doi.org/10.1080/15017410701758005

Macdonald, S. J., & Clayton, J. (2013). Back to the future, disability and the digital divide. *Disability and Society*, 28(5), 702–718. https://doi.org/10.1080/09687599.2012.732538

Mike, D. G. (1996). Internet in the schools: A literacy perspective. *Journal of Adolescent & Adult Literacy*, 40(1), 4–13. https://www.jstor.org/stable/30012106

Miller, S. M. (2008). The effect of frequency and type of internet use on perceived social support and sense of well-being in individuals with spinal cord injury. *Rehabilitation Counseling Bulletin*, 51(3), 148–158. https://doi.org/10.1177/0034355207311315

Office of Communications (Ofcom). (2013). Disabled Consumers' Ownership of Communications Services. A Consumer Experience Report. http://stakeholders.ofcom.org.uk/binaries/research/media-literacy/1515282/Disabled_consumers_use_of_communications_services.pdf

Oliveira, A. D. A., & Eler, M. M. (2017). Strategies and Challenges on the accessibility and interoperability of e-government web portals: A case study on Brazilian Federal Universities. *Proceedings – International Computer Software and Applications Conference*, 1, 737–742. https://doi.org/10.1109/COMPSAC.2017.222

Oliver, M. (2013). The social model of disability: Thirty years on. *Disability and Society*, 28(7), 1024–1026. https://doi.org/10.1080/09687599.2013.818773

Raghavendra, P., Newman, L., Grace, E., & Wood, D. (2015). Enhancing social participation in young people with communication disabilities living in rural Australia: Outcomes of a home-based intervention for using social media. *Disability and Rehabilitation*, 37(17), 1576–1590. https://doi.org/10.3109/09638288.2015.1052578

Ritchie, H., & Blanck, P. (2003). The promise of the Internet for disability: a study of on-line services and web site accessibility at Centers for Independent Living. *Behavioral Sciences & the Law*, 21(1), 5–26. https://doi.org/10.1002/bsl.520

Salmerón, L., Gómez, M., & Fajardo, I. (2016). How students with intellectual disabilities evaluate recommendations from internet forums. *Reading and Writing*, 29(8), 1653–1675. https://doi.org/10.1007/s11145-016-9621-4

Seymour, W., & Lupton, D. (2004). Holding the line online: Exploring wired relationships for people with disabilities. *Disability and Society*, 19(4), 291–305. https://doi.org/10.1080/09687590410001689421

Shin, S.-K. (2019). The convergence of technology and welfare: Effect of the development of ICT on the work environment and job placement for people with disabilities. *Journal of Digital Convergence*, 17(7), 417–422. https://doi.org/10.14400/JDC.2019.17.7.417

Sik-Lanyi, C., & Orbán-Mihálykó, É. (2019). Accessibility testing of European health-related websites. *Arabian Journal for Science and Engineering*, 44(11), 9171–9190. https://doi.org/10.1007/s13369-019-04017-z

Smedema, S. M., & McKenzie, A. R. (2010). The relationship among frequency and type of internet use, perceived social support, and sense of well-being in individuals with visual impairments. *Disability and Rehabilitation*, 32(4), 317–325. https://doi.org/10.3109/09638280903095908

Swain, J., & French, S. (2000). Towards an affirmation model of disability. *Journal of Disability & Society*, 15(4), 569–582. https://doi.org/10.1080/09687590050058189

The Union of the Physically Impaired Against Segregation & The Disability Alliance [UPIAS]. (1975). Fundamental Principles of Disability. https://disability-studies.leeds.ac.uk/wp-content/uploads/sites/40/library/UPIAS-fundamental-principles.pdf

US Department of Commerce. (2000, October). Falling through the Net: Toward Digital Inclusion. A Report on Americans' Access to Technology Tools. https://www.ntia.doc.gov/files/ntia/publications/fttn00.pdf

Vicente, M. R., & López, A. J. (2010). A multidimensional analysis of the disability digital divide: Some evidence for internet use. *Information Society*, 26(1), 48–64. https://doi.org/10.1080/01615440903423245

Web Accessibility Initiative [WAI]. (n.d.). Introduction to Web Accessibility. What Is Web Accessibility? https://www.w3.org/WAI/intro/accessibility.php

Wong, A. W. K., Chan, C. C. H., Li-Tsang, C. W. P., & Lam, C. S. (2009). Competence of people with intellectual disabilities on using human-computer interface. *Research in Developmental Disabilities*, 30(1), 107–123. https://doi.org/10.1016/j.ridd.2008.01.002

World Health Organization. (n.d.). WHO Health Topics. Disabilities. https://www.who.int/topics/disabilities/en/

World Health Organization. (2011). World Report on Disability. www.who.int/about/licensing/copyright_form/en/index.html

World Health Organization. (2013). *How to use the ICF: A practical manual for using the International Classification of Functioning, Disability and Health (ICF)*. Geneva: WHO. https://www.who.int/classifications/drafticfpracticalmanual.pdf

7 Health 4.0 for the elderly

New challenges and opportunities for a smart system

Francesco Schiavone, Stefano Tagliaferri, Gaetano Cafiero, Michela De Rosa, and Rosa De Angelis

Introduction

The advances associated with Industry 4.0 have had a huge impact on healthcare technologies (collectively known as Health 4.0). The new paradigm that is emerging in this area involves not only connecting medical devices but rather marks out an important path for developing and interlinking intelligent health data systems with the aim to extract knowledge useful for addressing emerging social challenges. As a direct consequence of demographic changes along with improved access to healthcare services, the demand for care services is on the rise. The question therefore arises as to how to meet the needs of patients and at the same time fit well in the social, political, and economic context of reference (Sneha and Straub, 2017). The demographic changes coupled with advances in medical science present several critical challenges in terms of cost and quality of healthcare, which implies the need for a new paradigm in health services and processes. In this perspective, the use of ICT in healthcare promises to enhance the quality, efficiency, and effectiveness of health service management (De Rosis and Vainieri, 2017). A health information system based on a remotely collected set of well-organised and reliable real-time data can provide tangible support in implementing evidence-based treatment methods (Azimi et al., 2017).

Health professionals and other stakeholders involved in the provision of health services to the elderly are called upon to move toward a new awareness in decision-making which should reflect the evaluation of the best practices in the management of elderly care. In this approach, it is important to optimise the care of all patients through an appropriately designed system that facilitates delivering patient-oriented care and to assess its quality. The transformative impact of new technologies on healthcare is likely to produce an interconnected health ecosystem based on a focus on people, empowering the actors involved in the healthcare system with a view to co-creating new value for the wellbeing of the elderly (The European House-Ambrosetti, 2019).

However, despite all the potential benefits, the actual implementation of digital transformation (DT) in healthcare services faces a number of barriers. Some of them involve limited interest in and readiness to accept new

DOI: 10.4324/9781003144403-7

technologies, while other barriers are associated with the reference context from which the prerequisites for effective change are missing. In this perspective, the present contribution aims to emphasise the significant role that DT, as part of the broader paradigm of Health 4.0, has to play in the healthcare sector in a context in which new opportunities for the development and implementation of digital models inevitably collide with social, political, and economic barriers. At present, each and every actor in the system should acknowledge that DT is the keystone for sustainable growth in the healthcare sector and should contribute to creating conditions conducive to its full and actual implementation.

The ageing population and the digital transformation: An outline of the social background

As people live longer, population ageing is becoming one of the most critical phenomena that characterise the 21st century (Czaja et al., 2019). Improvements in public health, advances in medicine, and the positive economic and social developments have contributed to enhancing people's wellbeing and quality of life, even if socio-economic differences still persist. While on the one hand longevity undoubtedly represents a great achievement, since it testifies to the steadily improving living conditions and progress in medicine, on the other, it may well turn into a threat for the immediate future unless it is counterbalanced by a renewed capacity to devise adequate, systematic, and timely health policy interventions that involve research, the well-being of the elderly taking into consideration the evolution of the very concept of ageing (Kielland Aanesen and Borras, 2013). Countries have very different demographic trajectories - some populations are ageing rapidly, even shrinking; as a result, their workforce as a proportion of the total population is due to decrease (PwC, 2016). In 2019, there were 703 million persons aged 65 years or over worldwide. The number of older people is projected to double to 1.5 billion in 2050 (WHO, 2020). Specifically, the share of the population aged 65 years or over increased from 6% in 1990 to 9% in 2019, and this proportion is projected to rise further to 16% by 2050. The world's largest populations in this age bracket live in Asia and Europe (cf. Figure 7.1) (UNO, 2019).

Specifically, considering the top 10 countries with the greatest percentage of elderly people (65 years old and over), Japan is the country with the highest presence of 28%, which translates into 35.58 million. In Italy, the elderly account for 23% of the population, followed by Finland, Greece, Portugal, Germany, and Bulgaria - each with more than 21%. The top 10 is concluded by Croatia, Latvia, and France, which register less than 21% each (Figure 7.2) (UNO, 2019).

The rapid ageing of the population is associated with a significant increase in the prevalence of chronic diseases, which entails the need for continuous supervision and intensive contact with health and social care centres in order to ensure a healthy and sustainable lifestyle in compliance with the quality

Figure 7.1 People aged 65 or over in world's 50 most populous countries.

Source: Own study based on World Population Prospects 2019.

standards applicable to the care of the elderly (Abdi et al., 2018). In 2014, the World Health Assembly requested the Director-General to develop a comprehensive global strategy and action plan on ageing and health as a significant step towards establishing a framework of shared principles for the

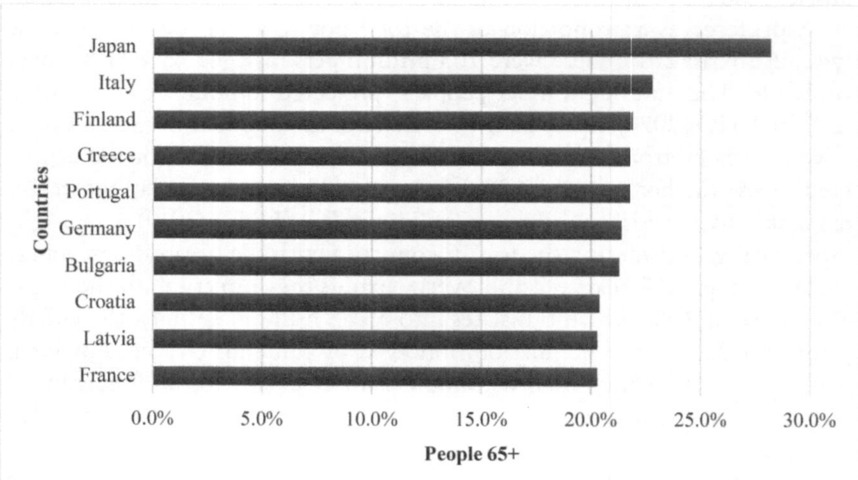

Figure 7.2 Top 10 countries with the highest percentage of people aged 65 or older.

Source: Own study based on World Population Prospects 2019.

Member States. In a long-term perspective, it is expected to be the main blueprint for a world in which everyone can live a long and healthy life. By 2020, the strategy had achieved its second goal - to establish evidence and partnerships necessary to support a Decade of Healthy Ageing from 2020 to 2030.

As the number of older people requiring care and support increases, every country will need to have an integrated system of long-term care in place. Its main objective should be to help older people maintain the best possible level of functional ability in order to allow them to live with dignity as well as enjoy their basic human rights and fundamental freedoms. Moreover, considering the fact that their health needs will inevitably become more complex and chronic, a transformation is required in the way that health systems are designed to ensure feasible access to integrated patient-centred services. In most care contexts, however, taking into account the social, economic, and political conditions will demand fundamental changes in the way care is organised, funded, and delivered across the health and social sectors.

In the context of Health 4.0, DT, which involves a combination of information, computing, communication, and connectivity technologies (Vial, 2019), can play an essential role. The shift to an increasingly digital world that we are witnessing today is swiftly changing the ways in which global industries experience new business models and growth. The healthcare sector can derive several advantages from the opportunities offered by the new paradigm (Reis et al., 2018). The DT opens up a range of opportunities leading to value creation at local, regional, and national levels from a multi-stakeholder perspective. Proper implementation of e-health has shown to improve co-operation among the service providers and fosters partnership between healthcare organisations. Accordingly, the shift to an increasingly digital world is also rapidly changing the ways in which the healthcare industry experiences new business models and growth. Various actors of the healthcare ecosystem (patients, pharmaceutical companies, hospitals, public agencies, and many more) contribute to it through several forms of innovation (García-Holgado et al., 2019). DT is significantly enhancing the healthcare as experienced by both professionals and patients, especially in supporting its operational efficiency and the quality of medical services provided; nonetheless, the challenges it is facing should not be underestimated (Farahani et al., 2018).

Health 4.0 systems in elderly care

Health 4.0 applications harness technological progress in order to more effectively respond to the needs of patients and in the process, to overcome the barriers of traditional systems with modern technologies of information and communication (Shah and Chircu, 2018). New smart digital solutions have the potential to support the healthcare system by empowering individuals to have more control over monitoring their health (Catalyst, 2017). A wide range of services, such as communication, consultation, monitoring, diagnostics, and training, maintain user autonomy and improve the quality of available care. A key role among the technologies dedicated to the elderly is played by remote assistance systems. Generally, considering the services provided, they can be divided into three main categories:

- Support is delivered via information and communication technology (ICT).
- Support is delivered via the monitoring of health parameters and vital signs.
- Safety and security monitoring, such as gas sensors, and flood and fire detectors.

The term health-related information and communication technologies (HRICT) refers to systems or devices that often depend on microprocessors used to collect, process, display, and communicate information. These forms of technology include devices such as desktop computers, smartphones, smartwatches, and tablets (Dupuis and Tsotsos, 2018). ICT can provide assistance to many older people who face social isolation due to age-related declines in health and mobility, loss of partner, etc. It can allow them to keep in touch with the outside world, take advantage of social assistance, participate in a variety of activities, and boost their self-confidence. Web-connected ICT provides new communication capabilities by promoting higher levels of interaction, facilitating access to digital information and services than its non-web-connected counterparts. The purpose of using ICT tools is to give the patient the opportunity to remain safely under constant medical supervision in a friendly environment. The supervision is carried out by teleconsultation/videoconference between the patient and the doctor, the nurse, or other healthcare professionals in order to monitor for possible worrying changes in vital signs, syncope, and other potentially dangerous situations. The patient has access to their primary care physician, as well as to specialists, nurses, and other health professionals regardless of their place of residence, whereas the necessary examinations can be performed virtually at any time of the day or night. Direct and speedy access to qualified health professionals without having to leave home or endure long waiting times makes telemedicine modules an extremely promising and affordable solution for the elderly and the disabled. The advent of and advances in wearable technologies have opened the door to developing innovative and practical elderly care devices. Human activity recognition (HAR) can provide continuous monitoring of the activities of an elderly person (Hassan et al., 2018). It already plays an important role in people's daily lives owing to its ability to generate high-level knowledge about human activity from raw sensor inputs. It can be divided into two categories: vision-based recognition and sensor-based recognition.

- Vision-based systems use captured images or recorded video sequences to monitor the activities of the elderly and, unlike contact-based activity recognition systems, have a non-intrusive nature - ordinary users are not required to wear different and uncomfortable devices on different parts of their body; this system is limited to specific environments in which such visual disturbances can be controlled with a video recorder (Beddiar et al., 2020)
- Sensor-based systems focus on motion data relayed from smart sensors such as accelerometers, gyroscopes, Bluetooth devices, and sound sensors (Chen and Shen, 2017)

Moreover, the current mainstream Health 4.0 systems devised specifically with senior citizens in mind include wearable technologies with care functions, such as smartwatches/smartphones and smart clothing. Some of the latter can recognise physical activity and monitor physiological vital signs, whereas others can detect a disease early. Wearable technologies can be improved to pinpoint the patient's exact location indoors and outdoors, which would be useful if the patient was alone and needed immediate help. ICT also includes artificial intelligence (AI), which is used to collect and process data on patient status from electronic health records and other sources to aid the diagnostic process. If AI becomes the foundation for health technologies, it can fundamentally transform elderly care facilities and practices (Amin et al., 2021). Falls, deteriorating health, and emergencies can be anticipated and prevented by feeding algorithms with data from monitoring systems and sensors. AI has the potential to optimise care processes, increase the quality of life of end users, and enable them to lead an active, healthy, and independent life. By combining large data sets from electronic health records and care documentation, monitoring, and surveillance systems as well as smart wearable sensors with the best available empirical evidence, AI systems could fulfil the promise of the so-called P4 (Shin et al, 2018) or predictive, personalized, preventive, and participatory medicine (Jenkins and Maayan, 2013). It empowers patients by allowing them to play an active role in the process and also gives them at least partial control over their health data (Jayaratne et al., 2019). To sum up, Health 4.0 may offer elderly people a broad range of benefits. The awareness of being constantly monitored instils a greater sense of security in the elderly, who can benefit from remote assistance while remaining in a familiar and comfortable environment. At the same time, remote assistance allows them to maintain their independence and continue to live in their own homes.

One of the key attributes of telemedicine systems is electronic connectivity, which transcends time and distance barriers. With telecare technologies, elderly people enjoy almost instant access to a series of geographically and functionality disparate health providers without having to travel to distant places, and at times that are convenient both for themselves and healthcare professionals. Physicians in various practice locations can have ready access to efficient tools for clinical decision-making (Perera et al., 2021).

The implementation of digital transformation in elderly care: Critical issues to consider

Considering the benefits brought about by the new smart tools and their main users, various barriers to healthcare delivery are set to be broken by the optimal utilisation of digital technologies. Over the next few decades, older adults will become an increasingly larger segment of technology consumers, hence their acceptance of innovative technologies in routine healthcare processes is a key success factor for governments, technology suppliers, and healthcare providers as well as other groups of healthcare stakeholders (Ali et al., 2021). The ease of use and user interface design choices play a crucial role in their experience of the system: The goal should be to offer a device that can be as intuitive as possible, while keeping in mind that older adults may have limited information-processing capabilities. They tend to be more easily distracted than younger ones, more memory-constrained, and process information more slowly, taking on average about twice as long for basic mental and physical activities to complete. However, the most critical challenge is how to communicate the instructions on the use of digital solutions to their intended end users. In any case, clear and simple instructions will be needed in consideration of individual differences in the learning process, self-efficacy, learning anxiety, motivation to learn, cognitive ability, and enthusiasm for a specific topic. It is essential to understand whether the healthcare technology offered is perceived as interesting and necessary. Its successful deployment will depend on selecting feasible technologies, relevance to the needs of the elderly, appropriate instruction and training, and understanding the differences in cognition, motor control, technology experience, and motivation. Education and training of all the service users, its availability, and the acceptance of necessary technology have been suggested as possible bottlenecks that need to be resolved before e-health can be fully implemented globally. More noteworthy is the fact that despite the broad coverage of e-health, considerable inequity in access to it still persists (Viswanath and Kreuter, 2007). This is attributed to low technology literacy in middle- and low-income countries. Moreover, individuals in those countries have been reported less likely to seek health information online (Gibbons et al., 2011; Viswanath, 2006; Zach et al., 2012), which may be due to poverty or low levels of education. The existing empirical research has already provided a number of relevant insights in this respect. For example, geographical location and language proficiency are significant predictors of digital technology adoption. Behavioural or attitudinal factors (e.g. lack of trust, lack of time, lack of support, or lack of interest) have also been shown to limit the use of e-health services. Even though digital technologies pervade all aspects of our lives, a 'digital divide' has been observed between the young and the elderly. For these reasons, it is important not only to understand the benefits associated with Health 4.0 but also to recognise the barriers that the elderly people encounter in using these technologies.

First, the adoption of DT faces physical barriers that include changes in motor, cognitive, and sensory abilities. Age-related changes in fine motor control and coordination due to diseases such as arthritis may significantly affect an individual's ability to physically interact with technology by making it more difficult for older adults to use the input devices currently in use such as a mouse or a keyboard that often accompany assistive devices (Czaja and Lee, 2002). Cognitive impairment refers to the problems of elderly with such functions as thinking, reasoning, memory, or attention span.

Sensory changes may cause some of the greatest barriers to the use of technology by older adults; in fact, people with visual or auditory impairments will find it challenging to use new technology. Moreover, representatives of this age group usually prefer personal communication with health professionals, which means that the elimination of face-to-face contact may create a perception of reduced social interaction in the older person's life. Another barrier may be posed by the prospect of spending money: Pensioners may fear the high costs of purchasing computer equipment or other electronic devices. Despite the health benefits made possible by telecare services, older people are often unwilling to invest in home health monitoring systems. On their part, professionals need to develop specific skills to deliver better care to older people. Many of these skills are associated with digital information processing as part of deeper learning based on analytical, complex reasoning, problem-solving, and teamwork. It is essential that health professionals should critically review their actions, keep abreast of new developments by reading specialist literature, and engage in ongoing professional development. Having said that some health professionals have concerns about e-health services. One of them has to do with patient safety since a malfunctioning device may generate incorrect patient information, offer misleading advice, or even prompt harmful decisions (Fernando et al., 2004). Exactly how secure and private is the information stored using DT remains a hotly debated topic. Health professionals are also responsible for concerns related to the confidentiality and security of patient data, which can be yet another major obstacle to the use of e-health services by patients. Not all the systems are considered as sufficiently secure (Car et al., 2007), given the fact that the data stored in them may be subject to unauthorised modification, which may result in critical errors in the evaluation process. Several studies point to the fact that the internet does not actually supersede face-to-face consultation but rather serves as a supplementary dispensable service (Sanders et al., 2015), which continues to depend on enabling technology that supports the relations between patients and well-skilled clinicians.

A new empowerment paradigm for elderly healthcare

Recent progress in ICT, sensor networks, and wired and wireless home networking has led to significant advancements in home automation for remote health monitoring. E-health offers a number of benefits for both the patients and health professionals in the delivery of healthcare. A major one involves patient empowerment (Kontos et al., 2014) in that healthcare providers can communicate with patients easily and more frequently, and address their health concerns even if they are in different locations. More effective and efficient healthcare services would be delivered to more patients, providing feasible access to information and self-care (Scholz, 2015).

In this way, e-health helps to avoid unnecessary referrals, hospital visits, and admissions. It is of proven benefit in improving the efficiency of healthcare practitioners (Car et al., 2007) because patient information can be easily accessed and decisions can be made earlier (Wade et al., 2010), "reducing waiting time in clinics and the time of burdensome consultations" (Jennett et al., 2003).

Several studies support the effectiveness of e-health in reducing the time to diagnosis, ensuring access of individuals to health services in remote areas, and improving quality of life and patient satisfaction (McLean et al., 2013). Ammenwerth and Shaw (2005) also argue that e-health is expected to reduce the medical error rate due to its capacity to improve "the record-keeping, retrieval, and sharing of patients' information" (Pagliari et al., 2007). This technology needs to be supported by an interactive platform for integrating the collected data to be shared with health services. The availability of data and technical support are both critical elements needed to enhance evidence-based decision-making, monitoring, and evaluation.

The complexity of the demographic health profiles of the elderly and their specific needs requires a greater sophistication in equipment and technologies. In the case of the elderly, it is particularly important to consider person-centeredness, usability, and accessibility of e-health technologies to ensure that meaningful data is captured, and relevant feedback is provided.

Moreover, in light of the relevance of technology from the value co-creation perspective, as discussed in Chapter 8, it is possible to consider e-health as a means of integrating and optimising the resources exchanged as well as creating new insights. In order to increase and improve patient engagement, e-health is not limited to simply providing the technical infrastructure but rather considers the social aspects associated with the development of new practices that foster patient autonomy. Patients become 'co-producers of services' and 'partial employees' in the health service delivery process due to their active role in managing the own care plans (Mende, 2019). The professional-patient relationship in the healthcare system is enhanced by the DT that contributes to providing self-service and feedback cycles (Gray et al., 2013), typical features of a healthcare industry that is becoming increasingly patient-centred.

On their part, decision-makers in the health sector should be encouraged to manage better ICT platforms, strive towards the creation of competence centres in digital healthcare, build a digital space shared among all the actors of the ecosystem, and support the development of digital healthcare and value co-creation (Botti and Monda, 2020). In this sense, public decision-makers and standard setters should be induced to stimulate active citizenship through actor engagement and to lay out the conditions for a participatory governance model. As will be discussed in Chapter 12, the definition of new patient-centred social norms is required, such as the democratisation of the health service; more specific e-health law to clarify the roles, rights, and responsibilities of the various actors involved (Geissbuhler, 2013); the dematerialisation of pharmaceutical prescriptions; remote monitoring; and access to health documentation through technology. The actual implementation of the new paradigm requires healthcare organisations to devise appropriate investment strategies taking into account the financial resources available (Dobrev et al. 2008); public-private partnerships in developing health policies are also encouraged.

Table 7.1 Health 4.0 for the elderly: main findings

Evidence

- Demographic data indicates that the proportion of senior citizens in the total population is set to increase worldwide. The number of older adults is projected to double to 1.5 billion by 2050.
- Digitalisation in the healthcare sector is revolutionising the way health conditions are prevented, treated, and managed. Health 4.0 has an increasing impact on care delivery and offers the opportunity to address the next frontier of healthcare by shifting the focus from treatment to prevention. Therefore, healthcare, which requires ever new and more advanced solutions, continues to present one of the most significant social and economic challenges worldwide.

Problem

- Elderly patients tend to have complex health needs due to the fact that they usually suffer from a range of conditions and diseases. As life expectancy is increasing, providing the best care and constant support to an ageing person through remote monitoring and home care is not a simple task.

Solution

- Health 4.0 can make a difference in contexts where the physician and the patient cannot meet face to face. It has already successfully addressed the issues of access, efficiency, and quality of a range of healthcare processes by overcoming the problems of physical distance and access to heterogeneous health data sources.

Barriers	*Needs*
• <u>*Users*</u>: Physical barriers related to cognitive skills and attitudes; economic barriers due to a limited budget to access digital solutions. • <u>*Providers:*</u> Misperception of interests; lack of training for new digital solutions.	• Support to the elderly in developing digital skills. • Creation of digital solutions that correspond to the actual skills and capabilities of the elderly. • Policymakers and standard setters must support active citizenship through actor engagement and lay down the conditions for a participatory governance model.

Source: Own study.

Conclusions

To sum up, the use of e-health services depends on enabling technology-supporting relations between patients and competent medical staff, which are the main drivers of the new, patient-oriented healthcare paradigm involving sustainable value co-creation. On their part, hospitals and decision-makers must identify and act on the drivers of successful implementations, while governments should support the development of e-health programs by providing an adequate framework for medical jurisdiction, liability, and reimbursement for e-health services. Health professionals should try to incorporate this new digital culture in their day-to-day work and to assume a key role in supporting patients in self-management (cf. Table 7.1).

References

Abdi, J., Al-Hindawi, A., Ng, T., and Vizcaychipi, M. P. (2018). Scoping review on the use of socially assistive robot technology in elderly care. *BMJ Open*, *8*(2), e018815.

Ali, M. A., Alam, K., Taylor, B., and Ashraf, M. (2021). Examining the determinants of e-health usage among elderly people with disability: The moderating role of behavioural aspects. *International Journal of Medical Informatics*, *149*, 104411.

Amin, H., Weerts, J., Brunner-La Rocca, H. -P., Knackstedt, C., and Sanders-van Wijk, S. (2021). Future perspective of heart failure care: Benefits and bottlenecks of artificial intelligence and ehealth. *Future Medicine*. 10, 1–5.

Ammenwerth, E., and Shaw, N. T. (2005). Bad health informatics can kill – is evaluation the answer? *Methods of Information in Medicine*, *44*(01), 1–3.

Azimi, I., Rahmani, A. M., Liljeberg, P., and Tenhunen, H. (2017). Internet of things for remote elderly monitoring: A study from user-centered perspective. *Journal of Ambient Intelligence and Humanized Computing*, *8*(2), 273–289.

Beddiar, D. R., Nini, B., Sabokrou, M., and Hadid, A. (2020). Vision-based human activity recognition: A survey. *Multimedia Tools and Applications*, *79*(41), 30509–30555.

Botti, A., and Monda, A. (2020). Sustainable value co-creation and digital health: The case of trentino e-health ecosystem. *Sustainability*, *12*(13), 5263.

Car, J., Koshy, E., Bell, D. and Sheikh, A. (2007). Telephone triage in out of hours call centres. *BMJ*, *337*, e1167.

Catalyst, N. E. J. M. (2017). What is patient-centered care? *NEJM Catalyst*, *3*(1), 1–3.

Chen, Y., and Shen, C. (2017). Performance analysis of smartphone-sensor behavior for human activity recognition. *IEEE Access*, *5*, 3095–3110.

PwC (2016). Five megatrends and their implications for global defense & security. *Ausgabe November, S*, *1*, 1–32.

Czaja, S. J., Boot, W. R., Charness, N., and Rogers, W. A. (2019). *Designing for older adults: Principles and creative human factors approaches*. Boca Raton, FL: CRC press.

Czaja, S. J., and Lee, C. C. (2002). Designing computer systems for older adults. In J. Jacko and A. Sears (eds.), *Handbook of human-computer interaction*. Mahwah, NJ: Lawrence Erlbaum and Associates.

De Rosis, S., and Vainieri, M. (2017). Incentivizing ICT in healthcare: A comparative analysis of incentive schemes in Italian Regions. *International Journal of Healthcare Management*, *10*(1), 1–12.

Dobrev, A., Jones, T., Stroetmann, V., Stroetmann, K., Artmann, J., Kersting, A., Kasiri, N., Zegners D., and Lilischkis, S. (2008). Sources of financing and policy recommendations to Member States and the European Commission on boosting e-health investment. Final report of the Financing e-health study.

Dupuis, K., and Tsotsos, L. E. (2018). Technology for remote health monitoring in an older population: A role for mobile devices. *Multimodal Technologies and Interaction, 2*(3), 43.

Farahani, B., Firouzi, F., Chang, V., Badaroglu, M., Constant, N., and Mankodiya, K. (2018). Towards fog-driven IoT e-health: Promises and challenges of IoT in medicine and healthcare. *Future Generation Computer Systems, 78*, 659–676.

Fernando, B., Savelyich, B. S., Avery, A. J., Sheikh, A., Bainbridge, M., Horsfield, P., and Teasdale, S. (2004). Prescribing safety features of general practice computer systems: Evaluation using simulated test cases. *BMJ, 328*(7449), 1171–1172.

García-Holgado, A., Marcos-Pablos, S., and García-Peñalvo, F. J. (2019). A model to define an e-health technological ecosystem for caregivers. In *World Conference on Information Systems and Technologies* (pp. 422–432). Cham: Springer.

Geissbuhler, A. (2013). Lessons learned implementing a regional health information exchange in Geneva as a pilot for the Swiss national e-health strategy. *International Journal of Medical Informatics, 82*(5), e118–e124.

Gibbons, M. C., Fleisher, L., Slamon, R. E., Bass, S., Kandadai, V., and Beck, J. R. (2011). Exploring the potential of Web 2.0 to address health disparities. *Journal of Health Communication, 16*(Suppl 1), 77–89.

Gray, P., El Sawy, O. A., Asper, G., and Thordarson, M. (2013). Realizing strategic value through center-edge digital transformation in consumer-centric industries. *MIS Quarterly Executive, 12*(1), 1–17.

Hassan, M. M., Uddin, M. Z., Mohamed, A., and Almogren, A. (2018). A robust human activity recognition system using smartphone sensors and deep learning. *Future Generation Computer Systems, 81*, 307–313.

Jayaratne, M., Nallaperuma, D., De Silva, D., Alahakoon, D., Devitt, B., Webster, K. E., and Chilamkurti, N. (2019). A data integration platform for patient-centered e-healthcare and clinical decision support. *Future Generation Computer Systems, 92*, 996–1008.

Jenkins, S. L., and Maayan, A. (2013). Systems pharmacology meets predictive, preventive, personalized and participatory medicine. *Pharmacogenomics, 14*(2), 119–122.

Jennett, P. A., Affleck, H. L., Hailey, D., Ohinmaa, A., Anderson, C., Thomas, R., Young, B., Loenzetti, D., and Scott, R. E. (2003). The socio-economic impact of tele-health: A systematic review. *Journal of Telemedicine and Telecare, 9*(6), 311–320.

Kielland Aanesen, H. A. and Borras, J. (2013). E-Health: The future service model for home and community healthcare. *2013 7th IEEE International Conference on Digital Ecosystems and Technologies (DEST).* Menlo Park, CA, 172–177.

Kontos, E., Blake, K. D., Chou, W. Y. S., and Prestin, A. (2014). Predictors of e-health usage: Insights on the digital divide from the Health Information National Trends Survey 2012. *Journal of Medical Internet Research, 16*(7), e172.

McLean, S., Sheikh, A., Cresswell, K., Nurmatov, U., Mukherjee, M., Hemmi, A., and Pagliari, C. (2013). The impact of tele-healthcare on the quality and safety of care: A systematic overview. *PLoS One, 8*(8), e71238.

Mende, M. (2019). The innovation imperative in healthcare: An interview and commentary. *AMS Review, 9*(1–2), 121–131.

Pagliari, C., Detmet, D., and Singleton, P. (2007). *Electronic personal health records emergence and implications for the UK: A report to the Nuffield Trust.* London: The Nuffield Trust.

Perera, M. S., Halgamuge, M. N., Samarakody, R., and Mohammad, A. (2021). Internet of Things in healthcare: A survey of telemedicine systems used for elderly people. In G. Marques, A.K. Bhoi, V.H.C. de Albuquerque, K.S., Hareesha (eds.), *IoT in healthcare and ambient assisted living*. Singapore: Springer.

Reis, J., Amorim, M., Mel ã o, N., and Matos, P. (2018). *Digital transformation: A literature review and guidelines for future research*. Cham: Springer.

Sanders, K., Sáanchez Valle, M., Viñaras, M., and Llorente, C. (2015). Do we trust and are we empowered by "Dr. Google"? Older Spaniards' uses and views of digital healthcare communication. *Public Relations Review, 41*(5), 794–800.

Scholz, N. (2015). *ehealth – Technology for Health* (pp. 1–8). European Parliamentary Research Service, EPRS. Briefing.

Shah, R., and Chircu, A. (2018). IoT and AI in healthcare: A systematic literature review. *Issues in Information Systems, 19*(3), 33–41.

Shin, M. S., Lee, H. Y., Kim, J. S., and Ki, J. H. (2018). Design of intelligent healthcare support system applying machine learning. *International Journal of Advanced Scientific Technologies in Engineering and Management Sciences, 111*, 73–84.

Sneha, S., and Straub, D. (2017). E-Health: Value proposition and technologies enabling collaborative healthcare. *Proceedings of the 50th Hawaii International Conference on System Sciences*. pp. 920–929.

The European House-Ambrosetti (2019). Meridiano Sanità. *XIV Rapporto 2019*. https://eventi.ambrosetti.eu/forum-meridiano-sanita-14/wp-content/uploads/sites/107/2019/11/ReportMS14-2019-rev_rid.pdf

UNO. (2019). *World Population Prospects 2019*. Department of Economic and Social Affairs. New York.

Vial, G. (2019). Understanding digital transformation: A review and a research agenda. *The Journal of Strategic Information Systems, 28*(2), 118–144.

Viswanath, K. (2006). Public communications and its role in reducing and eliminating health disparities. In G. E. Thomson, F. Mitchell, and M. B. Williams (eds). *Examining the health disparities research plan of the National Institutes of Health: Unfinished business*. Washington DC: Institute of Medicine.

Viswanath, K., and Kreuter, M. W. (2007). Health disparities, communication inequalities, and e-health. *American Journal of Preventive Medicine, 32*(5), S131–S133.

Wade, V., Karnon, J., Elshaug, A., and Hiller, J. E. (2010). A systematic review of economic analyses of tele-health services using real time video communication. *BMC Health Services Research, 10*(1), 233.

WHO (2020). World Population Ageing 2019. ST/ESA/SER.A/444. New York: United Nations, Department of Economic and Social Affairs.

Zach, L., Dalrymple, P. W., Rogers, M. L., and Williver-Farr, H. (2012). Assessing internet access and use in a medically underserved population: implications for providing enhanced health information services. *Health Information & Libraries Journal, 29*(1), 61–71.

8 Co-creation in Health 4.0

Norbert Laurisz

Introduction

Co-creation is usually defined in general terms as the involvement of stakeholders in the creation of new products and services, the key stakeholders in this process being consumers. The opening up of market operators to broad cooperation with a view to increasing the effectiveness of their activities, improving the quality, and expanding their range of products has become a hallmark of the modern economy. Going beyond the group of contractors and experts (i.e. the supply side of the production process) and expanding the group of participants in the creative process to include the recipients (i.e. the clients/consumers) mean that the creative process ceases to be a closed and exclusive domain of the supply side. Expanding the group of participants in the creation process increases the number of opinions and visions and, as a result, significantly democratises the entire process, which obviously introduces both the advantages and disadvantages of democratisation into the rather hermetic conventional creation process. The former significantly improves the adaptive capacity and effectiveness of businesses in the areas of products (by tailoring them better to the needs and expectations of their recipients) and processes (adjusting the creation process and management methods to the changing market conditions).

The changing market conditions, its growing flexibility in terms of the range of products and thus the ability of consumers choose, compare, and as a result, pick a different product or supplier, puts increased pressure on enterprises to look for solutions that would render the product creation process more flexible to tailor their offer and features of individual products to consumer needs and expectations to the greatest extent possible. Co-creation has become a way of addressing this requirement in a systematic rather than incidental manner.

Companies invariably look for more permanent solutions that will help them to gain a competitive advantage over the other market players. Modifications introduced to the production process or to the products offered on the market are intended to ultimately ensure that consumers derive the highest possible satisfaction from their use (Vargo et al., 2008). It is expected

DOI: 10.4324/9781003144403-8

that as a result, he or she would be less inclined to give up its consumption and to place more trust in the product, the company, and the brand. The search for such solutions is costly and time-consuming, hence the key factor is to choose and implement the one that will lead to the best result. In other words, it is expected to help deliver a product that will guarantee the consumer the highest possible satisfaction (Vargo & Lusch, 2004). Attempts to address this issue include a search for ways to increase the adaptability of companies themselves in the context of the changing market conditions as well as the capacity to better tailor their offer to consumer needs and expectations (Ritzer & Jurgenson, 2010).

Particularly important in this context are the ever-changing consumer expectations and their social make-up, especially in terms of age, which is discussed in more detail in the chapter devoted to the problems faced by the ageing society. These factors in particular force the creators to modify the way in which they operate, including attempts to influence the attitudes of the intended recipients of their products, which, in the case of the elderly and Health 4.0, is even considered desirable. Facilitating adaptation and acceptance of modern healthcare solutions is becoming a key challenge for Health 4.0 product developers.

In order to address the needs of the growing group of senior consumers, who tend to distrust new technologies, as well as the evolving market conditions, companies increasingly need to take into account their opinions and not only develop a niche for their products but above all tailor what they offer to the expectations of the target recipients. As a result, the trend to change the business model or the product creation strategy is becoming evident. It affects a variety of industries and sectors, including the public and the social one, although it seems that in the latter, the impact of the opinions of the final beneficiaries has always been present (Laurisz, 2019).

This phenomenon is known as the "prosumer society" (Ritzer & Jurgenson, 2010), and the approach that puts the consumer at the centre of corporate action is termed "consumer centrism" (Prahalad & Ramaswamy, 2004). Today's consumers take a much more active role in the product development process, whereas the opening up of markets and the evolution of expectations have led to the emergence of consumer-actors who have become active market players and who expect the products offered to precisely meet their needs. This attitude has a bearing on the market, especially the sales stage and the product's longevity, including its update timeline (Galvagno & Dalli, 2014; Ramaswamy & Ozcan, 2013; Vargo et al., 2008).

In the changing business model, it is the consumer rather than the company that is regarded as the key element in the development of modern products, services, and concepts (Vargo & Lusch, 2004). This is especially true for personalised and technology-based goods, i.e. all Health 4.0 products, as they have high acceptance and adaptation thresholds, which can be lowered by involving patients in the creation process (Arief et al., 2013; Wildenbos et al., 2018). At the same time, recent advances in technology and biomedical research affect the approach to the delivery of therapy and the creation of both institutional solutions and treatment tools. The so-called P4 medicine is becoming a paradigm of the future, which, within a coherent model, combines four key elements of modern healthcare: personalised treatment, predictive medicine, prevention, and treatment with active patient participation. The use of cutting-edge technologies in combination with innovative procedures allows for therapies to be very precisely tailored and targeted, e.g. by matching pharmaceuticals to an individual patient's profile rather than the disease; performing predictive diagnostics in order to detect diseases before symptoms appear, thus shifting the burden of medical interventions from remediation to prevention (Hood & Flores, 2012). Central to the implementation of P4 medicine is personalisation and strong patient engagement from diagnosis and therapy to testing novel solutions. Both trends clearly demonstrate that the future business model and the future medical model will be based on co-creation and will involve strong product personalisation.

Modern technologies and personalised solutions have become a natural environment for the development of co-creation. This is due to the fact that co-creation turns the consumer into an active partner in the creation process and into a source of knowledge, experience, and inspiration. This relationship and change affect both the consumer and the company, as a result of which the behaviours of both entities change. Companies modify the process of creating innovative solutions or improvements, while consumers become innovators and change agents (Ramaswamy & Gouillart, 2010; Ramaswamy & Ozcan, 2014). This is true for every sector but is perhaps most evident in the field of healthcare and modern Health 4.0 solutions due to the two-sided pressure to engage the consumer in the creation process described above.

This chapter sees co-creation as a way to improve the quality of products and increase the effectiveness of the entire process of delivering Health 4.0 products. Specifically, it focuses on the impact of individual actors on the process and on its individual stages in the context of engaging consumers (patients).

Co-creation in healthcare and Health 4.0

In the 20th century, stakeholders used to be treated as passive participants in the product creation process. The consumer was a target to be reached rather than a partner in product development. The boundary between design/creation and consumption - between the sphere of production and the sphere of consumption - was very clearly drawn. The predominant belief that products in the area of health should be created by professionals led to a widespread disregard of the opinions of stakeholders, especially patients. Technological progress in the 21st century has occasioned a change in the approach to business as well as to the role of stakeholders in it. In today's economy, stakeholders are perceived as active contributors, while consumers become key partners in product development. A shift in the business model towards patient-centricity and co-creation is beginning to be felt across the health sector, especially in Health 4.0 (Palumbo, 2015, 2017).

While consumer engagement in an open market is usually marketing and sales driven - as the solutions are ultimately designed to deliver increased impact and value in this particular area (Bhalla, 2010) - in the case of Health 4.0 products, the aim of co-creation is much less commercial. Ensuring functionality and obtaining relevant feedback from patients and health professionals gain prominence instead. In these markets, co-creation noticeably promotes involvement in the process of creating and/or testing new Health 4.0 technologies (Eysenbach, 2008). The production and market outcomes are positive, but most importantly, the efficiency of the entire process improves, while the likelihood of error or incorrect/unintended use markedly decreases.

The key participants in co-creation in Health 4.0 are stakeholders. Their specific roles depend on the product and the way in which the entire creation process is aligned with information flows (Hsu, 2016; Mantzana et al., 2007; Ramaswamy & Gouillart, 2010; Ramaswamy & Ozcan, 2014; Voorberg et al., 2015). These two qualities determine the sustainability of solutions and their systems developed with Health 4.0 in mind (Eysenbach, 2008). A particularly important aspect is the application of specialist knowledge and combining it with the views and experience of health professionals as well as with the experiences and often subjective feelings of patients (Mair et al., 2012).

Until recently, patients used to be regarded as passive recipients of services provided to them by healthcare professionals. For a long time, healthcare developed independently of patients, in line with the then prevailing logic of cooperation between producers and healthcare professionals. However, the mounting costs of health services, and the pressure to improve both therapy success rates and patient satisfaction necessitated changes in the way production and services are managed as well as new business model based on more efficient and cost-effective solutions throughout the healthcare sector. This has become especially evident in the context of Health 4.0, for which the assimilation barrier often remains quite high (Chanchaichujit et al., 2019).

In the search for effective solutions, co-creation appears to render the process of developing new products and services cheaper and better tailored to patients' needs. The implementation of new solutions in healthcare compared with other sectors is a particularly sensitive process. As such, activities that invite patient participation in the creation process, especially those that strongly involve them throughout, enable the healthcare sector to take advantage of patient knowledge, experience, and perspectives to create personalised products. Research shows that co-creation improves the quality and efficiency of healthcare services, increases trust in healthcare, enhances patient satisfaction, reduces the costs of therapy and equipment, fosters prevention, ensures the relevance of medical research, and increases patient satisfaction and adherence to treatment regimens (Botti & Monda, 2020). For active dialogue and collaboration to occur, physicians, healthcare organisations, providers, and consumers must become equal partners focused on issues of common interest (Elg et al., 2012). As shown by the literature review on health service development in general, patients are usually a source of knowledge for companies; the latter, however, as a rule fail to involve them in the creation process (Crawford et al., 2002). The situation is different in Health 4.0, where manufacturers make extensive use of patients' knowledge and experience; moreover, their involvement at different product development stages is even expected (Alkhaldi et al., 2014; Chanchaichujit et al., 2019; Palumbo, 2017; Zayyad & Toycan, 2018).

Actors

The most commonly used terminologies and classifications in the literature divide actors in the health sector into regulators, providers, payers, suppliers, and patients (Bessant et al., 2012). This division makes it possible to discuss the issue of value creation and the phenomenon of co-creation from a functional perspective, although it obviously does not fully reflect the complexity of this sector, such as the dual role of health professionals, who, depending on circumstances, are either providers or consumers of Health 4.0 products - in the latter case, they should be grouped together with patients (Mantzana et al., 2007).

Apart from the characteristics of the different actors, an important aspect is the issue of barriers and factors that cause resistance to the implementation of Health 4.0. Participants in the process of creating healthcare products will naturally tend to behave and act with a view to slowing down or even blocking the changes. This result from the game of interests that characterises complex systems, the routine processes, or spheres of influence of individual actors in the process, the boundaries of which may be radically altered by the implementation of new Health 4.0 systems and solutions. Moreover, the natural inertia of complex systems will negatively affect the pace of implementation of novel solutions.

Regulators

In any project, regulators invariably operate at a level above production and implementation. They are not directly or indirectly involved in value creation or the production process, yet their contribution is significant since they provide the framework for the operation of the entire system and its individual components, while leaving open the formal possibility of renegotiating these rules. Regulators, such as the Ministry of Health, set the overall scene for creating solutions, build the foundations for the subsequent activities to be carried out, and supervise the entire system (Kaplan & Babad, 2011; Mantzana et al., 2007; Ramaswamy & Ozcan, 2014). Regulators set the boundaries and establish the rules of the system, but given that the sector in question is highly socially sensitive, it is impossible to create a sustainable healthcare system without an active participation of stakeholders in the decision-making process (Kaplan & Babad, 2011). As the creators of new spaces for the development of innovative solutions in Health 4.0, regulators hold sway over the whole sector and it is their responsibility to create the formal and functional conditions for novel solutions (Harrison, 2014). From this perspective, they devise provisions intended first of all not to restrict the system's capacity to develop.

Yet another level, with a different profile, is occupied by the Agencies for Health Technology Assessment (HTA). Decision-making on new technologies in healthcare requires professional decision support; therefore, HTA agencies have been established in many countries and entrusted with the task of scrutinising new technologies to provide objective information on their utility and effectiveness as well as the potential consequences of their implementation. The International Network of Agencies for Health Technology Assessment (INAHTA) was set up to make the assessment process more efficient and to increase its reach. This network currently includes 51 agencies that support decision-making in healthcare systems that cover over a billion people.

Providers

As was already mentioned, providers can be considered as typical representatives of the supply side of the system since they provide, suggest, and persuade the patient to use certain products. On the other hand, they often are consumers of their own products and services, which gives them a dual role in the Health 4.0 market (Harrison, 2014; Kaplan & Babad, 2011). This group consists of physicians, nurses, and organisations, such as hospitals or nursing homes. It specifically affects the quality and adaptability of products since it acts as an individual or institutional provider, a consultant possessed of a high level of relevant knowledge and specialisation, and as a consumer or a closest advisor to consumers (Bryson et al., 2017; Kazadi et al., 2016; Mantzana et al., 2007). Its high-level expertise combined with the ability to take into account patients' opinions makes it a key partner in the process of developing new solutions (Mair et al., 2012). In the context of Health 4.0, its representatives determine the actual ultimate success of the proposed systems and solutions. Their ability to anticipate patients' needs combined with specialist knowledge and broad experience enables them to reliably evaluate new devices, treatments, therapies, monitoring devices, etc.

In the case of health services in the broadest sense, the role of health professionals may change, depending on the type and purpose of the product. Physicians and hospital employees working together with patients may form a group of end users, or they may operate a given product independently, and, as a result, they may become the end users of a given solution. The latter applies, in particular, to databases, monitoring applications, and platforms for disease identification or therapy. In such cases, the patient does not appear as a consumer at all – the role of consumer/end user is instead played by the provider.

In the case of providers, possible resistance to new solutions is associated, among others, with the emergence of new administrative procedures or the need to learn how to use new software or equipment. This is frequently compounded by the prospect of changes to the current personnel structure, as new technologies tend to be adopted more quickly by younger people, which disrupts the established hierarchies in the medical profession and, in turn, arouses opposition from influential actors. Efforts to collect patient data complete with diagnostic and therapeutic information may be blocked for similar reasons. The resistance of the environment is intensified by the prospect of unrestricted access to (information on) diagnosis and treatment, which undermines the competitiveness of individual entities (physicians, hospitals, therapeutic centres, etc.). From a healthcare perspective, this would improve the efficiency of the whole system, but from an individual perspective, it is dangerous for providers as making certain information public has a negative effect on their competitiveness (Hermes et al., 2020).

Payers

Payers as a group exert a significant impact on the development directions of the sector as a whole and on individual projects. In any given system, a proportion of payers maintain direct relationships with regulators – for publicly funded systems, European countries have the highest proportion of health spending in public finance. Although these systems are shaped in different ways – healthcare financing may be separated e.g. from the group of budget expenditure – in the system, they belong in the same group of redistributive financial flows (classified as national health insurance). In contrast, non-public payers are private health insurance providers. Regardless of the funding system, the role of each payer is important in maintaining the cohesion and viability of the health system. It is generally accepted, however, that the role of payers remains passive, especially in the case of statutory health insurance (SHI) (Kaplan & Babad, 2011).

In the context of Health 4.0, the impact of payers is not easy to determine. Undoubtedly, they have an indirect impact on whether or not certain solutions devised by the health sector are ultimately adopted, but this secondary role, despite its important function in the sector, makes it impossible to include payers in the group of key actors in the product creation process (Mair et al., 2012). The payers' influence is thus limited to fundholding, i.e. they do not participate in co-creation. However, modern healthcare encourages the co-creation of new products with a view to reducing the operating costs or new insurance products, which, without systemic changes, may push financial flows towards new Health 4.0 solutions, especially in the private sector (Ewert & Evers, 2014). In contrast, a very important source of funding that makes a key difference in the development of Health 4.0 solutions is public or private grants directly earmarked for this kind of activity (Mair et al., 2012). The prevalence of public funding in the creation of new products necessary for development became particularly evident in the context of the recent coronavirus pandemic. State funds allocated to research on the virus and development of a cure or vaccine underpinned the financial efforts of the entire sector. It is worth noting that in the case of most Health 4.0 solutions, even if they are devised by private entities, the process is strongly supported by public funds, which, interestingly, occurs not only in the European countries but also in the USA (Mazzucato, 2011).

Whether or not Health 4.0 solutions are ultimately taken up by payers depends on financial and procedural reasons, as is the case with regulators. Complexity resulting from the presence of numerous participants within a single system, who implement highly diverse activities as part of a huge number of therapies, has led to the development of a specialised financing formula based on the insurance system. This has a strong stabilising effect on therapies as well as diagnostic and treatment methods. The consolidated procedures, approved under the current legal provisions and internal regulations, are often implemented regardless of whether better alternative methods exist. As a result, the payers discourage the application of new solutions by at least initially refusing to reimburse the costs of novel solutions. Thus, the presence of established procedures within the healthcare system and the adoption of cost-effectiveness as an important benchmark of therapy evaluation slow down the implementation of Health 4.0 products due to the tenacity of the existing procedures and the economic aspect. Therefore, new solutions that reduce the costs of therapies and diagnostics are more likely to be incorporated into the system than more expensive ones, even though they may be more effective than the existing ones (Kellermann & Jones, 2013).

Suppliers

Suppliers as a group of actors comprise creators/inventors, manufacturers, and distributors as well as universities, pharmaceutical companies, medical device companies, information and communications technology (ICT) companies, and pharmacies. Suppliers are an enterprising group with the means and capacity to engage in activities resulting in the development, creation, and marketing of modified or completely new products. Unquestionably, their role in the creation of Health 4.0 products is crucial, as they initiate and coordinate the entire process and decide on the scale of stakeholder involvement (Harrison, 2014).

Providers constitute a reservoir of inspiration and manufacturing capacity that often requires market-based incentives. By acting in concert, regulators and payers create a space for action and provide an extensive array of incentives. Suppliers, by using their own creative facilities or cooperating on a larger scale, develop solutions that can later be found on the market. However, the specificity of products offered under Health 4.0 means that they need to go beyond the previous collaboration boundaries to significantly involve end users in the process of creating new solutions (Valderas et al., 2016). This implies a significant increase in the involvement of both patients and providers in Health 4.0. From a contemporary management perspective, suppliers engage stakeholders, with a particular focus on consumers, in each successive stage of product development.

Supplier attitudes and behaviours also affect the pace of adaptation and implementation of Health 4.0 products. According to qualitative research findings, from the perspective of consumers - both physicians and patients - the solutions offered are often insufficiently user-friendly (Kellermann & Jones, 2013). Other problems include poor technical support, which leaves physicians or patients to fend for themselves with technical issues that may arise (Kruse et al., 2017), including hardware quality, which affects the operation of some Health 4.0 apps (Meskó et al., 2017). For example, the sensors on smartphones on which apps are intended to run often vary in quality, which may result in inaccurate and/or different readings (Hermes et al., 2020).

Patients

Patients are the largest and the most diverse group since they alone or together with health professionals are the end users of most Health 4.0 products. When confronting Health 4.0 solutions with patients' needs, health professionals begin to play a dual role. This is due to the fact that it is usually the physician who decides or advises the patient to use a given product. For this reason, health professionals - who together with patients create demand - are a key link in this process. Patients evaluate the functionality of a given product, while the provider is actually responsible for its substantive aspect. These two actors shape the demand for Health 4.0 products (Alkhaldi et al., 2014). In the case of preventive health products, the patient group may or may not create demand together with the health professionals. Demand for the latter group of products usually depends on positive opinions of other users, which also constitutes a factor that fosters co-creation as a form of involvement in creating solutions compatible with the needs and expectations of the consumer.

Both the medical and economic literature emphasise patient empowerment understood as using patients' knowledge and experience in the process of creating solutions for Health 4.0 and making them an important fixture in the whole process (Anderson & Funnell, 2010; Elg et al., 2012). As a result, business practice shows that the participation of patients involved in the creation process is steadily growing, which contributes to the increasing efficiency of Health 4.0 products (Harrison, 2014; Valderas et al., 2016). By proposing a classification of patient involvement in the health product creation process (more on this in the chapter devoted to application areas of Health 4.0 solutions), it was possible to assess the scale of involvement that optimises the product creation pathway both from the perspective of the type of product and the specific stage of the creation process (Palumbo, 2017). The analysis discussed here shows that in the context of Health 4.0 products, empowering patients and simultaneously involving them in product development increase the efficiency of each stage of the process. This is particularly evident when moving from the testing stage to implementation and upgrading, which is particularly relevant from the perspective of Health 4.0 solutions.

In the patient group, the mechanism that hinders the acceptance and eventual use of modern Health 4.0 products stems from technological anxiety, which points to a certain similarity in attitudes between patients, physicians, and other health professionals. In this context, a key element is population ageing, which most strongly raises the acceptance threshold for modern healthcare solutions (Arief et al., 2013; Wildenbos et al., 2018). The other important aspect is the problem of access to of sensitive data. The proposal that data on health status, past and current diseases, therapies prescribed, etc., should be widely available erects a psychological barrier to a widespread adoption of Health 4.0 systems and solutions. Moreover, granting access to such data to public entities, market players, insurance institutions, and financial institutions often associated with them may have a major negative impact on the private lives of patients. This is exacerbated by the fact that, as Hermes et al. (2020) note, unlike institutional actors, patients find it difficult to access such data. This strongly suggests that trust in public authorities and/or market actors is limited (Anderson & Funnell, 2010).

In summary, the backgrounds, perceptions, and fears of actors involved in the development of Health 4.0 products and medical products in general widely differ. However, since their interests and goals converge, the factors that foster the motivation for broad cooperation under the co-creation formula should be more easily acceptable than those in the case of classic market-oriented products. The analysis of potential resistance to the implementation of Health 4.0 solutions reveals that the response to the actors' fears should involve close cooperation between them and their active participation in the process of creating Health 4.0 products, especially since, as research shows, even if a given product is accepted and approved by all of them, it may remain unused for a variety of reasons (Kane & Labianca, 2011). In such cases, actively engaging providers and patients in testing and giving feedback and thus in the process of product development and improvement will facilitate the acceptance and assimilation of Health 4.0 products.

Co-creation vs. product development stages in Health 4.0

Healthcare as a system is by no means homogeneous, hence it is not easy to discuss individual stages of this process in a way that corresponds to the various forms of activity within Health 4.0. However, stakeholder analysis allows us to propose a unified classification and to adopt the models established for the subsequent analysis (Freeman, 2010). The approach in question is based on a modified Life Cycle Development classification, taking into account the technical and formal possibilities of participation of consumers and other stakeholders in each of these stages, as well as the specificity of each stage and its importance in the process of developing Health 4.0 products (Alkhaldi et al., 2014; Bhalla, 2010; Bryson et al., 2017; Galvagno & Dalli, 2014; Harrison, 2014; Hsu, 2016; Mair et al., 2012; Urueña et al., 2016; Zayyad & Toycan, 2018).

Each stage is important from the perspective of a unified Health 4.0 development process; moreover, other steps or sub-stages may be included in it (e.g. needs analysis) - they are thus considered to be intrinsic elements of each stage or any specific one proposed under this division. Thus, the following stages of the Health 4.0 product development process have been identified: (1) planning; (2) design; (3) implementation/delivery; and (4) maintenance.

Planning

Planning together with the incubation stage constitutes the initial step in developing any solution and crucially informs major product creation and implementation decisions. Consequently, it is necessary to develop a logical and feasible path for the whole process and to consider all of its constituents - those that are its "natural" components, such as strategy, schedule, budget, supplies, logistics, etc., and the immeasurable ones, which may or may not occur, such as potential risks, barriers and limitations, the impact of the environment, etc. In the context of the entire process, it is extremely important to analyse the input of consumers and their possible impact on the intended final product, its implementation, and maintenance stages (Freeman, 2010; Harrison, 2014).

Research suggests that in the case of Health 4.0 products, a key element of this stage involves a detailed analysis of consumer opinions, which helps to make the subsequent stages of creation more efficient, which, in turn, improves the entire process (Alkhaldi et al., 2014). Consumer participation in the planning stage of the entire Health 4.0 product development process promotes the long-term development of the entire project, ensures its stability, and enhances its adaptability (Urueña et al., 2016). Patient involvement in this stage brings practical and conceptual assistance to the development of solutions in what is known as in-depth product customisation (Kaplan & Babad, 2011). The patient involved in the planning stage shows his or her point of view, often different from that of the originator's original intentions, which allows the creators to modify their vision and adapt the implemented project to the requirements of individual needs and personalised therapies (Bryson, 2004; Harrison, 2014).

Design

This is the stage in which the assumptions and visions from the planning stage begin to materialise, incorporating the knowledge about the process and the product itself. It follows up on the findings of panel discussions with consumers and considers the possible risks and problems associated with product development (Freeman, 2010; Hsu, 2016; Ramaswamy & Gouillart, 2010). Engaging consumers (patients) in this stage permits the original assumptions to be reviewed before the testing stage thanks to the confrontation of designers and manufacturers with user feedback. In the previous production process that did not involve co-creation, this stage offered no opportunities to verify the originally adopted assumptions. Co-creation in Health 4.0 permits these assumptions to be confronted with the experiences of patients whose unique knowledge and experiences may be unavailable to the creators, such as those arising from therapy, understanding age-related limitations of sensory perception, digital exclusion, adaptation and accommodation difficulties, etc. (Bryson, 2004; Harrison, 2014; Ramaswamy & Ozcan, 2013; Wildenbos et al., 2018).

Patient involvement in this stage increases the effectiveness of manufacturers' decisions and changes the patient/physician relationship with the supplier, which makes the next stage, i.e. product implementation, more effective. As a result, considering the end users' opinions, concerns, and experiences facilitates developing a more functional product that is more closely aligned with patient needs (Wildenbos et al., 2018). Research shows that co-creation improves the efficiency of this stage and the subsequent ones. Thanks to patient involvement it is possible to design and deliver a better product (Ramaswamy & Gouillart, 2010).

Implementation/delivery

From a management perspective, this is the most difficult stage in the creation process, the main problem being the transition from the internal stage when the product must stand comparison with others available on the market. Many companies struggle to overcome the barriers inherent in this transition (Freeman, 2010; Urueña et al., 2016). A key issue at this stage is how to effectively evaluate the research findings and make the necessary improvements to the way the product is marketed, priced, serviced, etc. Therefore, collaboration with patients and health professionals is crucial, as their feedback ultimately determines the demand for a given medical products (Gaddi et al., 2014). Co-creation in this stage significantly increases the efficiency of implementation thanks to better tailored solutions and better and more efficient customer service (Mair et al., 2012).

At such an early stage, the main problem is associated with the high costs of product and process modifications. This is particularly evident in the case of Health 4.0 and constitutes one of the reasons why so many projects are cancelled in their pilot or testing stages (Alkhaldi et al., 2014; Valderas et al., 2016). Usually, the reasons include technical glitches or insufficient collaboration with physicians and patients to convince them to use a given product (Mair et al., 2012). Co-creation in the implementation stage allows for a significant reduction in testing costs, offers an invaluable opportunity to persuade patients and health professionals to use an often-unfamiliar Health 4.0 solution, and improves customer service (Alkhaldi et al., 2014).

Maintenance

At this stage, it is crucial to maintain the long-term functionality of the product and the company's ability to update/upgrade it. This requires constant monitoring of the market, the product, and consumer needs (Freeman, 2010).

There is a range of problems that may arise at this stage, especially in the context of Health 4.0, ranging from the technical, functional, upgrade, and adaptation-related ones to ethical or aesthetic issues, which prompts manufacturers to work closely with end users (Zayyad & Toycan, 2018). Maintaining implementation outcomes and extending product usability requires robust user support. In Health 4.0, two influential sources of recommendations emerge. On the one hand, it is the patients themselves, who, often despite the views of health professionals, pressure the latter to use certain products, therapies, etc. (Urueña et al., 2016). On the other, physicians and health professionals recommend a particular product based on patients' opinions and their own experience.

The co-creation model, thanks to ongoing collaboration with physicians and patients, permits the providers to respond quickly to the changing conditions and user expectations, as well as recognise the reasons behind changes in demand for a new technology product (Keeys & Huemann, 2017). Co-creation in the maintenance stage stabilises the entire development process and extends the product's lifespan (Zayyad & Toycan, 2018). From this perspective, patient engagement should be a priority for Health 4.0 companies (Urueña et al., 2016).

Challenges in the development of Health 4.0 and co-creation

When discussing Health 4.0 products, what we have in mind are cutting-edge solutions that will transform the reality as we know it in the near future. Most of them are currently being tested, a smaller proportion is being used, but in addressing the expected challenges, it is where we seek solutions to our current and future problems in the area of health and beyond. Health 4.0 is a complex field with many different solutions and tools that primarily include mobile applications and big data analytics, artificial intelligence, the Internet of Things (IoT), wearables, and blockchain technologies (Thuemmler & Bai, 2017). It is hoped that these tools will serve to counter the dangerous trends in the lives of societies and will themselves contribute to social and economic change on an unimaginable scale (more on this in the chapter on technologies in Health 4.0). The tabulated findings of literature review presented below highlight the main trends and challenges facing healthcare today and in the future (Table 8.1).

Table 8.1 Future trends in healthcare

Trends	*Determinants*
Increasing number of patients	Population ageing Rising incidence of civilisation or lifestyle diseases
Increasing costs	Growing demand for medical and care services Decreasing numbers of physicians and carers Increasing number of available treatments for chronic diseases
Increasing use of technology	Development of internet and telecommunication technology Development of IoT Development of AI
Increasing amount of information	Development of diagnostics Comprehensive databases of all disease entities AI-enabled diagnostics
Change in patient position	Raising the profile of consumer choice Increased say in the choice of treatment, physician, and form of insurance
Changes in the delivery of some medical services	A significant proportion of diagnostics shifted to networks Fragmented medical consultations Hospitals defined for difficult cases
Pressure on innovation	Search for tools that aid the diagnosis, monitoring, and data collection on patients and diseases Drive to reduce the costs of indirect medical services
The state taking over private medical care	In countries with predominantly private care or non-public insurance, increasing importance of the state or public guarantees for financing healthcare
Expanding additional health insurance options	Rising healthcare costs shifted to the state A proportion of healthcare costs shifted to the patient

Sources: André (2019), Garson & Levin (2001), Thakur et al. (2012).

In the face of changing social and economic circumstances, countries find themselves under increasing pressure to modify their public policies. In this context, healthcare is subject to the most far-reaching modifications, as the current global social trends affect health and social security to the greatest extent. Undoubtedly, the most important of these trends - and, at the same time, a factor that drives changes in the design of public health services that require a different approach to the creation of Health 4.0 products - is population ageing (Arief et al., 2013). Thanks to advances in healthcare, life expectancy is increasing, a trend that is expected to be sustained in the future. This effect, combined with declining birth rates, will contribute to even faster population ageing. The drastic increase in the proportion of older people in the population will soon lead to a major reorientation of social and health policy with an impact on producers and providers of services alike. The market for health services will change in response to a strong pressure to implement solutions that provide older people with longer autonomy and self-reliance in health and personal terms as well as ensure appropriate supervised care (Wildenbos et al., 2018). This will help address the already present social phenomena, such as the need for older people to remain active in society and at work, inefficiencies in care and pension systems that do not permit them to benefit from a full range of services available on the market, and the growing number of older people living alone who need care and/or supervision.

When analysing patients' ability to adapt to technological change, it appears that age constitutes a key determinant of their reluctance to use modern solutions. Most studies show that this reluctance increases with age, even if technology serves to improve or stabilise health (Wildenbos et al., 2018); moreover, the higher the technological sophistication, the stronger the reluctance to use modern health solutions (Rogers & Fisk, 2010). As a result, the existing way of developing modern medical products and services faces a demand barrier in the groups that need them the most. Thus, the determining factor for the applicability of Health 4.0 products is not their quality or usability but older people's perception and motivation to use new technologies in treatment and care (Zhou & Salvendy, 2018). In this context, an interesting classification of barriers to user acceptance and adoption of Health 4.0 products was proposed by Holzinger, and Rogers and Fisks. In their research, they identified the following aspects key to the acceptance of Health 4.0 products (Holzinger et al., 2007):

1 Cognition is associated with cognitive ability, ease of use, and, in technical and procedural terms, cognitive fit, serviceability, and testability. The most common problem is that products tend to be designed "by the young for the young" who rarely takes into consideration older people's language or technology skills.
2 Physical ability includes all the age-related limitations that may affect an individual's ability to use new technologies. One commonly cited example is the problem with operating smartphone apps due to restricted joint range of movement or declining fine motor skills.
3 Perception related to the declining acuity of the senses, mainly vision and hearing.
4 Motivation pertains to two issues: (1) Producers and/or providers rarely do their best to demonstrate the possibilities and benefits of using their products, and (2) how to convince older persons that they can indeed independently "cope with" the technology in question. A way of addressing it requires engaging older people in one of the product development stages, e.g. testing.

As can be gleaned from the above, apart from the purely physical aspects, the key adaptation barriers include familiarity with the technology, its positive perception, a belief that it is helpful and meets the needs of an older person. In other words, the user fit of Health 4.0 and the pro-consumer orientation of a given solution significantly increase the likelihood of its acceptance and, ultimately, assimilation (Arief et al., 2013; Wildenbos et al., 2018). In this context, the research findings confirm that involving patients in the development of Health 4.0 products by considering their opinions and needs successfully addresses the problem of assimilation.

In response to the mounting challenges associated with social change, modern health products and services must be more flexible and better tailored to consumer expectations. Priya Nambisan and Satish Nambisan proposed a solution in the form of flexible and varied models of co-creation in health-care, both in its current version and that known as Health 4.0. Their matrix comprises 4 different models of co-creation, which can be further aggregated. These models include Partnership, Open Source, Support Group, and Diffusion (Figure 8.1) (Nambisan & Nambisan, 2009).

In the case of Partnership, the authors emphasise greater innovation in the existing and new solutions, the reduction of innovation costs, and the development of trust between providers and patients through transparent innovation creation and testing procedures. The Open Source model focuses on a better alignment of emerging innovations with market needs, a growing potential for innovation participants in the process, and the opening of health-care entities to the initiatives of their non-medical partners and consumers themselves, which sometimes entails handing over the management side of the process to non-health professionals. The Support Group model stipulates

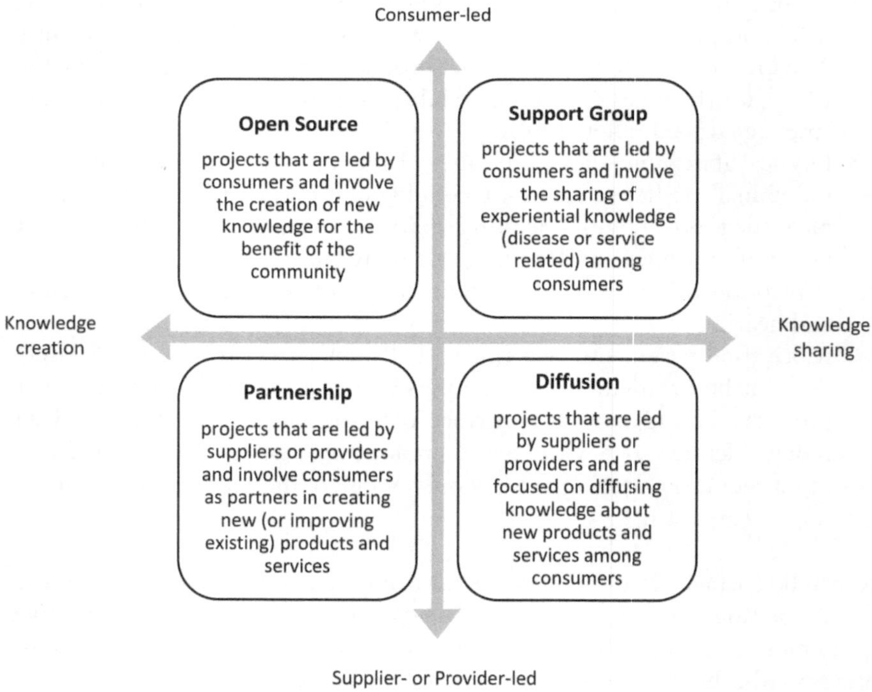

Figure 8.1 Models of consumer value co-creation in healthcare.

Source: Nambisan & Nambisan (2009).

making expert know-how available in the innovation process, optimising the cost, and medical knowledge of patient-oriented innovations. The Diffusion model is associated with positive perceptions and a high level of acceptance of the solutions and providers themselves by patients and other stakeholders but, most importantly, a long-term capacity of the former to work with patients on new and existing healthcare and Health 4.0 solutions. All these models have a strong potential for adaptation as their shape and nature can change at different levels, making it possible to apply a range of models within a single development process.

As the foregoing discussion shows, co-creation generates two major groups of benefits. First, there are qualitative benefits associated with the innovation itself. Thanks to the emergence of new solutions in the process of co-creation, suppliers introduce products and services which can be easily assimilated, are well suited to the needs of patients and/or physicians, and are characterised by a high level of innovation, while the time to market becomes shorter. This is particularly evident in the case of beta versions in the life cycles of products (testing). The other group of benefits involves relations with partners and consumers. The involvement of partners, especially patients and health professionals, fosters a psychological bond based on trust. This increases interest in cooperation, promotes innovation and knowledge flows among the partners, and from a market perspective, links consumers with the manufacturer through a sense of loyalty and trust in product and service quality.

Conclusions

Changes that affect the market, the relations between producers and consumers, as well as those resulting from the technological revolution, alter the social and economic landscape. In this context, it appears that a successful response to this challenge should consist in introducing appropriate creation models into the production process. In the context of Health 4.0 products and beyond, co-creation appears to be a solution that can meet the challenges of the future market. The modern healthcare system must improve the flexibility of the creation process while increasing the adaptability and assimilability of Health 4.0 products. However, a much wider use of co-creation is needed to make the regulatory sphere and health policy more flexible, apart from the production aspect itself. An equally important aspects of co-creation are the factors that hinder change or make it more difficult to choose optimal pathways from the perspective of the entire health system as well as the patient. This is particularly true of the assimilation of Health 4.0 products intended for use beyond the existing practices (Hermes et al. 2020).

Co-creation has introduced the consumer-patient into industrial relationships. Health 4.0 products as well as the health system in general require moving away from the traditional model of care to that based on multi-level collaboration and active patient participation. For such collaboration to be possible, however, the consumer should be recognised as a partner of the other actors involved in the creation process. From this perspective and in the context of possible future activities of policymakers, the idea of co-creation should be promoted throughout the health sector. This will involve redefining the role of the patient in the healthcare system. Interestingly, in the case of Health 4.0 products, the redefinition of the patient's role is already well underway with the patient becoming a key element in the process of creating modern solutions. What the process in question needs is an infrastructure and institutional environment that will permit a systemic implementation of new solutions based on ICT or biotechnology, which are characterised by strong personalisation, predictive capacity, and active patient participation. In the case of Health 4.0, this reorientation is subject to pressure from two sides: on the one hand, from producers, and, on the other, from patients and health professionals. Even though it appears to be occurring naturally and in an unforced manner, institutional support would help accelerate and consolidate this process by extending it to the entire sector. Conversely, failure to act systemically in the context of relentless technological progress, which increasingly affects healthcare, may lead to implementation difficulties, lack of stability of the already implemented actions, and reduce the effectiveness of the entire system. A concerted implementation of co-creation in the said system should be viewed as a response to the needs resulting from medical and technological challenges.

References

Alkhaldi, B., Sahama, T., Huxley, C., & Gajanayake, R. (2014). Barriers to implementing eHealth: A multi-dimensional perspective. *Studies in Health Technology and Informatics, 205*, 875–879.

Anderson, R. M., & Funnell, M. M. (2010). Patient empowerment: Myths and misconceptions. *Patient Education and Counseling, 79*(3), 277–282. https://doi.org/10.1016/j.pec.2009.07.025

André, A. (2019). *Conclusion: Future Trends for Our Health-Care System* (pp. 103–106). https://doi.org/10.1007/978-3-319-98216-8_10

Arief, M., Hai, N. T. T., & Saranto, K. (2013). Barriers to and advantages of e-health from the perspective of elderly people: A literature review. *Finnish Journal of EHealth and EWelfare, 5*(2–3), 50–56.

Bessant, J. R., Künne, C., & Möslein, K. (2012). *Opening Up Healthcare Innovation: Innovation Solutions for a 21st Century Healthcare System*. London: AIM Research.

Bhalla, G. (2010). *Collaboration and Co-creation: New Platforms for Marketing and Innovation* (2011 edition). New York: Springer-Verlag:.

Botti, A., & Monda, A. (2020). Sustainable value co-creation and digital health: The case of Trentino eHealth ecosystem. *Sustainability, 12*(13), 5263. https://doi.org/10.3390/su12135263

Bryson, J. (2004). What to do when stakeholders matter. *Public Management Review, 6*(1), 21–53. https://doi.org/10.1080/14719030410001675722

Bryson, J., Sancino, A., Benington, J., & Sørensen, E. (2017). Towards a multi-actor theory of public value co-creation. *Public Management Review, 19*(5), 640–654. https://doi.org/10.1080/14719037.2016.1192164

Chanchaichujit, J., Tan, A., Meng, F., & Eaimkhong, S. (2019). *Healthcare 4.0: Next Generation Processes with the Latest Technologies*. Singapore: Springer Nature Singapore.

Crawford, M., Rutter, D., Manley, C., Weaver, T., Bhui, K., Fulop, N., & Tyrer, P. (2002). Systematic review of involving patients in the planning and development of health. *BMJ (Clinical Research Ed.)*, *325*, 1263. https://doi.org/10.1136/bmj.325.7375.1263

Elg, M., Engström, J., Witell, L., & Poksinska, B. B. (2012). Co-creation and learning in health-care service development. *Journal of Service Management*, *23*, 328–343. https://doi.org/10.1108/09564231211248435

Ewert, B., & Evers, A. (2014). An ambiguous concept: On the meanings of co-production for healthcare users and user organizations? *VOLUNTAS: International Journal of Voluntary and Nonprofit Organizations*, *25*(2), 425–442. https://doi.org/10.1007/s11266-012-9345-2

Eysenbach, G. (2008). Medicine 2.0: Social networking, collaboration, participation, apomediation, and openness. *Journal of Medical Internet Research*, *10*(3). https://doi.org/10.2196/jmir.1030

Freeman, R. E. (2010). *Stakeholder Theory: The State of the Art*. Cambridge: Cambridge University Press,.

Gaddi, A., Gaddi, A., & Manca, M. (Eds.). (2014). *EHealth, Care and Quality of Life*. Springer-Verlag. https://www.springer.com/gp/book/9788847052529

Galvagno, M., & Dalli, D. (2014). Theory of value co-creation: A systematic literature review. *Managing Service Quality: An International Journal*, *24*(6), 643–683. https://doi.org/10.1108/MSQ-09-2013-0187

Garson, A., & Levin, S. A. (2001). Ten 10-year trends for the future of healthcare: Implications for academic health centers. *Ochsner Journal*, *3*(1), 10–15.

Harrison, J. S. (2014). *Strategic Management of Healthcare Organizations: A Stakeholder Management Approach*. New York: Business Expert Press.

Hermes, S., Riasanow, T., Clemons, E., Böhm, M., & Krcmar, H. (2020). *The Digital Transformation of the Healthcare Industry: Exploring the Rise of Emerging Platform Ecosystems and Their Influence on the Role of Patients*. https://doi.org/10.1007/s40685-020-00125-x

Holzinger, A., Searle, G., & Nischelwitzer, A. (2007). On some aspects of improving mobile applications for the elderly. In C. Stephanidis (Ed.), *Universal Access in Human Computer Interaction. Coping with Diversity* (pp. 923–932). Springer: Berlin Heidelberg.

Hood, L., & Flores, M. (2012). A personal view on systems medicine and the emergence of proactive P4 medicine: Predictive, preventive, personalized and participatory. *New Biotechnology*, *29*(6), 613–624. https://doi.org/10.1016/j.nbt.2012.03.004

Hsu, Y. (2016). A value co-creation strategy model for improving product development performance. *Journal of Business & Industrial Marketing*, *31*(5), 695–715. https://doi.org/10.1108/JBIM-11-2014-0221

Kane, G., & Labianca, G. (2011). Is avoidance in health-care groups: A multilevel investigation. *Information Systems Research*, *22*, 504–522. https://doi.org/10.1287/isre.1100.0314

Kaplan, R. M., & Babad, Y. M. (2011). Balancing influence between actors in healthcare decision making. *BMC Health Services Research*, *11*, 85. https://doi.org/10.1186/1472-6963-11-85

Kazadi, K., Lievens, A., & Mahr, D. (2016). Stakeholder co-creation during the innovation process: Identifying capabilities for knowledge creation among multiple stakeholders. *Journal of Business Research*, *69*(2), 525–540. https://doi.org/10.1016/j.jbusres.2015.05.009

Keeys, L. A., & Huemann, M. (2017). Project benefits co-creation: Shaping sustainable development benefits. *International Journal of Project Management, 35*(6), 1196–1212. https://doi.org/10.1016/j.ijproman.2017.02.008

Kellermann, A., & Jones, S. (2013). What it will take to achieve the as-yet-unfulfilled promises of health information technology. *Health Affairs (Project Hope), 32*, 63–68. https://doi.org/10.1377/hlthaff.2012.0693

Kruse, C. S., Mileski, M., & Moreno, J. (2017). Mobile health solutions for the aging population: A systematic narrative analysis. *Journal of Telemedicine and Telecare, 23*(4), 439–451. https://doi.org/10.1177/1357633X16649790

Laurisz, N. (2019). The role of stakeholders in development of social economy organizations in Poland: An integrative approach. *Administrative Sciences, 9*(4), 74. https://doi.org/10.3390/admsci9040074

Mair, F. S., May, C., O'Donnell, C., Finch, T., Sullivan, F., & Murray, E. (2012). Factors that promote or inhibit the implementation of e-health systems: An explanatory systematic review. *Bulletin of the World Health Organization, 90*(5), 357–364. https://doi.org/10.2471/BLT.11.099424

Mantzana, V., Themistocleous, M., Irani, Z., & Morabito, V. (2007). Identifying healthcare actors involved in the adoption of information systems. *European Journal of Information Systems, 16*(1), 91–102. https://doi.org/10.1057/palgrave.ejis.3000660

Mazzucato, M. (2011). The entrepreneurial state. *Soundings, 49*. https://doi.org/10.3898/136266211798411183

Meskó, B., Drobni, Z., Bényei, É., Gergely, B., & Gyorffy, Z. (2017). Digital health is a cultural transformation of traditional healthcare. *MHealth, 3*, 38–38. https://doi.org/10.21037/mhealth.2017.08.07

Nambisan, P., & Nambisan, S. (2009). Models of consumer value co-creation in healthcare. *Healthcare Management Review, 34*, 344–354. https://doi.org/10.1097/HMR.0b013e3181abd528

Palumbo, R. (2015). Contextualizing co-production of healthcare: A systematic literature review. *International Journal of Public Sector Management, 29*, Published on-line ahead of print. https://doi.org/10.1108/IJPSM-07-2015-0125

Palumbo, R. (2017). *The Bright Side and the Dark Side of Patient Empowerment: Co-creation and Co-destruction of Value in the Healthcare Environment*. https://doi.org/10.1007/978-3-319-58344-0

Prahalad, C. K., & Ramaswamy, V. (2004). Co-creation experiences: The next practice in value creation. *Journal of Interactive Marketing, 18*(3), 5–14. https://doi.org/10.1002/dir.20015

Ramaswamy, V., & Gouillart, F. (2010, October 1). Building the co-creative enterprise. *Harvard Business Review*. https://hbr.org/2010/10/building-the-co-creative-enterprise

Ramaswamy, V., & Ozcan, K. (2013). Strategy and co-creation thinking. *Strategy and Leadership, 41*. https://doi.org/10.1108/SL-07-2013-0053

Ramaswamy, V., & Ozcan, K. (2014). *The Co-Creation Paradigm*. Stanford University Press.

Ritzer, G., & Jurgenson, N. (2010). Production, consumption, prosumption the nature of capitalism in the age of the digital 'prosumer'. *Journal of Consumer Culture – J CONSUM CULT, 10*, 13–36. https://doi.org/10.1177/1469540509354673

Rogers, W. A., & Fisk, A. D. (2010). Toward a psychological science of advanced technology design for older adults. *The Journals of Gerontology: Series B, 65B*(6), 645–653. https://doi.org/10.1093/geronb/gbq065

Thakur, R., Hsu, S. H., & Fontenot, G. (2012). Innovation in healthcare: Issues and future trends. *Journal of Business Research – J BUS RES, 65*. https://doi.org/10.1016/j.jbusres.2011.02.022

Thuemmler, C., & Bai, C. (2017). Health 4.0: How virtualization and big data are revolutionizing healthcare. In *Health 4.0: How Virtualization and Big Data are Revolutionizing Healthcare* (p. 254). https://doi.org/10.1007/978-3-319-47617-9

Urueña, A., Hidalgo, A., & Arenas, Á. E. (2016). Identifying capabilities in innovation projects: Evidences from eHealth. *Journal of Business Research, 69*(11), 4843–4848. https://doi.org/10.1016/j.jbusres.2016.04.041

Valderas, J. M., World Health Organization, World Health Organization, & Department of Service Delivery and Safety. (2016). *Patient Engagement*. Geneva: World Health Organization.

Vargo, S. L., & Lusch, R. F. (2004). Evolving to a new dominant logic for marketing. *Journal of Marketing, 68*(1), 1–17. https://doi.org/10.1509/jmkg.68.1.1.24036

Vargo, S. L., Maglio, P. P., & Akaka, M. A. (2008). On value and value co-creation: A service systems and service logic perspective. *European Management Journal, 26*(3), 145–152. https://doi.org/10.1016/j.emj.2008.04.003

Voorberg, W. H., Bekkers, V. J. J. M., & Tummers, L. G. (2015). A systematic review of co-creation and co-production: Embarking on the social innovation journey. *Public Management Review, 17*(9), 1333–1357. https://doi.org/10.1080/14719037.2014.930505

Wildenbos, G., Peute, L., & Jaspers, M. (2018). Aging barriers influencing mobile health usability for older adults: A literature based framework (MOLD-US). *International Journal of Medical Informatics, 114*, 66–75. https://doi.org/10.1016/j.ijmedinf.2018.03.012

Zayyad, M. A., & Toycan, M. (2018). Factors affecting sustainable adoption of e-health technology in developing countries: An exploratory survey of Nigerian hospitals from the perspective of healthcare professionals. *PeerJ, 6*, e4436. https://doi.org/10.7717/peerj.4436

Zhou, J., & Salvendy, G. (2018). Human Aspects of IT for the Aged Population. *Acceptance, Communication and Participation: 4th International Conference, ITAP 2018, Held as Part of HCI International 2018, Las Vegas, NV, USA, July 15–20, 2018, Proceedings*. Springer.

9 The implementation of new technologies in Health 4.0 in selected countries

Michał Żabiński

Introduction

Technology pervades almost all the spheres of human life and organisation of society, hence its presence and association with most areas of our activity no longer surprises us. It affects us in our work, especially its remote form as a consequence of the ongoing severe acute respiratory syndrome coronavirus 2 (SARS-Cov-2), known as COVID-19 pandemic; in our homes - the smart home concept is still being developed; in transportation - as the idea of autonomous vehicles; in entertainment - where mobile technologies are particularly important; the potential of new technologies has also been noticed by the state, to mention only the concept of smart cities; and, last but not least, in medicine understood broadly as the healthcare system (Aceto et al., 2020; Jayaraman et al., 2020). This process, in its current stage known as Health 4.0, is extremely dynamic - almost every day brings us the realisation of new visions taken straight out of science fiction films (Lopes et al., 2019). The aim of this chapter is to review the key aspects of technology development in the health sector using examples from selected countries.

Health 4.0 in the world today

Technological advances in broadly conceived healthcare and the revolutionary changes to its system (Sharma et al., 2019), which we are currently witnessing, began in the 1970s. From the 1970s to the 1990s, progress was associated with the implementation of IT systems in the health sector. In the following decades, solutions such as electronic health records (EHR) and networked electronic databases were introduced and gained in popularity. This period is referred to as Health 2.0. Early 21st century saw breakthrough developments in implant technology, knowledge about the human genome and the beginnings of sweeping integration of health information and electronic document flow as well as the first applications of wearable technologies. This period is referred to as Health 3.0 (Chanchaichujit et al., 2019; Sharma et al., 2019). This topic is covered in more detail in Chapter 2: Transition from Telemedicine and e-Health to Health 4.0.

DOI: 10.4324/9781003144403-9

The emergence and rise of Industry 4.0 and its conceptual framework led to the adoption in the literature of the term Health 4.0 to emphasise the consequences of technological transformation for the healthcare system (Aceto et al., 2020; Sharma et al., 2019). They involve, among other things, the integration of the Internet of Things (IoT) with data collection systems, artificial intelligence in the area of analytics, and the use of blockchain technologies for building patient records (Lopes et al., 2019). The successive stages of technological development outlined above as applicable to the healthcare system can thus be categorised as follows (Chen et al., 2020; Sharma et al., 2019):

- Health 1.0 - paternalistic care
- Health 2.0 - reactive care
- Health 3.0 - proactive care
- Health 4.0 - predictive care

New technologies now affect almost every single component of this system (Sharma et al., 2019). Changes are taking place in medical procedures, therapies, innovation in medicines, therapy outcome monitoring, or more broadly, in the conduct of medical research, and in the administrative apparatus of the healthcare system (Jayaraman et al., 2020; Lopes et al., 2019).

In Health 4.0, one may identify four dominant systems and solutions that set the direction and pace of change (Chanchaichujit et al., 2019):

1. IoT and wearable devices
2. Blockchain technology
3. Artificial intelligence
4. Big data and mobile applications

Health 4.0 involves the use and development of existing technologies in new areas as well as the so-called emerging technologies, i.e. completely new solutions, which, apart from those mentioned above, include autonomous robots, 3D printing technologies, augmented virtual reality, and telemedicine (Jayaraman et al., 2020; Sharma et al., 2019).

The pace at which these advances affect healthcare systems worldwide varies. According to estimates by McKinsey, the implementation of the above-mentioned technologies may lead to a significant reduction in national healthcare costs in most Organisation for Economic Co-operation and Development (OECD) countries (Chen et al., 2019). Moreover, Health 4.0 may contribute to reducing the number of diagnostic errors and transaction costs thanks to streamlined management of medical devices, remote patient, and medication monitoring, while ensuring better quality of health services (Aceto et al., 2020; Chute & French, 2019).

Some of the technological solutions considered part of Health 4.0 are already widely used in highly developed countries. These technologies include cloud computing (e.g. AirView - a cloud-based system that enables clinicians to obtain a better picture of their patients' health by remotely monitoring and adjusting the settings of their medical devices, now used in many countries worldwide; cf. Allen, 2021). Another increasingly popular standard are the EHR also known as digital patient medical records (Jayaraman et al., 2020). A number of new systems are still being tested and are awaiting the right application (Jayaraman et al., 2020; Sharma et al., 2019).

Vital links in the healthcare system, where Health 4.0 systems are particularly prominent, are hospitals. However, they adopt new technologies at different rates, as was revealed by the findings of the Digital Maturity Assessment of Hospitals conducted by the Healthcare Information and Management System Society (HIMSS). The study - the Electronic Medical Record Adoption Model (EM RAM) - has been carried out worldwide since 2005 (Taylor et al., 2020). The HIMSS EM RAM standard looks at the degree of digital maturity in terms of digitalisation of medical records rated on a scale of 0–7 (where: 0 = very limited digitisation, and 7 = completely digital working environment). Several thousand hospitals in different countries worldwide have been subject to this assessment (HIMSS Analytics, 2017). Currently, only a few dozen hospitals in Europe are thought to have reached stages 6 or 7, including in (HIMSS Analytics, 2021):

- Portugal: 2 stage 6 hospitals, 1 stage 7 hospital;
- Spain: 3 stage 6 hospitals;
- Austria, Belgium, Denmark, Ireland, Germany, Russia, Slovenia, Switzerland: 1 stage 6 hospital each;
- UK: 5 stage 6 hospitals, 2 stage 7 hospitals;
- Netherlands: 1 stage 6 hospital, 2 stage 7 hospitals; and
- Italy: 6 stage 6 hospitals.

In this respect, US hospitals definitely stand out, since more than 30% of them qualify at least as stage 6 (Chen et al., 2019). This example illustrates how early we currently are in the process of implementing Industry 4.0 concepts in the healthcare system.

Another important indicator of the implementation of Health 4.0 principles is the World Index of Healthcare Innovation, which is a comprehensive ranking of national healthcare systems in terms of quality, choice, science and technology, and fiscal sustainability compiled by the US think tank The Foundation for Research on Equal Opportunity (Roy, 2020). The ranking, which currently covers 31 countries, is informed by a wide array of indicators divided into four main groups: (1) Quality, (2) Choice, (3) Science & Technology, and (4) Fiscal Sustainability. Currently, the five top-ranked countries are Switzerland, Germany, the Netherlands, the USA, and Ireland (cf. Table 9.1).

However, in Science & Technology, which includes sub-indices such as Health Digitisation and Medical Advances, the top five includes the USA, Denmark, the Netherlands, Sweden, and the United Kingdom (Table 9.2). There is a clear gap between the first-ranking USA (score 75.14) and the

Table 9.1 Top 10 countries in the World Index of Healthcare Innovation 2020 ranking: overall rank

Overall rank	*Country*	*Overall tier*	*Overall score*	*Quality*	*Choice*	*Science & technology*	*Fiscal sustainability*
1	Switzerland	Excellent	59.56	73.35	46.53	47.28	71.06
2	Germany	Excellent	59.28	60.99	47.95	46.90	81.28
3	Netherlands	Excellent	59.14	65.70	50.42	49.97	70.46
4	USA	Excellent	54.96	59.71	57.65	75.14	27.33
5	Ireland	Excellent	54.48	67.07	41.77	40.71	68.39
6	Israel	Good	51.14	63.89	43.20	38.79	58.69
7	Singapore	Good	50.37	55.77	46.84	47.98	50.89
8	Czech Republic	Good	49.80	52.22	40.80	27.39	78.78
9	Belgium	Good	49.65	56.55	39.23	44.89	57.95
10	Taiwan	Good	49.19	57.15	46.42	25.28	67.90

Source: https://freopp.org/

other countries (52.63; 49.97; 49.72, 49.39, respectively). Countries in the top five in the overall ranking, which did not make the top five in Science & Technology, were Switzerland (47.28), Germany (46.90), and Ireland (40.71). Particularly interesting are the scores for Germany, where the concept of Industry 4.0 was born, and Japan, one of the three largest medical technology markets in the world (US International Trade Administration, 2020), which came last (31st) in the overall ranking, whereas in Science & Technology, it ranked fifth from the bottom (23.31), along with South Korea (last but one with a score of 18.83), even though both countries are popularly considered to have well-developed high-tech industries and robust economies (Roy, 2020). This ranking does not provide a clear answer as to how advanced each country is in terms of implementing Health 4.0, but it does provide some guidance.

Table 9.2 Top 10 countries in the World Index of Healthcare Innovation 2020 rankings: Science & Technology

Science & technology rank	*Country*	*Overall rank*	*Overall tier*	*Overall score*	*Science & technology*
1	USA	4	Excellent	54.96	75.14
2	Denmark	14	Good	47.59	52.63
3	Netherlands	3	Excellent	59.14	49.97
4	Sweden	15	Good	47.40	49.72
5	United Kingdom	13	Good	47.78	49.39
6	Singapore	7	Good	50.37	47.98
7	Switzerland	1	Excellent	59.56	47.28
8	Germany	2	Excellent	59.28	46.90
9	Finland	23	Moderate	43.65	46.78
10	Belgium	9	Good	49.65	44.89

Source: Own study based on https://freopp.org/

At present, new Digital Health Technologies (DHTs) with a breakthrough potential are being tested and experimented with. Nevertheless, this is a long-term process, currently in a relatively early stage (Taylor et al., 2020), in which security issues are extremely important (Castro e Melo & Faria Araújo, 2020). For that reason, the state plays a special role as a regulator to guarantee the safety of the newly-developed systems by devising admissibility criteria for the use of technology and laying down the conditions for its commercialisation and testing (Iizuka & Ikeda, 2019). For this reason, development in this area proceeds much more slowly and technology migration between countries is much more complicated (Castro e Melo & Faria Araújo, 2020).

Due to the diversity of the technological systems and solutions and the areas of their application, they can be classified in terms of their nature and the extent to which they require regulation, and thus the complexity of the process of state approval of technologies to be used in the health sector. Technological solutions implemented in the healthcare system can be thus divided into three basic groups (Stephens et al., 2021):

1 Medical Devices - all kinds of medical devices that include a software component as well as themselves are software;
2 DHTs - Medical Information and Communication Technologies (MICT); and
3 Wellness Technologies - technologies and products intended to restore health and promote a healthy lifestyle, but which do not meet the definition of a medical device.

The last group of devices does not require registration in order to be released on the market, while the products in the first one require thorough research and testing as well as legislative action prior to being approved for use in the healthcare sector (Jayaraman et al., 2020).

Selected examples of achievements of various countries in Health 4.0

The transfer of solutions from the world of Industry 4.0 to the medical environment commonly referred to as Health 4.0 or Healthcare 4.0, proceeds at different speeds. This point is illustrated by the following four examples of countries representing four continents, where technological advancement is thought to have a large impact on the development of the healthcare industry.

The USA

The country ranks fourth in the World Index of Healthcare Innovation, but first in Science & Technology (Girvan & Roy, 2020c). This is not surprising given that US healthcare spending in 2019 totalled $3.8 trillion or 17.7% of the country's gross domestic product (GDP) (NHE Fact Sheet, 2020). Even though this is the highest level of healthcare spending in the world, its quality varies widely (Raine et al., 2016; Schulte et al., 2020). However, the country continues to be a world leader in new medical technologies (Girvan & Roy, 2020c).

An important factor that affects progress in the area of Health 4.0 is the advancement of the legislative process for the implementation of new technologies in healthcare. As early as in 1996, the Health Insurance Portability and Accountability Act (HIPAA) was passed, which regulated the introduction of IT (digitalisation) in healthcare. In 2003, the Medicare Modernization Act was adopted, enabling digital prescriptions, and 2009 saw the adoption of the Health Information Technology for Economic and Clinical Health Act, which aimed to popularise the EHRs. In 2004, a federal agency - the National Coordinator for Health IT - was established to bring together and co-fund private and public efforts to advance digital health technology (Edmunds et al., 2016). Americans have thus created institutional conditions that promote the rapid development of technologies and their deployment in medicine.

In the area of medical devices, a breakthrough occurred in 2017 with the approval by the US Food and Drug Administration of the first digital medicine Abilify MyCite (Cosgrove et al., 2020). The capsule contains an ingestible sensor that sends a signal confirming that the medication has been taken to be picked up by a smartphone or computer app. As a result, the attending physician receives real-time information about his/her patient's adherence to the medication regime (Flore, 2020). This heralds the development of a new approach to treatment based on digital pills - a combination of medicines and measuring/monitoring devices designed to aggregate and transmit data about individual patients. As a result, their medication habits can be monitored and therapy outcomes can be assessed more effectively (Martani et al., 2020).

In DHTs, the USA boasts the most widespread implementation of the concept of digital hospital management known as smart hospital technologies. According to the HIMSS EMRAM ranking, more than 30% of American hospitals qualify as stage 6 or 7 (Chen et al., 2019), which reflects the country's leading position in this field.

A solution that combines digital health and wellness technologies are the virtual health services, which promise to be an important step towards improving the quality and accessibility of healthcare services, especially in non-urbanised, sparsely populated and poorly connected areas where distance significantly affects the quality and cost of access to healthcare (Schulte et al., 2020). Thanks to new technologies emerging as part of Industry 4.0, the range of medical services that can be provided remotely is constantly expanding. Mobile applications, videoconferencing, and home-installed sensors can be combined into a single coherent system which enables remote patient monitoring and/or virtual medical visits, thus reducing costs, improving quality and access to health services. Apart from diagnostics, the virtual health technology allows for remote monitoring by tracking vital signs, which is particularly important for chronically ill patients or senior citizens who require supervised care, and enables ongoing adjustment of medicine dosage and therapy, which reduces the risk of life-threatening events and increases the chances of delivering urgent medical care when needed (Schulte et al., 2020).

To date, the Office of Advancement of Tele-health has established 12 regional and 2 national federally funded tele-health resource centres (TRCs). Their mission is to provide assistance and support in technology assessment, implementation of new technologies, technical assistance, and support in the fundraising process to healthcare providers interested in implementing virtual healthcare (Schulte et al., 2020). TRCs are part of a centralised programme to develop virtual health across the USA. This is a feature specific to this country and is related to its federal structure.

Germany

This is the country that gave name to and charted the initial course of Industry 4.0 (Yang & Gu, 2021). On top of that, it is EU's only truly global economy. It ranks second in the World Index of Healthcare Innovation, but eighth in Science & Technology (Girvan & Roy, 2020b), which is somewhat surprising. In the area of Health 4.0, Germany is less advanced compared to other highly developed countries (Berghöfer et al., 2020, p. 916; Mattauch, 2017, p. 13; Steinhauser, 2019). Based on the Digital Economy and Society Index, the country ranks close to the EU-28 average (DESI Composite Index, 2020) in terms of digital technology adoption, which is paradoxical as it is the third largest health technology market in the world (US International Trade Administration, 2020).

The slow pace of legislative change significantly hampers the introduction of Health 4.0 in Germany. In 2019, the Improvement in Healthcare Provision through Digitalisation and Innovation Act was passed. It permitted widespread use of mobile apps, online video consultations, and the creation of secure database networks (Digital Healthcare Act [DVG], 2019; Dittrich et al., 2020). However, Germany had already taken the first steps to implement innovations in the health sector - since 2016, its healthcare Innovation Fund programme initiated by the federal government has supported the development and dissemination of integrated healthcare (Berghöfer et al., 2020). Between 2016 and 2020, this programme funded about 380 different projects in New Forms of Care and Healthcare Research. Originally, it was expected to run until 2019; however, it was extended until 2024 (Berghöfer et al., 2020; Gemeinsamer Bundesausschuss, 2021).

An interesting illustration of Germany's problems with the implementation of Health 4.0 is the development of telemetric care networks. Healthcare, due to its specificity, is subject to extensive regulation; consequently, both public institutions as decision-making organisations and the applicable legal provisions strongly determine what can be done in this area (Steinhauser, 2019). Although telemedicine is classified as a Digital Health Technology with a moderate level of implementation difficulties due to legal regulations, in Germany, these represent a major barrier to development. Accordingly, most telemedicine projects undertaken in Germany in recent years have not progressed beyond the pilot stage due to the lack of support from public institutions (Steinhauser, 2019). However, where commitment and institutional support were present, sustainable results were achieved. A good example is the TEMPiS project (Telemedic Pilot Project for Integrative Stroke Care) conducted with the participation of 19 Bavarian hospitals. Its success is in no small measure due to the involvement of the Bavarian government (Steinhauser, 2019).

Japan

The case of Japan is full of contradictions. As one of the richest countries in the world, it tends to be associated with cutting-edge technologies, yet surprisingly it came only 31st in the overall ranking compiled by the World Index of Healthcare Innovation. This is interesting since Japan is considered one of the most developed countries in terms of healthcare, with health spending accounting for 10.2% of its GDP (Raghavan et al., 2021). It should be noted, however, that its final position was significantly affected by its last place in Fiscal Sustainability (where it scored 0 due to its high level of public debt) and only 28th in Science & Technology (Roy, 2020).

The plan for implementing the principles of Industry 4.0 in the healthcare system was part of Japan's Revitalisation Strategy of 2013 (Raghavan et al., 2021). Another effort to that end was the Industrial Value Chain Initiative of 2015, which involved 30 corporations, including companies such as Panasonic and Mitsubishi. The next step was the adoption in 2019 of the Society 5.0 concept - a system designed to further integrate cyberspace with the physical space. This is to be achieved by implementing the idea of Industry 4.0 across all the branches of the Japanese economy, including its health system (Yang & Gu, 2021). However, as studies show, so far, little progress has been made in this area. For example, the country ranks only 30th out of 31 countries in the World Index of Healthcare Innovation in implementing EHR (Girvan & Roy, 2020a).

Japan has the world's fastest ageing population, hence implementing information and communication technologies (ICT) in the healthcare system, i.e. DHTs and Wellness Technologies, is particularly pressing (Obi et al., 2013; Raghavan et al., 2021). However, these systems require a better understanding of the needs of the elderly to be properly tailored as well as appropriately designed promotional and dissemination activities (Iizuka & Ikeda, 2019). In Japan, the first steps in in the area of e-health were made in the 1990s with the adoption of the Healthcare Information System Strategy. This document provided a blueprint for the development of the electronic medical records (EMRs) system, which was formally implemented in 1999 (Obi et al., 2013). In the early 21st century, the e-Japan strategy was adopted, one of whose priorities was to digitise the healthcare system and develop telemedicine (Obi et al., 2013). The Japan Association of Medical Informatics subsequently approved a new five-tier EMR system for widespread use in hospitals (Raghavan et al., 2021). A Tier 1 EMR system means activities at the level of a single unit - a hospital ward. A Tier 3 system means hospital-wide EMR implementation, whereas Tier 5 means EMR interoperability between facilities and includes access to patient care information. Barriers to further development of this system include, on the one hand, state concerns about data security and, on the other, the costs of implementing these systems by hospitals (Raghavan et al., 2021). As regards DHTs, Japan has a well-developed cloud infrastructure, both in the public and private sectors, but progress in this area was possible mostly due to state involvement and well-designed sectoral policies (Raghavan et al., 2021). This example shows the important role played by the state in the dissemination of DHTs.

Perhaps the best example of Wellness Technologies is the Person-centred Open Platform for Wellbeing (PeOPLe), which links and integrates citizens' health data generated throughout their lives and gives both health professionals and patients easy access to the necessary information. In 2017, a law was passed governing the use of big data for the purpose of such activities. The cloud-based version of the PeOPLe platform is also being developed and is expected to be operational by 2025 (Raghavan et al., 2021). This clearly shows how lengthy the process of creating appropriate legislation, testing, and implementing new technology can be.

In the area of Medical Devices, which is considered the most demanding in terms safety, outcome assessment and legislation, Japan is undertaking a range of robotisation efforts. Cyberdyne, which was the first company to develop and commercialise a device that brings technology from the field of robotics and cybernetics into a wearable medical/healthcare device, serves as an excellent example. The Hybrid Assistive Limb (HAL) developed by Cyberdyne, is essentially a robot which can improve, support, and/or enhance a person's physical functions. It is intended to be worn primarily by people with mobility difficulties and is now also available outside Japan in the EU and the USA, among others (Iizuka & Ikeda, 2019). As part of developing and commercialising the technology, Cyberdyne had to conduct relevant clinical trials to verify the usefulness, efficacy and safety of their device, but the most significant problem was posed by legislative constraints due to the fact that the pace of legal change lagged far behind the development of new technologies (Iizuka & Ikeda, 2019). This example, while demonstrating success in implementing solutions that represent Health 4.0, shows how challenging it is to adapt laws, safety norms, and standards for industry, the absence or archaic nature of which delays the process of adapting Industry 4.0 technologies to the needs of Health 4.0.

Australia

In the World Index of Healthcare Innovation, the country ranked 11th, whereas in the area of Science & Technology it came only 26th out of 31 countries (Dornauer, 2020). Interestingly, Australia has implemented a range of public activities in the area of Industry 4.0 and is involved in numerous international projects in the field of Health 4.0 (Stephens et al., 2021). The reason for its fairly low position in the World Index of Healthcare Innovation ranking is the limited use of new technologies in the public system. This is, however, partly due to the high share of the private sector in the healthcare system - as many as 44% of Australians rely on private health insurance (Dornauer, 2020).

Officially, the concept of Industry 4.0 was adopted by the Australian government in 2017 with the establishment of a network of Australian universities and private companies tasked with creating and implementing digital technology solutions (Yang & Gu, 2021). From the state's perspective as a regulator, the DHTs implementation process is primarily based on risk assessment and performance measurement and is geared towards regulatory harmonisation in an international context to enable the development of transnational solutions, thereby increasing the rate of uptake of new and innovative applications in the sector (Stephens et al., 2021).

To achieve this goal, the Australian government established MTPConnect – an organisation responsible for monitoring the adaptation of the legal framework to the new context arising from the implementation of new medical technologies. It takes into consideration the perspectives of the different actors in this process: technology developers, regulators (political actors responsible for public policies), industry representatives, including medical and pharmaceutical companies, and users of new technologies. The said organisation evaluates activities, identifies the challenges and problems - regulations that need to be adapted or changed due to the lack of compatibility with the new technologies (Stephens et al., 2021).

In the area of Medical Devices, clinical trials are currently underway to market intestinal gas detection capsules for use in gastroenterology for real-time examination using wireless communication technology. This system is the fruit of research conducted at the Royal Melbourne Institute of Technology (RMIT). Planet Innovation, an engineering consultancy firm, was engaged to work out how and to what extent the novel technology can be commercialised. This collaboration led to the founding of a consortium Atmo Biosciences to commercialise the solution. Efforts to market it are ongoing in both Australia and the USA (Stephens et al., 2021).

In DHTs, a digital patient monitoring platform, Vitalic Medical, is being developed with the aim to provide better nursing care in hospitals. The platform consists of sensors and devices that monitor a patient's condition, an application for mobile devices, and risk assessment software, which, using a system of algorithms, makes the decision to send a nurse to a particular patient. The venture is being carried out by Ramsay Healthcare - a private hospital network, the largest institution of its kind in Australia. The platform is currently being tested in a hospital setting in order to obtain the necessary validation and approvals leading to its commercial roll-out in Australia, the USA, and Europe (Stephens et al., 2021).

An example of Wellness Technology is the Cardihab service developed for cardiac rehabilitation, currently in its early stages of clinical trials. It combines several technologies: the IoT, wearable devices, big data, and mobile applications. The platform aims to increase cardiac patients' engagement in rehabilitation, including the all-important issue of adherence to the prescribed regimens. It is based on a smartphone app and expands the options of home rehabilitation. The physician and the patient can keep in touch without having to visit the rehabilitation clinic, which is expected to facilitate supervision of the rehabilitation process (Stephens et al., 2021).

Conclusions

The examples discussed above illustrate the complexity of issues surrounding the implementation of Industry 4.0 concepts in the healthcare system. Advancements in this field are hampered by two main challenges: the costs of developing and testing new technologies, and legislative strictures associated with potential risks to health and life. These challenges are interrelated; as a consequence, the development of new technologies in healthcare proceeds much more slowly than in the other sectors of the economy. At the same time, the question of social inequalities in access to innovative healthcare technologies remains open.

The foregoing review shows that the moderate pace of uptake of technological advancements by the health sector is due to the need to reliably assess their impacts and outcomes in the long term; in other words, to protect human health and life. The challenge consists in developing new systems and testing them before they are released for use; moreover, due to different standards and formats, substantial financial outlays are required to ensure that novel solutions approved in one country can be replicated elsewhere. Given the cost-intensive nature of research, the lengthy testing and validation period as well as the potential health risks, it is necessary to involve the state in the implementation of new technologies in healthcare. Cooperation between private and public entities should involve financing, models of action, and the provision of an institutional framework to facilitate the process. The fact that Germany and Japan - both highly developed and technologically advanced countries - have problems with transferring knowledge and technology to healthcare serves to prove that systemic public-private solutions must be sought to remove at least the major barriers to progress in this area. However, since the said technology may pose risks to health and life, the implementation of new systems and solutions in healthcare will necessarily proceed more slowly than in other sectors of the economy, where such risks do not exist.

References

Aceto, G., Persico, V., & Pescapé, A. (2020). Industry 4.0 and Health: Internet of Things, Big Data, and Cloud Computing for Health 4.0. *Journal of Industrial Information Integration, 18*, 100129. https://doi.org/10.1016/j.jii.2020.100129

Berghöfer, A., Göckler, D. G., Sydow, J., Auschra, C., Wessel, L., & Gersch, M. (2020). The German Healthcare Innovation Fund – An Incentive for Innovations to Promote the Integration of Healthcare. *Journal of Health Organisation and Management, 34*(8), 915–923. https://doi.org/10.1108/JHOM-05-2020-0180

Castro e Melo, J. A. G. de M. e, & Faria Araújo, N. M. (2020). Impact of the Fourth Industrial Revolution on the Health Sector: A Qualitative Study. *Healthcare Informatics Research, 26*(4), 328–334. https://doi.org/10.4258/hir.2020.26.4.328

Chanchaichujit, J., Tan, A., Meng, F., & Eaimkhong, S. (2019). *Health 4.0: Next generation processes with the latest technologies*. Springer, Singapore. https://doi.org/10.1007/978-981-13-8114-0

Chen, B., Baur, A., Stepniak, M., & Wang, J. (2019). *Finding the future of care provision: The role of smart hospitals*. McKinsey & Company.

Chen, C., Loh, E.-W., Kuo, K. N., & Tam, K.-W. (2020). The Times they Are a-Changin' – Health 4.0 Is Coming! *Journal of Medical Systems, 44*(2), 40. https://doi.org/10.1007/s10916-019-1513-0

Chute, C., & French, T. (2019). Introducing Care 4.0: An Integrated Care Paradigm Built on Industry 4.0 Capabilities. *International Journal of Environmental Research and Public Health, 16*(12), 2247. https://doi.org/10.3390/ijerph16122247

Cosgrove, L., Karter, J. M., McGinley, M., & Morrill, Z. (2020). Digital Phenotyping and Digital Psychotropic Drugs. Mental Health Surveillance Tools That Threaten Human Rights. *Health Hum Rights, 22*(2), 33–39.

DESI Composite Index. (2020). *Data Visualisation Tool – Data & Indicators*. https://digital-agenda-data.eu/charts/desi-composite#chart={%22indicator%22:%22desi_sliders%22,%22breakdown%22:{%22desi_1_conn%22:5,%22desi_2_hc%22:5,%22desi_3_ui%22:3,%22desi_4_idt%22:4,%22desi_5_dps%22:3},%22unit-measure%22:%22pc_desi_sliders%22,%22time-period%22:%222020%22}

Digital Healthcare Act (DVG). (2019, December 3). [Federal Ministry of Health]. Federal Ministry of Health. Digital Healthcare Act (DVG).

Dittrich, F., Albrecht, U.-V., von Jan, U., Malinka, C., Ansorg, J., Jung, J., Back, D. A., & AG Digitalisierung. (2020). The Digital Healthcare Act – A Turning Point in the German Digitisation Strategy? Results of a Survey in Orthopaedics and Trauma Surgery. *Zeitschrift für Orthopädie und Unfallchirurgie*. https://doi.org/10.1055/a-1141-4274

Dornauer, M. (2020, June 2). Australia: #11 in the World Index of Healthcare Innovation. *OppBlog*. https://freopp.org/australia-health-system-profile-11-in-the-world-index-of-healthcare-innovation-164225723e08

Edmunds, M., Peddicord, D., & Frisse, M. E. (2016). The Evolution of Health Information Technology Policy in the United States. In C. A. Weaver, M. J. Ball, G. R. Kim, & J. M. Kiel (Eds.), *Healthcare information management systems* (pp. 139–162). Springer International Publishing. https://doi.org/10.1007/978-3-319-20765-0_8

Flore, J. (2020). Ingestible Sensors, Data, and Pharmaceuticals: Subjectivity in the Era of Digital Mental Health. *New Media & Society*. https://doi.org/10.1177/1461444820931024

Gemeinsamer Bundesausschuss. (2021). The Innovation Fund and the Innovation Committee of the Federal Joint Committee. https://innovationsfonds.g-ba.de/

Girvan, G., & Roy, A. (2020a, June 26). Japan: #31 in the World Index of Healthcare Innovation [FREOPP]. *OppBlog*. https://freopp.org/japan-health-system-profile-31-in-the-world-index-of-healthcare-innovation-b401ff41e549

Girvan, G., & Roy, A. (2020b, September 4). Germany: #2 in the World Index of Healthcare Innovation [FREOPP]. *OppBlog*. https://freopp.org/germany-health-system-profile-2-in-the-world-index-of-healthcare-innovation-14b0953e9f82

Girvan, G., & Roy, A. (2020c, September 5). United States: #4 in the World Index of Healthcare Innovation. *OppBlog*. https://freopp.org/united-states-health-system-profile-4-in-the-world-index-of-healthcare-innovation-b593ba15a96

HIMSS Analytics. (2017). EMRAM: A Strategic Roadmap for Effective EMR Adoption and Maturity. *HIMSS Analytics*. https://www.himssanalytics.org/europe/electronic-medical-record-adoption-model

HIMSS Analytics. (2021). Provider Maturity Achievement. Stage 6 & 7 Provider Achievement Map. *HIMSS Analytics*. https://www.himssanalytics.org/europe/stage-6-7-achievement

Iizuka, M., & Ikeda, Y. (2019). Regulation and Innovation Under Industry 4.0: Case of Medical/Healthcare Robot, HAL by Cyberdyne. Working Paper Series UNU-MERIT. https://doi.org/10.13140/RG.2.2.35788.97928

Jayaraman, P. P., Forkan, A. R. M., Morshed, A., Haghighi, P. D., & Kang, Y. (2020). Health 4.0: A Review of Frontiers in Digital Health. *WIREs Data Mining and Knowledge Discovery*, *10*(2). https://doi.org/10.1002/widm.1350

Lopes, J. M., Marrone, P., Pereira, S. L., & Dias, E. M. (2019). Health 4.0: Challenges for an Orderly and Inclusive Innovation [Commentary]. *IEEE Technology and Society Magazine*, *38*(3), 17–19. https://doi.org/10.1109/MTS.2019.2930265

Martani, A., Geneviève, L. D., Poppe, C., Casonato, C., & Wangmo, T. (2020). Digital Pills: A Scoping Review of the Empirical Literature and Analysis of the Ethical Aspects. *BMC Medical Ethics*, *21*(1), 3. https://doi.org/10.1186/s12910-019-0443-1

Mattauch, W. (2017). *Digitising European industries—Member states profile: Germany (digitising European industries)*. European Commission. https://ec.europa.eu/futurium/en/system/files/ged/de_country_analysis.pdf

NHE Fact Sheet. (2020, December 16). [A federal government website]. *Centers for Medicare & Medicaid Services*. https://www.cms.gov/research-statistics-data-and-systems/statistics-trends-and-reports/nationalhealthexpenddata/nhe-fact-sheet

Obi, T., Ishmatova, D., & Iwasaki, N. (2013). Promoting ICT innovations for the ageing population in Japan. *International Journal of Medical Informatics*, *82*(4), e47–e62. https://doi.org/10.1016/j.ijmedinf.2012.05.004

Raghavan, A., Demircioglu, M. A., & Taeihagh, A. (2021). Public Health Innovation through Cloud Adoption: A Comparative Analysis of Drivers and Barriers in Japan, South Korea, and Singapore. *International Journal of Environmental Research and Public Health*, *18*(1), 334. https://doi.org/10.3390/ijerph18010334

Raine, R., Fitzpatrick, R., Barratt, H., Bevan, G., Black, N., Boaden, R., Bower, P., Campbell, M., Denis, J.-L., Devers, K., Dixon-Woods, M., Fallowfield, L., Forder, J., Foy, R., Freemantle, N., Fulop, N. J., Gibbons, E., Gillies, C., Goulding, L., … Zwarenstein, M. (2016). Challenges, Solutions and Future Directions in the Evaluation of Service Innovations in Healthcare and Public Health. *Health Services and Delivery Research*, *4*(16), 1–136. https://doi.org/10.3310/hsdr04160

Roy, A. (2020, June 17). Introducing the FREOPP World Index of Healthcare Innovation. *FREOPP*. https://freopp.org/wihi2020-505b1b60bce6

Schulte, A., Majerol, M., & Nadler, J. (2020, July). Narrowing the Rural-Urban Health Divide. Bringing Virtual Health to Rural Communities. Deloitte Review, The Essence of Resilient Leadership. Business Recovery from COVID-19 (Issue 27), 79–93.

Sharma, D., Singh Aujla, G., & Bajaj, R. (2019). Evolution from Ancient Medication to Human-Centered Health 4.0: A Review on Healthcare Recommender Systems. *International Journal of Communication Systems*, e4058. https://doi.org/10.1002/dac.4058

Steinhauser, S. (2019). Network-Based Business Models, the Institutional Environment, and the Diffusion of Digital Innovations: Case Studies of Telemedicine Networks in Germany. *Schmalenbach Business Review*, *71*(3), 343–383. https://doi.org/10.1007/s41464-019-00076-9

Allen, S. (2021). *Global healthcare outlook 2021. Accelerating industry change*. Deloitte Insight. Deloitte Development LLC. https://www2.deloitte.com/global/en/insights/industry/health-care/global-health-care-outlook.html.

Stephens, A., Pregelj, L., Smith, A., & Hine, D. (2021). *Adaptive regulation for digital health: Enhancing Australia's regulation system*. Department of Industry, Science, Energy and Resources, Australian Government, Australia.

Taylor, K., Properzi, F., Bhatti, S., & Ferris, K. (2020). *Digital transformation. Shaping the future of European healthcare*. Deloitte LLP. https://www2.deloitte.com/content/dam/Deloitte/nl/Documents/public-sector/deloitte-nl-shaping-the-future-of-european-healthcare.pdf

US International Trade Administration. (2020, October 7). *Germany—Country Commercial Guide. Healthcare and Medical Technology*. https://www.trade.gov/knowledge-product/germany-healthcare

Yang, F., & Gu, S. (2021). Industry 4.0, a Revolution That Requires Technology and National Strategies. *Complex & Intelligent Systems*. https://doi.org/10.1007/s40747-020-00267-9

10 The key factors of the healthcare system's adaptiveness for Health 4.0

Marek Ćwiklicki

Introduction

The aim of this chapter is to discuss the main factors that influence the receptiveness of the healthcare system to Health 4.0. Previous analyses (Ćwiklicki et al., 2020) pointed to the lack in the literature of commonly agreed upon factors that are important for the implementation of advanced medical technology solutions, but suggested that such factors can be derived from adaptive capacity theory. These include (1) human capital, (2) social capital, (3) information and communication technology (ICT), (4) financial resources, (5) legal regulations, and (6) governance. They also map out the areas of threats and problems of development in Health 4.0 discussed in more detail in Chapter 15.

The chapter is thus divided into six corresponding sections, in which the suggested parameters to be met by the main factors enabling the use of Health 4.0 solutions in the healthcare system are discussed. The examples provided draw on an in-depth literature review and their main focus is on issues without which successful implementation of Health 4.0 is unlikely to be possible.

Human capital

Human capital is defined as a set of competencies and skills to use technological solutions, which in this case represent the domain of Health 4.0. In particular, it refers to the so-called digital literacy of young people and adults. These competencies also include the knowledge of medical terminology, which allows them to navigate the systems and solutions dedicated to health. Apart from the skills themselves, this concept also includes psychological factors, such as the perception that Health 4.0 tools and techniques ensure the security of transmitted information.

The main areas listed above play a key role in e-health literacy understood as "the ability to seek, find, understand, and appraise health information from electronic sources and apply the knowledge gained to addressing or solving a health problem" (Norman & Skinner, 2006). In their model, Norman and Skinner included the following skills: information, learning, media, computer, health, and traditional literacy. This set in the context of Health 4.0 is

DOI: 10.4324/9781003144403-10

still relevant, but with a greater emphasis on science, technology, and health, as evidenced by research findings on students' self-assessment of digital competence, which show a clear link between the daily performance of digital activities and perceptions of higher digital competencies in other areas (Martzoukou et al., 2020). What it means is that whether or not an individual can employ Health 4.0 tools effectively depends on their regular use of other IT solutions. The limited use of e-health solutions by senior citizens has been well documented (Berkowsky & Czaja, 2018) and is further discussed in Chapter 10. However, studies among adults have shown not only increasing digital competencies in this age but group but also, which I would like to emphasise, that older adults are much less reluctant to use new technology (Xie, 2012). According to other studies among adolescents, higher levels of e-health competence tend to be associated with taking health-promoting actions. Therefore, medical platforms should be designed in a way that meet the needs of young people with higher levels of digital literacy who seek health-related information on their own (Gazibara et al., 2020).

In light of the above, digital health skills are crucial for the widespread adoption of Health 4.0 tools in society. However, as research indicates, they mostly result from self-initiated actions by users, mainly young people with Internet access, and accompany the implementation of e-health. It contributes to the popularisation of more advanced Health 4.0 solutions, for example the growing use of information technology and the popularity of health services based on the Internet of Things (IoT) (Martínez-Caro et al., 2018).

Nevertheless, a review of research on e-health competencies reveals a lack of association between such skills and health status as well as the need to update the popular scales used for assessing digital health competencies due to the emergence of new technologies (Watkins & Xie, 2014).

Naturally, skills requirements for Health 4.0 may not necessarily translate into rising demand for specialised knowledge due to the design of user-friendly solutions using advanced technology, such as the life alert bracelet or the artificial intelligence behind chatbots. Moreover, some Health 4.0 technologies do not require any special patient competencies, such as the sensor-enabled tablets, the sensor patch (BioStamp) or other wearable biosensors (Ray et al., 2019).

On the other hand, the availability of digital health information has huge implications for the competencies of health professionals. For example, it was possible to anticipate the successive waves of SARS-Cov-2 infection from online search trends (Venkatesh & Gandhi, 2020). Novel complex technological solutions should be thus broadly embraced not only by physicians and nurses but also by other healthcare stakeholders. Previous research on the development of e-health solutions indicated differences in the perception of benefits due to their roles as initiators rather than beneficiaries of such tools and solutions (Duplaga et al., 2013).

This observation points to a broader context of developing appropriate competencies contributing to the adoption of Health 4.0 systems, since the latter affect not only patients but also those who operate these technologies, namely health professionals. This, in turn, depends on an appropriately designed system of training and continuous education. Self-efficacy, which is determined by proficiency derived from experience, is considered a key factor of digital competence (Pourrazavi et al., 2020). Self-confidence contributes to more frequent use of online technologies, which are perceived as a gateway to better use of tools based on online platforms.

Specific activities aimed at developing competencies that resonate with Health 4.0 are not particularly different in kind from other targeted upgrades of competencies across society. What is important in this case is the specificity of the health sector. The measures used as predictors of Health 4.0 adaptiveness may include the proportion of population using e-services; the number of available health platforms; the number of patients, doctors, and nurses equipped with the competencies needed to use internet technologies more effectively; campaigns promoting the use of e-health resources; or medical procedures in which advanced medical technology is used. Human capital in healthcare is discussed in more detail in Chapter 13.

Social capital

In the context of Health 4.0, social capital is understood as the behaviours, attitudes, and propensities that govern the acceptance and use of advanced medical technologies. Social capital influences the willingness to collaborate in the virtual space, for example, in a question-and-answer exchange of information on online communities (Zhang et al., 2017). Habits influence the pattern of online activities, such as searching for information. One study showed that health information queries were mostly directed to institutional and non-institutional sites (about 17% each) with a much smaller proportion addressed to social networks (average 5%) (De Sousa & Almeida, 2016).

The model that best explains consumer behaviour towards health information technology (HIT) is the Technology Acceptance Model (TAM; cf. Tao et al., 2020). In its simplest form, it comprises factors such as perceived usefulness, perceived ease of use, attitude, and acceptance understood as the behavioural intention that ultimately leads to the use of a given technology (Holden & Karsh, 2010). A synthesis of research on TAM in health showed that attitude was replaced by social influence/subjective norms, whereas the behavioural intention to use by control or facilitating conditions (ibid.).

Patient safety is worth mentioning as one of the social factors that affect attitudes to HIT (Sittig et al., 2020). Even a service as simple as electronic medical appointment booking requires patients' trust in the security of their personal data (Xie et al., 2020). Apart from patients, physicians and nurses are also concerned about HIT. A study on the preliminary factors that cause resistance to HIT showed that potential dissatisfaction and loss of professional autonomy had a serious impact on the perception of risks posed by the technology used (Alohali et al., 2020).

Accordingly, it can be said that the perceived usefulness of Health 4.0 along with ease of use affect the behavioural intention directly associated with the use itself. Due to the fact that these factors vary from one health technology to another, formulating unequivocal standards across the board is currently impossible. Further research to that end is needed, such as the previously cited study on participation in online forums.

Social capital also influences the commitment of members of society to initiate and engage in activities related to the promotion of Health 4.0. This is the core content of Chapter 14, which discusses examples of community initiatives to use the above-mentioned technologies for health purposes.

Information and communication technology

ICT refers to the infrastructure necessary for the transmission of data, or more specifically in the context of Health 4.0, health data. Since infrastructure is also common to other non-medical services, it can be said to include

> phone lines, fibre trunks and submarine cables, T1, T3 and OC-xx, ISDN, DSL and other high-speed services … as well as satellites, earth stations and teleports, … telecommunications, electricity, access to computers, a number of Internet hosts, a number of ISPs (Internet service providers) and available bandwidth and broadband access.
>
> (Wickramasinghe et al., 2004)

The focus is thus on enabling the transmission of electronic information and refers to broadly defined information infrastructure. Studies on the relationship between ICT and e-health (e.g. Tavares, 2018) employ data on the following indicators (ITU, 2020):

- Fixed network (e.g. basic-rate Integrated Services Digital Network [ISDN] subscriptions)
- Mobile network (e.g. mobile cellular telephone subscriptions per 100 inhabitants)
- Traffic (e.g. domestic fixed-to-fixed telephone traffic, in minutes)
- Prices (e.g. fixed-broadband cap, in GB)
- Revenue/Investment (e.g. annual investment in fixed [wired]-broadband services)
- Employees (e.g. full-time equivalent telecommunication employees, total)
- Internet (e.g. dial-up Internet subscriptions)
- Broadband (e.g. active mobile-broadband subscriptions per 100 inhabitants)
- ICT Household (e.g. percentage of households with electricity, percentage of households with Internet)
- Broadcasting (e.g. multichannel TV subscriptions)
- Quality of service (e.g. mobile cellular unsuccessful call ratio)

Taken together, they form the so-called ICT Development Index, which consists of ICT readiness, ICT intensity or the degree of ICT use in society, ICT skills in general concerning education as proxy measures for ICT-related skills (ITU, n.d.). Since ICT skills issues belong to the previously presented Health 4.0 adaptiveness factors, they will not be discussed in this section. On the basis of the main constituents of the ICT Development Index it can be concluded that the greater the access to information technology (e.g. the number of telephone subscribers, the number of cell phones, the number of households with computers) and the use of this technology (e.g. the number of active cable and mobile broadband subscriptions), the higher the adaptiveness of Health 4.0.

The issue of appropriate technology is particularly important for countries with less economic potential (Lewis et al., 2012).

ICT infrastructure should also secure the data transmitted by it, which has to do with the sharing of information across different applications and systems (Bossuyt et al., 2017).

Considering ICT in the context of health led to the coining of a new term - 'HIT' - which is defined as electronic health data and their use not only by patients or physicians but also by researchers (Detmer, 2003; Zayas-Cabán et al., 2020). Studies have shown that the use of HIT alters the proportion of activities in the workload of nurses in that the latter require more time to document medical events, but make fewer errors (Moore et al., 2020). However, positive outcomes do not automatically follow from the implementation of advanced technologies alone. For these to occur, it is necessary to secure appropriate staffing, funding, and education to sustain the use of technology that supports the electronic health record technology (Baillieu et al., 2020).

The importance of being able to work with electronic health records was underscored by the SARS-Covid-2 pandemic. Telephone consultations, electronic record keeping, vaccination referrals, etc. proved their utility in slowing the spread of the virus. As a result, publications on adapting health information technology to pandemic-induced hardships highlight the broader support offered by advanced web-based techniques (Singh et al., 2020). This includes regulations related to patient identification and social norms, e.g. consent to the processing of personal data by a variety of organisations and institutions (Sittig & Singh, 2020). The social factor is discussed separately.

Financial resources

The topic of funding is discussed in Chapter 11, so here we shall focus only on the basic issues regarding this adaptiveness factor. Cutting-edge technologies tend to be expensive - this is due in part to the outlays required to create them, which have not yet been recouped, not to mention yielding a return, and a reduced willingness to risk further investment (Fleming et al., 2011). This raises the issue of financial support by public and private financial institutions. A good example of this is the case of telemedicine in France (Ohannessian et al., 2020), which involved not only funding but also the improvement of IT infrastructure (billing software) and training to encourage the use of telemedicine. This shows that the general receptiveness to Health 4.0 tools benefits from the co-occurrence of a number of positive and mutually reinforcing contributing factors, not least of them being the availability of various sources of funding for technological solutions at the stages of prototyping, technology development, implementation, and maintenance leading to their long-term use.

Legal regulations

Legal regulations refer to the legislative conditions that encourage the widespread use of Health 4.0 technologies. They are discussed in more detail in Chapter 12, hence only their key aspects shall be highlighted here. The extent of regulation applicable to e-health in its broadest sense is related to the requirements that must be met by institutions that store health records/data, patient consent, access to and updating of resources, archiving and reuse of health data, and the exchange of health data between systems (Milieu, 2014).

The literature primarily emphasises the importance of data security, especially when information is being exchanged between systems. Guaranteeing the privacy of data, especially those stored in cloud-hosted systems, is a factor that significantly affects patients' trust in using new technologies (Xu, 2019). According to the TAM mentioned above, this factor determines the use of technology. As one may expect, the issue of personal data security affect not only the domain of Health 4.0. Good examples include the EU General Data Protection Regulation (GDPR) and previous e-commerce regulations, such as EU Directive 2000/31/EC (Callens, 2010).

Another aspect to be mentioned is the physician-patient relationship as mediated by information technology, especially the issues of provision of appropriate health services and responsibility for the consequences of remote consulting (Silverman, 2003). In the context of telemedicine, another form of Health 4.0, which has been present and operational for quite some time, data privacy is emphasised. The regulations in force specify the parties affected, namely the providers of devices with relatively short lifespans and the health professionals using them (Nittari et al., 2020).

The diversity in regulation across countries is well illustrated by data from Europe. Around 80% of the member states have passed laws securing patient health data, but only about 50% of them regulate individual access to them as well as permit the individuals concerned to choose the extent of data sharing (Peterson et al., 2016).

In summary, the key parameters of this enabler of Health 4.0 adaptiveness include health data security, the exchange of such data between electronic health record systems as well as access by health professionals and the patients themselves.

Governance

In general, this factor subsumes leadership, autonomy, decision-making capacity, political capital, formal and informal institutions determining regional planning, innovation, and participation (Lemos et al., 2013). It is strongly associated with social capital, but is capable of exerting a more profound impact on reality. It is also linked with regulations, since all the actions of public institutions are mandated by legislation. In particular, it concerns the adoption of acts governing national e-health development policies and Health 4.0 solutions.

The coordination and management of new health technologies can be analysed on two levels. The first one is made up of companies offering advanced solutions, which, with the participation of social organisations and public institutions responsible for healthcare, are tested, piloted, and then applied on a local basis. The second one emerges when these move to the national level and require institutional support from central government. An example is the establishment of The Office of the National Coordinator for Health Information Technology located within the US Department of Health and Human Services, with responsibilities, among other things, for implementing and using the most advanced health information technology and electronic exchange of health information (Ricciardi et al., 2013).

Conclusions

This chapter reviews the key determinants of adaptiveness of Health 4.0. Each of them affects individuals, businesses, and governments to varying degrees. Moreover, they interpenetrate to a much greater degree than most would like to admit; to wit, regulation cannot be considered separately from funding, as the law sets the framework within which the application of new health technologies is deemed admissible. Likewise, human capital without a reference to social capital cannot fully explain the process of implementation of Health 4.0, thus limiting the understanding of all the circumstances that affect the emergence of new technologies in the health sector.

Each of these factors comprises several criteria that can be employed to describe the readiness of the healthcare system to absorb new solutions. To clarify: each healthcare system has its own moment of inertia, despite which Health 4.0 tools can still be deployed, but the factors described in this chapter suggest that this will not be desirable in every instance, which has to do with the socio-economic development of a given country and the attitude of the national culture towards the adoption of innovation. At this point one may refer to previous research that provided guidelines for focusing activities around IT while ensuring good relationship with staff and relying on bottom-up approaches for implementation (Thakur et al., 2012).

These key determinants of the health system's capacity to absorb advanced technological solutions seem particularly relevant for a world affected by the

SARS-Cov-2 pandemic. Some authors regard them as crucial to the spread of digital innovations in health (Bayram et al., 2020), justifying their view by citing the need to steer in response to emerging issues and prepare for new challenges related to the many influences that new technologies, such as big data, bring to bear on society. It is also emphasised that despite the accelerated deployment of digital health innovation, problems of equal access to it still persist (Crawford & Serhal, 2020).

References

Alohali, M., Carton, F., & O'Connor, Y. (2020). Investigating the antecedents of perceived threats and user resistance to health information technology: A case study of a public hospital. *Journal of Decision Systems, 29*(1), 27–52. https://doi.org/10.1080/12460125.2020.1728988

Baillieu, R., Hoang, H., Sripipatana, A., Nair, S., & Lin, S. C. (2020). Impact of health information technology optimization on clinical quality performance in health centers: A national cross-sectional study. *PLOS ONE, 15*(7), e0236019. https://doi.org/10.1371/journal.pone.0236019

Bayram, M., Springer, S., Garvey, C. K., & Özdemir, V. (2020). COVID-19 digital health innovation policy: A portal to alternative futures in the making. *OMICS: A Journal of Integrative Biology, 24*(8), 460–469. https://doi.org/10.1089/omi.2020.0089

Berkowsky, R. W., & Czaja, S. J. (2018). Challenges associated with online health information seeking among older adults. In *Aging, Technology and Health* (pp. 31–48). Elsevier. https://doi.org/10.1016/B978-0-12-811272-4.00002-6

Bossuyt, P., Pouillon, L., Bonnaud, G., Danese, S., & Peyrin-Biroulet, L. (2017). e-Health in inflammatory bowel diseases: More challenges than opportunities? *Digestive and Liver Disease, 49*(12), 1320–1326. https://doi.org/10.1016/j.dld.2017.08.026

Callens, S. (2010). The EU legal framework on e-health. In E. Mossialos, G. Permanand, R. Baeten, & T. K. Hervey (Eds.), *Health Systems Governance in Europe* (pp. 561–588). Cambridge University Press. https://doi.org/10.1017/CBO9780511750496.014

Crawford, A., & Serhal, E. (2020). Digital health equity and COVID-19: The innovation curve cannot reinforce the social gradient of health. *Journal of Medical Internet Research, 22*(6), e19361. https://doi.org/10.2196/19361

Ćwiklicki, M., Klich, J., & Chen, J. (2020). The adaptiveness of the healthcare system to the Fourth Industrial Revolution: A preliminary analysis. *Futures, 122*, 102602. https://doi.org/10.1016/j.futures.2020.102602

De Sousa, A. P., & Almeida, A. M. (2016). Habits and behaviors of e-health users: A study on the influence of the interface in the perception of trust and credibility. *Procedia Computer Science, 100*, 602–610. https://doi.org/10.1016/j.procs.2016.09.201

Detmer, D. E. (2003). Building the national health information infrastructure for personal health, healthcare services, public health, and research. *BMC Medical Informatics and Decision Making, 3*(1), 1. https://doi.org/10.1186/1472-6947-3-1

Duplaga, M., Andrychiewicz, A., & Dańda, J. (2013). The opinions about e-health among nurses employed in hospitals located in an urban area in Poland. *CIN: Computers, Informatics, Nursing, 31*(6), 281–289. https://doi.org/10.1097/NXN.0b013e31828a0d98

Fleming, N. S., Culler, S. D., McCorkle, R., Becker, E. R., & Ballard, D. J. (2011). The financial and nonfinancial costs of implementing electronic health records in primary care practices. *Health Affairs, 30*(3), 481–489. https://doi.org/10.1377/hlthaff.2010.0768

Gazibara, T., Cakic, J., Cakic, M., Grgurevic, A., & Pekmezovic, T. (2020). Searching for online health information instead of seeing a physician: A cross-sectional study among high school students in Belgrade, Serbia. *International Journal of Public Health, 65*(8), 1269–1278. https://doi.org/10.1007/s00038-020-01471-7

Holden, R. J., & Karsh, B.-T. (2010). The technology acceptance model: Its past and its future in healthcare. *Journal of Biomedical Informatics, 43*(1), 159–172. https://doi.org/10.1016/j.jbi.2009.07.002

ITU. (2020). *List of indicators included in the World Telecommunication/ICT Indicators Database*. ITU. https://www.itu.int/en/ITU-D/Statistics/Documents/publications/wtid/WTID2020_ListOfIndicators_JulyEdition.pdf

ITU. (n.d.). *The ICT Development Index (IDI): Conceptual framework and methodology*. https://www.itu.int/en/ITU-D/Statistics/Pages/publications/mis/methodology.aspx

Lemos, M. C., Agrawal, A., Eakin, H., Nelson, D. R., Engle, N. L., & Johns, O. (2013). Building adaptive capacity to climate change in less developed countries. In G. R. Asrar & J. W. Hurrell (Eds.), *Climate Science for Serving Society* (pp. 437–457). Springer, Netherlands. https://doi.org/10.1007/978-94-007-6692-1_16

Lewis, T., Synowiec, C., Lagomarsino, G., & Schweitzer, J. (2012). e-Health in low- and middle-income countries: Findings from the Center for Health Market Innovations. *Bulletin of the World Health Organisation, 90*(5), 332–340. https://doi.org/10.2471/BLT.11.099820

Martínez-Caro, E., Cegarra-Navarro, J. G., García-Pérez, A., & Fait, M. (2018). Healthcare service evolution towards the Internet of Things: An end-user perspective. *Technological Forecasting and Social Change, 136*, 268–276. https://doi.org/10.1016/j.techfore.2018.03.025

Martzoukou, K., Fulton, C., Kostagiolas, P., & Lavranos, C. (2020). A study of higher education students' self-perceived digital competencies for learning and everyday life online participation. *Journal of Documentation, 76*(6), 1413–1458. https://doi.org/10.1108/JD-03-2020-0041

Milieu. (2014). *Overview of the national laws on electronic health records in the EU Member States and their interaction with the provision of cross-border e-health services* (Contract 2013 63 02). Milieu. https://ec.europa.eu/health/sites/health/files/e-health/docs/laws_report_recommendations_en.pdf

Moore, E. C., Tolley, C. L., Bates, D. W., & Slight, S. P. (2020). A systematic review of the impact of health information technology on nurses' time. *Journal of the American Medical Informatics Association, 27*(5), 798–807. https://doi.org/10.1093/jamia/ocz231

Nittari, G., Khuman, R., Baldoni, S., Pallotta, G., Battineni, G., Sirignano, A., Amenta, F., & Ricci, G. (2020). Telemedicine practice: Review of the current ethical and legal challenges. *Telemedicine and e-Health, 26*(12), 1427–1437. https://doi.org/10.1089/tmj.2019.0158

Norman, C. D., & Skinner, H. A. (2006). e-Health literacy: Essential skills for consumer health in a networked world. *Journal of Medical Internet Research, 8*(2), e9. https://doi.org/10.2196/jmir.8.2.e9

Ohannessian, R., Yaghobian, S., Duong, T. A., Medeiros de Bustos, E., Le Douarin, Y.-M., Moulin, T., & Salles, N. (2020). France is the first country to reimburse tele-expertise at a national level to all medical doctors. *Telemedicine and e-Health*, tmj.2020.0083. https://doi.org/10.1089/tmj.2020.0083

Peterson, C. B., Hamilton, C., & Hasvold, P. (2016). *From innovation to implementation: e-Health in the WHO European region*. WHO Regional Office for Europe.

Pourrazavi, S., Kouzekanani, K., Bazargan-Hejazi, S., Shaghaghi, A., Hashemiparast, M., Fathifar, Z., & Allahverdipour, H. (2020). Theory-based e-health literacy interventions in older adults: A systematic review. *Archives of Public Health*, *78*(1), 72. https://doi.org/10.1186/s13690-020-00455-6

Ray, T., Choi, J., Reeder, J., Lee, S. P., Aranyosi, A. J., Ghaffari, R., & Rogers, J. A. (2019). Soft, skin-interfaced wearable systems for sports science and analytics. *Current Opinion in Biomedical Engineering*, *9*, 47–56. https://doi.org/10.1016/j.cobme.2019.01.003

Ricciardi, L., Mostashari, F., Murphy, J., Daniel, J. G., & Siminerio, E. P. (2013). A national action plan to support consumer engagement via e-health. *Health Affairs*, *32*(2), 376–384. https://doi.org/10.1377/hlthaff.2012.1216

Silverman, R. D. (2003). Current legal and ethical concerns in telemedicine and e-medicine. *Journal of Telemedicine and Telecare*, *9*(1_suppl), 67–69. https://doi.org/10.1258/135763303322196402

Singh, R. P., Javaid, M., Haleem, A., Vaishya, R., & Bahl, S. (2020). Significance of health information technology (HIT) in context to COVID-19 pandemic: Potential roles and challenges. *Journal of Industrial Integration and Management*, *05*(04), 427–440. https://doi.org/10.1142/S2424862220500232

Sittig, D. F., & Singh, H. (2020). COVID-19 and the need for a national health information technology infrastructure. *JAMA*, *323*(23), 2373. https://doi.org/10.1001/jama.2020.7239

Sittig, D. F., Wright, A., Coiera, E., Magrabi, F., Ratwani, R., Bates, D. W., & Singh, H. (2020). Current challenges in health information technology–related patient safety. *Health Informatics Journal*, *26*(1), 181–189. https://doi.org/10.1177/1460458218814893

Tao, D., Wang, T., Wang, T., Zhang, T., Zhang, X., & Qu, X. (2020). A systematic review and meta-analysis of user acceptance of consumer-oriented health information technologies. *Computers in Human Behavior*, *104*, 106147. https://doi.org/10.1016/j.chb.2019.09.023

Tavares, A. I. (2018). e-Health, ICT and its relationship with self-reported health outcomes in the EU countries. *International Journal of Medical Informatics*, *112*, 104–113. https://doi.org/10.1016/j.ijmedinf.2018.01.014

Thakur, R., Hsu, S. H. Y., & Fontenot, G. (2012). Innovation in healthcare: Issues and future trends. *Journal of Business Research*, *65*(4), 562–569. https://doi.org/10.1016/j.jbusres.2011.02.022

Venkatesh, U., & Gandhi, P. A. (2020). Prediction of COVID-19 outbreaks using Google trends in India: A retrospective analysis. *Healthcare Informatics Research*, *26*(3), 175–184. https://doi.org/10.4258/hir.2020.26.3.175

Watkins, I., & Xie, B. (2014). e-Health literacy interventions for older adults: A systematic review of the literature. *Journal of Medical Internet Research*, *16*(11), e225. https://doi.org/10.2196/jmir.3318

Wickramasinghe, N., Fadlalla, A., Geisler, E., & Schaffer, J. (2004). A framework for assessing e-health preparedness. *AMCIS 2004 Proceedings*, *26*. http://aisel.aisnet.org/amcis2004/26

Xie, B. (2012). Improving older adults' e-health literacy through computer training using NIH online resources. *Library & Information Science Research*, *34*(1), 63–71. https://doi.org/10.1016/j.lisr.2011.07.006

Xie, H., Prybutok, G., Peng, X., & Prybutok, V. (2020). Determinants of trust in health information technology: An empirical investigation in the context of an online clinic appointment system. *International Journal of Human–Computer Interaction*, *36*(12), 1095–1109. https://doi.org/10.1080/10447318.2020.1712061

Xu, Z. (2019). An empirical study of patients' privacy concerns for health informatics as a service. *Technological Forecasting and Social Change, 143*, 297–306. https://doi.org/10.1016/j.techfore.2019.01.018

Zayas-Cabán, T., Chaney, K. J., & Rucker, D. W. (2020). National health information technology priorities for research: A policy and development agenda. *Journal of the American Medical Informatics Association, 27*(4), 652–657. https://doi.org/10.1093/jamia/ocaa008

Zhang, X., Liu, S., Chen, X., & Gong, Y. (Yale). (2017). Social capital, motivations, and knowledge sharing intention in health Q&A communities. *Management Decision, 55*(7), 1536–1557. https://doi.org/10.1108/MD-10-2016-0739

11 Financing Health 4.0

Jacek Klich

Introduction

The Fourth Industrial Revolution (4IR) brings with it and accelerates advances in the technologies used in the healthcare system as discussed in Chapter 3. These new technologies - especially innovative medicines - contribute to increasing treatment costs. The aim of this chapter is to analyse healthcare spending in the Organisation for Economic Co-operation and Development (OECD) countries between 2000 and 2019, taking into account out-of-pocket payments (OOP), and to identify the main drivers of healthcare cost growth. The author also charts the prospects for changes in the financing of healthcare systems in the context of Health 4.0 with a particular focus on human enhancement (HE), which is probably the most serious challenge posed to the financing of Health 4.0. The discussion concludes by showing that changes in the healthcare system will increase the share of OOP in total health expenditure and further stratify patient access to modern medicines and technologies.

Cost drivers in the healthcare sector

Even though the healthcare sector is already an important component of national economies, it is gaining its importance. Considering only the financial side of the healthcare system, it should be recalled that over the last 20-30 years, health expenditures have grown on average faster than the average economic growth rate. According to the World Health Organization (WHO) report, the growth in total health expenditure has averaged 6% compared to the average economic growth rate of 4% (WHO, 2019, p. 1). As the OECD estimates show, in 2017, approximately USD 7.8 trillion (or USD 1087 per capita) was spent on health globally (OECD, 2019, p. 5). Although most health expenditure projections anticipate its per capita growth to slow down somewhat in the coming years, it will still outpace economic growth by 2030. The OECD estimates that primary health spending will reach 10.2% of GDP by 2030, up from 8.8% in 2015 (Lorenzoni et al., 2019, p. 4). This is a global trend, and the SARS-CoV-2 pandemic will likely further reinforce this increase, since the almost universal growth in health spending is accompanied by weakening economic performance.

DOI: 10.4324/9781003144403-11

Increasing expenditure on healthcare is becoming a global problem. This is evidenced (albeit indirectly) by the three most important global challenges or tasks facing the healthcare sector identified in the second decade of the 21st century, namely: (1) improving the quality of healthcare services provided; (2) ensuring the affordability of health services (i.e. reducing their costs); and (3) expanding the reach of health services by improving access to healthcare (Godbole & Lamb, 2018, p. 4). It can be demonstrated that reducing health system costs will not only enable Task 2, but also contribute to the achievement of Task 3. This justifies the claim that reducing healthcare costs will contribute to addressing two of the three global challenges facing national health systems.

Rising healthcare costs are the subject of scrutiny in most countries worldwide, particularly in the USA. One reason for this is that both the total volume of health spending and its share in GDP are the highest in the world (see Table 11.1). As is emphasised in the literature, regrettably, this is not matched by treatment outcomes (Mahar, 2006). The efficiency of the US system has come under heavy criticism (Reinhardt, 2019). Time and again, it is pointed out that the rising costs of the US healthcare system result, among other things, from the overprovision of services (i.e. the performance of unnecessary ones), their inefficient provision, excessive administrative overheads, exorbitant prices as well as the untapped benefits of health promotion and disease prevention (Young et al., 2010). Excessive pricing, in turn, result from the introduction of modern technologies, medical equipment, and devices (Callahan, 2018) as well as medicinal products into the healthcare system. These findings also apply, albeit to varying degrees, to other countries.

The use of modern technologies and medicines in medical practice - especially in the first years of their application, when the economies of scale have not yet been achieved - contributes to increasing the costs of the healthcare system (to be discussed).

The OECD, in its latest modified model of healthcare costs estimates, lists the following key factors leading to increased costs: higher incomes (and concomitant higher patient expectations), supply side limitations, demographic changes, and technological progress (Lorenzoni et al., 2019, p. 8). Demographic changes are associated with increased life expectancy, which - in view of the changes in family models and the declining number of children - leads to an increase in the proportion of senior citizens in modern societies. This in turn, among other things, leads to increasing healthcare costs, since seniors (and children) represent the highest demand for healthcare services. Longer life expectancy further amplifies this demand.

An analysis of changes in national healthcare systems that occurred at the turn of the 20th and 21st centuries in the OECD countries leads to the conclusion that in some cases even all of the healthcare costs are shifted from collective to individual payers (Mamedov et al., 2019; Paolucci, 2011, p. 6). This is an important finding in the context of the projection of Health 4.0 financing, which is only emerging at present.

Table 11.1 Health spending and OOP spending in the OECD countries in 2000 and 2019 (per capita, USD)

Country	*Health spending 2000*	*Out of pocket 2000*	*Health spending 2019*	*Out of pocket 2019*	*Out of pocket 2019/2000*	*Health spending 2019/2000*	*Out of pocket/ spending 2000*	*Out of pocket/ spending 2019*
USA	4557	705	11,072	1150[a]	1.63	2.43	0.15	0.10
Switzerland	3325	1032	7732	2165	2.10	2.33	0.31	0.28
Luxembourg	3410	486	5558	544[a]	1.12	1.63	0.14	0.10
Germany	2894	352	6646	800	2.27	2.30	0.12	0.12
Iceland	2667	518	4811	744	1.44	1.80	0.19	0.15
Austria	2803	449	5851	1017[a]	2.27	2.09	0.16	0.17
Norway	2792	501	6647	950	1.90	2.38	0.18	0.14
France	2686	195	5376	477[a]	2.45	2.00	0.07	0.09
Netherlands	2646	292	5765	602	2.06	2.18	0.11	0.10
Canada	2451	407	5418	795	1.95	2.21	0.17	0.15
Denmark	2345	360	5568	729[a]	2.03	2.37	0.15	0.13
Belgium	2297	n/a	5428	972[a]	n/a	2.36	n/a	0.18
Sweden	2195	317	5782	788	2.49	2.63	0.14	0.14
Australia	2154	452	5187	845[b]	1.87	2.41	0.21	0.16
Italy	2030	537	3649	843	1.57	1.80	0.26	0.23
United Kingdom	1916	327	4653	717[a]	2.19	2.43	0.17	0.15
Japan	1851	295	4823	574[a]	1.95	2.61	0.16	0.12
Finland	1876	406	4578	798[a]	1.97	2.44	0.22	0.17
Ireland	1829	222	5276	619	2.79	2.88	0.12	0.12
New Zealand	1659	255	4204	520	2.04	2.53	0.15	0.12
Portugal	1600	400	3379	1005	2.51	2.11	0.25	0.30
Israel	1550	457	2932	597[a]	1.31	1.89	0.29	0.20
Spain	1523	371	3616	760[a]	2.05	2.37	0.24	0.21
Slovenia	1463	n/a	3224	439	n/a	2.20	n/a	0.14
Greece	1418	n/a	2384	826[a]	n/a	1.68	n/a	0.35
Czech Republic	1026	105	3428	450[a]	4.29	3.34	0.10	0.13

(Continued)

Table 11.1 Health spending and OOP spending in the OECD countries in 2000 and 2019 (per capita, USD) *(Continued)*

Country	*Health spending 2000*	*Out of pocket 2000*	*Health spending 2019*	*Out of pocket 2019*	*Out of pocket 2019/2000*	*Health spending 2019/2000*	*Out of pocket/ spending 2000*	*Out of pocket/ spending 2019*
Hungary	906	248	2222	578[a]	2.33	2.45	0.27	0.26
Korea	726	317	3384	1064	3.36	4.66	0.44	0.31
Slovak Republic	690	75	2354	405[a]	5.40	3.41	0.11	0.17
Poland	604	188	2230	471	2.51	3.69	0.31	0.21
Chile	591	253	2159	731	2.89	3.65	0.43	0.34
Lithuania	674	156	2638	835	5.35	3.91	0.23	0.32
Estonia	543	111	2579	618	5.57	4.75	0.20	0.24
Mexico	517	270	1154	474[a]	1.76	2.23	0.52	0.41
Latvia	464	221	1973	727[a]	3.29	4.25	0.48	0.37
Turkey	432	125	1337	214[a]	1.71	3.09	0.29	0.16
Colombia	n/a	n/a	1213	182[a]	n/a	n/a	n/a	0.15
OECD average	n/a	n/a	4224	n/a	n/a	n/a	n/a	n/a

[a] Data from 2018.

[b] Data from 2017.

Source: OECD (2021c).

The healthcare financing system, subject to constant government monitoring, also keeps changing. In the EU countries, where the insurance model predominates, healthcare financing reforms have focussed on improving premium collection, changing the mix of individual premium elements, merging (centralising) regional payers (sickness funds), expanding the scope of compulsory public health insurance, defining the basket of guaranteed services, and moving away from passive reimbursement for the health services provided (Thomson et al., 2009). Some EU countries, such as Slovenia, have shifted to a broader reliance on private health insurance (Thomson et al., 2009, p. 75). The increasing participation of the private sector in reforming healthcare system financing has also been observed outside the EU (Mamedov et al., 2019), including in countries where the healthcare model is based on private insurance, as is the case, e.g. in the USA (Barr, 2016). The private sector is also credited with growing significance in systems based on universal health insurance (Clarke et al., 2019). The increasing share of the private sector (private insurance) in health funding is also observable in the context of Health 4.0 financing.

According to the system of national health accounts (OECD/Eurostat/WHO, 2017), health expenditure measures the final consumption of health goods and services and reflects current spending on medical services and goods, public health and prevention programmes as well as the costs of the overall management and financing of healthcare delivery, regardless of the financing model. Subsidies paid to healthcare providers should also be subsumed under this category (OECD, 2020, p. 158).

In terms of the structure of healthcare financing, government-funded compulsory insurance schemes and compulsory health insurance financed by both public and private operators account for the largest share in the EU countries, together constituting almost three-quarters of total health expenditure in the EU countries (OECD, 2020, p. 162). It is significant that financial feasibility studies of these programmes focus on individual country analyses (Health Policy Project, 2015; Zeng et al., 2017) and regional programmes (Biggeri et al., 2018), but lack comparative analyses covering large groups of countries.

Health spending in the OECD countries in 2000–2019

The starting point for discussing the financing of the health systems in the OECD countries is a static picture of 2019. Figure 11.1 shows the amount of health spending calculated at purchasing power parity per capita and denominated in US dollars, including funds from universal health insurance (government programmes), supplementary insurance, and out-of-pocket (OOP) spending. In the OECD methodology, OOP are expenditures borne directly by households where neither public nor private insurance covers the full cost of a given health good or service. OOP spending includes cost-sharing and other expenditures borne directly by households, and should ideally

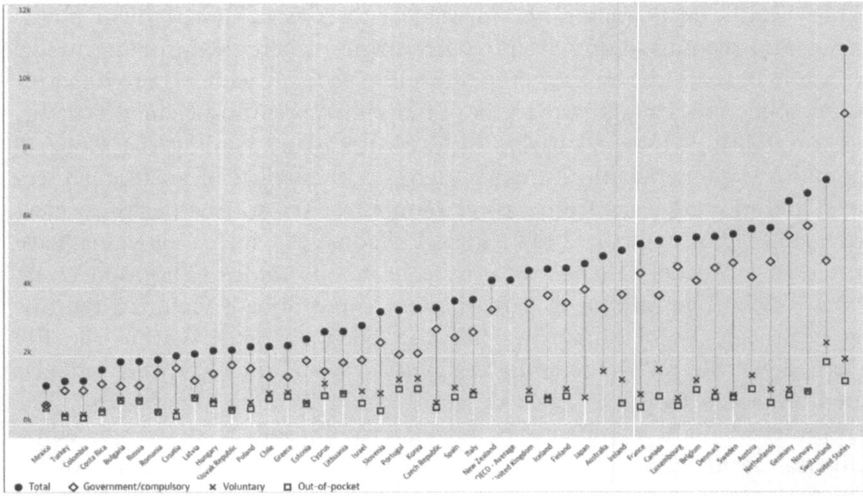

Figure 11.1 Health spending in the OECD countries: Total/Government/compulsory/ Voluntary/Out-of-pocket, US dollars/capita, 2019 or latest available.

Source: OECD (2021a).

also include estimates of informal payments made to providers by patients. The structure of OOP spending is dominated by expenditures on medicines and primary healthcare, which together account for about 2/3 of OOP. This is followed by spending on dental services (14%) and hospital care (11%) (OECD, 2019, p. 112). Figure 11.1 and Table 11.1 show that the amount of OOP spending in the OECD countries in 2019 does not show as much variation as is seen in the case of total health spending in the OECD countries. On average, across all the OECD countries, just over one-fifth of all health spending comes directly from patients (OECD, 2019, p. 112). This proportion should be considered substantial, with fairly high individual contributions recorded in Latvia, Chile, Greece, Lithuania, Portugal, Korea, and Spain, where health spending is lower than the OECD average (Table11.1).

The dynamics of OOP spending per capita in USD in the OECD countries from 2000 to 2019 are shown in Figure 11.2. The amounts vary substantially across countries: in 2019, it ranged from USD 2165 in Switzerland to USD 182 in Colombia.[1] Even in such a nested representation as Figure 11.2, it can be seen that patient OOP spending per capita increased in all the OECD countries during the period studied, although (as is evident when the figure is sufficiently zoomed in) the dynamics of this increase varies across countries and years, and the trend was not always upward. For example, Luxembourg and Lithuania reported a periodic decline in OOP spending (as did Poland in the last several years). The growth curves for Luxembourg and Greece, where OOP spending increases were relatively small between 2000 and 2019, are relatively flatter.

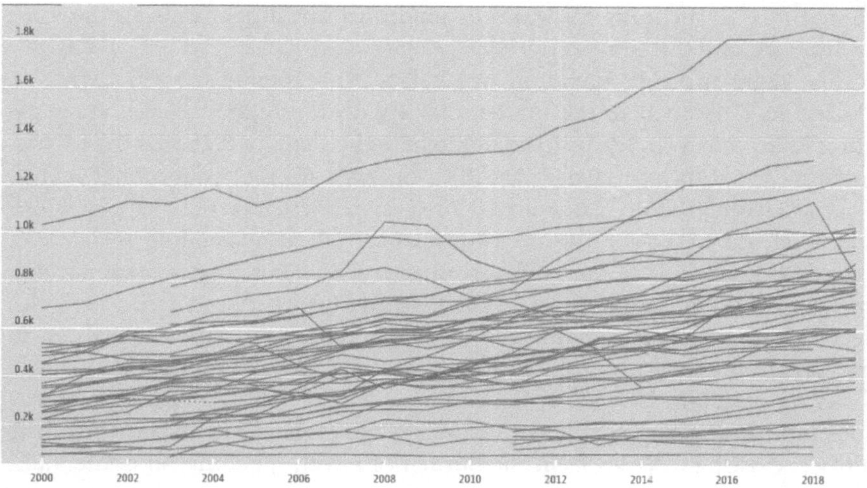

Figure 11.2 Out-of-pocket health spending per capita in the OECD countries 2000–2019 (USD).

Source: OECD (2021b).Detailed data on the growth of health spending and OOP spending per capita in the OECD countries between 2000 and 2019 can be found in Table 11.1.

The individual columns in Table 11.1 show, respectively, per capita health spending in 2000 and 2019 (Columns 2 and 4); OOP per capita in 2000 and 2019 (Columns 3 and 5); growth rate of OOP spending between 2019 and 2000 (Column 6); growth rate of health spending between 2019 and 2000 (Column 7); share of OOP spending in overall health spending in 2000 (Column 8); and share of OOP spending in health spending in 2019 (Column 9). The data indicate that in seven countries (Austria, France, Portugal, Czech Republic, Slovakia, Lithuania, and Estonia) the growth rate of OOP spending was higher than the growth rate of health spending between 2000 and 2019. It is also worth noting that the extent of this increase was the highest in Estonia, Slovakia, and Lithuania, or in countries where health expenditure per capita was lower than the OECD average in 2019. This may signify a comparatively higher financial burden on patients in comparison with the other OECD countries. This, in turn, may imply deteriorating access to health services in these countries. A comparison of the share of OOP patient spending in total health expenditure in 2000 and 2019 (Columns 8 and 9, respectively) leads to the conclusion that in seven countries (Austria, France, Portugal, Czech Republic, Slovakia, Lithuania, and Estonia), the share was higher in 2019 than in 2000. It is quite telling that post-socialist countries predominate in this group. It is also noteworthy that in 2019 compared to 2000, the largest decrease in the share of OOP spending in health expenditure was recorded by Turkey (by 44.8%), the USA (by 33.3%), and Poland (by 32.3%). Such a high position of Turkey and Poland in this league table reflects the fact that in both countries in 2019 the share of OOP spending in health expenditure was higher than in the USA (0.16; 0.21; and 0.10, respectively).

The share of OOP spending in total health expenditure was higher in Poland in 2019 than in the ten countries with the highest health expenditures in 2019 (except for Switzerland, where the share of 0.28 was the highest among the OECD countries). In 2019, in seven OECD countries (Mexico, Latvia, Greece, Chile, Lithuania, Korea, and Portugal), the share of OOP spending accounted for around a third of total health spending (41%, 37%, 35%, 34%, 32%, 31%, and 30%, respectively). These figures cannot but prompt a number of questions on the existing inequalities in access to health services in post-socialist countries and the potential for these inequalities to increase in the future.

As was noted in Chapter 1, the consequences of the 4IR increase inequalities in access to health services, which, when viewed in the context of the already existing differences in the burden of health spending on households, leads to the sad conclusion that these disparities are likely to increase in the emerging Health 4.0, since they are driven by technological progress.

Technological progress vs. health spending

The most important aspect of health spending and Health 4.0 is to examine the impact of technological progress on healthcare costs. In order to do so, one must start from the structure of health spending. In most countries, payments for treatment and rehabilitation services account for the majority of health costs, followed by medicines (especially in some Central and Eastern European countries) (OECD, 2020, p. 157). Exploring the impact of technology as a driver of health expenditure growth is a complex process due to the links between the former and other determinants such as income, the structure and health status of the population. Moreover, the impact of technological advances on health spending cannot be studied in isolation from the demand for health services, the policy context, and the broader institutional context that govern the implementation of new technologies.

Consequently, it is the relationship between supply and demand for new technologies and the institutional environment that determines the actual use of these technologies in healthcare. Technological progress is also accompanied by major qualitative changes which are also associated with costs and benefits. Technological progress in healthcare is understood as any change in products, procedures, and styles of medical practice that modifies the way health services are delivered (OECD, 2017). These advances can include new medicines (active substances), devices or services, new applications of existing technologies (such as the use of virtual reality in psychiatric treatment; cf. Suso-Ribera et al., 2022), new procedures or technologies (Chernew & Newhouse, 2012) as well as innovations in healthcare processes and delivery, such as, for example, the use of big data (European Commission 2014), bio-sensitive wearables, the use of smartphones or 3D printing (OECD,

2017). Technological advances may expand the range of healthcare goods and services offered, deliver innovations in care pathways and case management, and improve overall healthcare quality.

At this point it makes sense to look at the structure of patient OOP spending today and at the projections for the coming years, including the large share of medicines in total health spending. It is estimated that USD 1.25 trillion will be spent on medicines globally in 2019, which, compared to USD 887 billion spent in 2010, shows an unusually high increase. A conservative estimate puts it at USD 1.59 trillion in 2024 (Mikulic, 2020), but given the global experience with the SARS-Cov-2 pandemic it may very well be even higher. The most important medicine markets are the USA and Europe, with cancer and diabetes medicines (including insulin) dominating in the highest revenue-generating group. The USA and Europe also led the way in introducing innovative medicines (new active ingredients) between 2014 and 2018 (Mikulic, 2020).

Modelling quality improvement in terms of benefits obtained both inside and outside the healthcare system itself (e.g. impact on life expectancy, population ageing, productivity, and GDP) is a difficult task and to date, no macroeconomic models have satisfactorily managed to capture it. In their review of the literature on the impact of advanced technologies on health spending, Alberto Marino and Luca Lozenzoni (2019) focus on its cost side. The estimated effects of technological advances on health spending in the studies cited in their article vary significantly - from 10% to 75% of the observed annual increase in health spending, with most studies reporting values between 25% and 50%. Taking the average value reported in the literature - i.e. 35% - the authors estimate that in the OECD countries, between 1995 and 2015 modern technology accounted for about 1% of the annual growth in health expenditure. Assuming that technological progress will contribute to its further growth at a similar rate and taking into account the available projections, health spending is likely to increase by 0.9% annually until 2030 (Marino & Lorenzoni, 2019, p. 4). Converting percentage points into real money yields billions of USD.

Prospects for health financing in the context of Health 4.0

The above-mentioned developments - population ageing, increasing patient expectations, high costs of medicines, and new technologies used in health service delivery, as well as the phenomena presented in the previous chapters, including patient empowerment, active patient involvement in the process of creating new devices and applications used in healthcare (co-creation) - contribute to increased healthcare spending. Its high growth dynamics, which has persisted for decades in comparison to the dynamics of economic growth coupled with the high pace of technological progress, are a serious cause for concern with regard to the prospects of stable financing of health spending in the coming years and decades. After all, the market will see an increasing number of product and process innovations in the pharmaceutical industry, medical products and devices, and a matching supply of applications (some of which are fee-based) that make patients' lives easier. It can be safely assumed that some payers/insurers will be unwilling or unable to reimburse the costs of health services provided with the use of such innovations. Examples include the Argus II retinal prosthesis, the first implantable device to treat adults with advanced retinitis pigmentosa (FDA Approves World's First Artificial Retina, 2013), and the implantation of a computer chip into the brain of a paralysed patient to restore motor control to the injured upper extremity (Carey, 2016). Such and similar treatments - although they undeniably restore health - may be interpreted by the insurer's lawyers as HEs and thus excluded from the list of treatments reimbursed by the basic insurance.

These costs are thus increasingly likely to be borne by the patients (cf. cost shifting mentioned above). One may ask perversely: what is new about it? After all, for decades (if not centuries) we have experienced similar attitudes. Trying to capture the difference, one may focus on the exponentially increasing differences in the scale and pace of cost growth. In fact, it can be argued that the costs of health services driven by the dynamic development of technology will continue to rise at a pace that will appreciably limit access to health services for those who cannot contribute to their costs out of their own pocket. It can be assumed that access to state-of-the-art devices and technologies will increasingly be available to those patients whose income enables them to contribute towards or fully cover the costs of cutting-edge technologies which are not reimbursed by insurers under standard health insurance contracts. At present, a textbook example of such services is aesthetic medicine, where interventions - with very few exceptions - are paid for by the patients out of their own pockets.

Still, it is worth taking a broader look at this issue by invoking the *differentia specifica* of the 4IR, i.e. the blurring of the boundaries between man and machine and HE understood as natural, artificial, and technologically-enabled changes to the human body aimed at increasing the physical and mental capabilities of a human being, which were discussed in Chapter 1 on the 4IR and the healthcare system.

We also should bear in mind the fact that HE requires the adoption (and enforcement) of appropriate legal regulations (Almeida & Diogo, 2019) (these issues will be addressed in the next chapter), including the admissibility conditions for the use of human body enhancement technologies (Menuz et al., 2011). The literature on the subject raises a number of ethical issues associated with the implantation of advanced devices and applications in the human body (Jebari, 2013; Olarte-Pascual et al., 2021). Unsurprisingly, the extensive literature on HE lacks coverage of the financing of health services using expensive, highly advanced technologies that are not considered to be therapeutically beneficial.

In view of the above, it must be concluded that HE can only be financed by extra private health insurance with high premiums, or private OOP payments. This, in turn, will lead to widening gaps in access to both highly innovative and hence expensive therapies and HE options. As Cristina Olarte-Pascual and her team have shown, it is people's self-centredness that best explains their willingness to have advanced HE devices implanted (Olarte-Pascual et al., 2021); it can thus be suspected that HE will be very much in vogue in the future. Patients' own pockets are the most likely source of HE financing, whereas public funds for such procedures will be restricted to projects pursued in the military or space sectors (Szocik et al., 2019).

One of the consequences of such a scenario will be the widening and petrification of social disparities and increasing advantage of the rich over the poor, which may ultimately undermine social cohesion and order.

Characteristically, although the literature does identify the potential risks of increasing social inequality, including the emergence of a new social class - the unenhanced underclass (Wolbring, 2006) - these growing disparities are not analysed in terms of financing of health services considered to enhance human capabilities (Bateman et al., 2015; Buchanan, 2017; Koops et al., 2013).

It therefore seems that the issue of financing HE (and Health 4.0 with its intrinsic advances in new medicines, medical devices and equipment, and process innovations) should become the subject of in-depth analysis by policy makers and health sector managers.

Conclusions

For the past several decades, the growth rate in health spending has significantly outpaced the growth rate in the economy, and there is nothing to suggest that this trend will be reversed in the foreseeable future. Health systems are therefore beginning to experience serious and mounting problems in balancing their budgets. This is accompanied by an increasing share of households (and individual patients) in health financing. Experience in reforming health financing systems shows that in 2019 in seven OECD countries (Mexico, Latvia, Greece, Chile, Lithuania, Korea, and Portugal), the share of OOP patient spending in total health expenditure (per capita) was about 1/3. The rate of growth of the share of OOP spending in health financing per capita between 2000 and 2019 in countries such as Austria, France, Portugal, the Czech Republic, Slovakia, Lithuania, and Estonia was higher than the rate of growth of health spending, which strongly implies a shift of the financial burden to patients. Health services associated with HE will include a growing range of services and an increasing number of people who will finance such treatments from additional, expensive private insurance or from their own resources. All this will further increase the differences in access to healthcare, which may seriously undermine social cohesion (in the short term) and change the trajectory of human evolution as a species (in the long term).

These developments will force policy makers to lay down the rules and implement feasible mechanisms for providing HE services (starting with defining them) and to develop effective enforcement mechanisms for such regulations.

The added value of this chapter is that it compares the trends in the financing of health expenditures in the OECD countries with global trends in the context of financing HE, an issue that is rarely addressed in the literature.

Note

1 As Table 11.1 shows, the most recent data for Colombia are from 2017.

References

Almeida, M., Diogo, R. (2019). Human enhancement: Genetic engineering and evolution. *Evolution, Medicine, and Public Health*, 2019(1):183–189. https://doi.org/10.1093/emph/eoz026.

Barr, D.A. (2016). *Introduction to US Health Policy. The Organization, Financing, and Delivery of Healthcare in America*. Baltimore: Johns Hopkins University Press.

Bateman, S., Gayon, J., Allouche, S., Goffette, J., Marzano, M. (Eds.). (2015). *Inquiring into Human Enhancement. Interdisciplinary and International Perspectives*. Health, Technology and Society, Palgrave Macmillan.

Biggeri, M., Nannini, M., Putoto, G. (2018). Assessing the feasibility of community health insurance in Uganda: A mixed-methods exploratory analysis. *Social Science & Medicine, 200*:145–155. https://doi.org/10.1016/j.socscimed.2018.01.027.

Buchanan, A.E. (2017). Better than human: The promise and perils of biomedical enhancement. Oxford University Press.

Callahan, D. (2018). *Taming the Beloved Beast: How Medical Technology Costs Are Destroying Our Healthcare System*. Princeton: Princeton University Press.

Carey, B. (2016). Chip, implanted in brain, helps paralyzed man regain control of hand. *The New York Times*, April 13, 2016. https://www.nytimes.com/2016/04/14/health/paralysis-limb-reanimation-brain-chip.html, accessed 11.02.2021

Chernew, M.E., Newhouse, J. (2012). Healthcare spending growth. In Pauly, M.V., Mcguire, T.G., Barros, P.P. (Eds.). *Handbook of Health Economics*, Vol. 2: 1–43. Elsevier. https://doi.org/10.1016/B978-0-444-53592-4.00001-3.

Clarke, D., Doerr, S., Hunter, M., Schmets, G., Soucat, A., Paviza, A. (2019). The private sector and universal health coverage. *Bulletin of the World Health Organization, 97*(6), 434–435. https://doi.org/10.2471/BLT.18.225540

European Commission. (2014). *The use of big data in public health policy and research. Background document*. https://ec.europa.eu/health/sites/health/files/ehealth/docs/ev_20141118_co07b_en.pdf.

FDA Approves World's First Artificial Retina. (2013). American Society of Retina Specialists, Spring 2013. https://www.asrs.org/publications/retina-times/details/131/fda-approves-world-first-artificial-retina, accessed 19.02.2021

Godbole, N.S., Lamb, J.P. (2018). *Making Healthcare Green. The Role of Cloud, Green IT, and Data Science to Reduce Healthcare Costs and Combat Climate Change*. New York: Springer International Publishing AG, part of Springer Nature.

Health Policy Project. (2015). *A Health Insurance Feasibility Study in Afghanistan: Learning from Other Countries, a Legal Assessment, and a Stakeholder Analysis*. Washington, DC: Futures Group, Health Policy Project. https://www.healthpolicyproject.com/pubs/756_AfghanistanHealthInsuranceFeasibilitFINAL.pdf, accessed 16.02.2021.

Jebari, K. (2013). Brain machine interface and human enhancement – An ethical review. *Neuroethics*, 6:617–625. https://doi.org/10.1007/s12152-012-9176-2.

Koops, B-J., Lüthy, C.H., Nelis, A., Sieburgh, C., Jansen, J.P.M., Schmid, M.S. (Eds.). (2013). Engineering the human. In *Human Enhancement between Fiction and Fascination*. Berlin, Heidelberg: Springer-Verlag.

Lorenzoni, L., Marino, A., Morgan, D., James, C. (2019). Health spending projections to 2030: New results based on a revised OECD methodology. OECD Health Working Papers, No. 110. Paris: OECD Publishing. https://doi.org/10.1787/5667f23d-en.

Mahar, M. (2006). *Money-Driven Medicine: The Real Reason Healthcare Costs So Much*. London: Harper Collins e-book.

Mamedov, Z.F., Mamedova, S.K., Mirzaev, M.R. (2019). Characterisics of private financing of healthcare: New challenges and prospects. *ЭкОНОМикА и УпРАВлЕНиЕ/ Economics and Management*, *12*(170): 41–55. DOI: 10.35854/1998-1627-2019-12-41-55.

Marino, A., Lorenzoni, L. (2019). The impact of technological advancements on health spending: A literature review. OECD Health Working Papers, No. 113. Paris: OECD Publishing. https://doi.org/10.1787/fa3bab05-en.

Menuz, V., Hurlimann, T., Godar, B. (2011). Is human enhancement also a personal matter? *Science and Engineering Ethics 19*(1). DOI: 10.1007/s11948-011-9294-y. https://www.researchgate.net/publication/51518277_Is_Human_Enhancement_also_a_Personal_Matter, accessed 14.02.2021.

Mikulic, M. (2020). *Global spending on medicines 2010–2024*. Statista, May 25, 2020, https://www.statista.com/statistics/280572/medicine-spending-worldwide/, accessed 16.02.2021.

OECD. (2017). *New Health Technologies: Managing Access, Value and Sustainability*. Paris: OECD Publishing. http://dx.doi.org/10.1787/9789264266438-en.

OECD. (2019). *Health at a Glance 2019: OECD Indicators*. Paris OECD Publishing. https://doi.org/10.1787/4dd50c09-en.

OECD. (2020). *Health at a Glance: Europe 2020: State of Health in the EU Cycle*. Paris: OECD Publishing. https://doi.org/10.1787/82129230-en.

OECD (2021a). Total / Government/compulsory / Voluntary / Out-of-pocket, US dollars/capita, 2019 or latest available, https://www.oecd-ilibrary.org/social-issues-migration-health/health-spending/indicator/english_8643de7e-en; accessed 06.02.2021.

OECD (2021b). Out-of-pocket, US dollars/capita, 2000-2019 or latest available, https://www.oecd-ilibrary.org/social-issues-migration-health/health-spending/indicator/english_8643de7e-en; accessed 07.02.2021.

OECD (2021c).Total/Out-of-pocket, US dollars/capita, 2000-2019 or latest available, https://www.oecd-ilibrary.org/social-issues-migration-health/health-spending/indicator/english_8643de7e-en; accessed 14.02.2021.

OECD/Eurostat/WHO. (2017). A System of Health Accounts 2011: Revised Edition. Paris: OECD Publishing. http://dx.doi.org/10.1787/9789264270985-en.

Olarte-Pascual, C., Pelegrín-Borondo, J., Reinares-Lara, E., Arias-Oliva, M. (2021). From wearable to insideable: Is ethical judgment key to the acceptance of human capacity-enhancing intelligent technologies? *Computers in Human Behavior*, 114;106559. https://doi.org/10.1016/j.chb.2020.106559.

Paolucci, F. (2011). Healthcare financing and insurance. In *Options for Design*. Berlin, Heidelberg: Springer-Verlag.

Reinhardt, U. (2019). *Priced Out: The Economic and Ethical Costs of American Healthcare.* Princeton: Princeton University Press.

Suso-Ribera, C., Castilla, D., Martínez-Borba, V., Jaéna I., BotellaacRosa, C., Bañosb, R.M., García-Palaciosa, A. (2022). Technological interventions for pain management. *Reference Module in Neuroscience and Biobehavioral Psychology*, 2022. https://doi.org/10.1016/B978-0-12-818697-8.00009-1.

Szocik, K., Campa, R., Rappaport, M.B., Corbally, C. (2019). Changing the paradigm on human enhancements: The special case of modifications to counter bone loss for manned mars missions, *Space Policy, 48*:68–75. https://doi.org/10.1016/j.spacepol.2019.02.001.

Thomson, S., Foubister, T., Mossialos, E. (2009). Financing Healthcare in the European Union. Challenges and Policy Responses. European Observatory on Health Systems and Policies. Observatory Studies Series No.17.

WHO. (2019). *Public Spending on Health: A Closer Look at Global Trends.* World Health Organization. https://apps.who.int/iris/bitstream/handle/10665/276728/WHO-HISHGF-HF-WorkingPaper-18.3-eng.pdf?ua=1, accessed 18.01.2020.

Wolbring, G. (2006). The unenhanced underclass. In Miller, P., Wilsdon, J. (Eds.). *Better Humans? The Politics of Human Enhancement and Life Extension*, 122–128. London: Demos.

Young, P.L., Saunders, R.S., Olsen, L.A. (Eds.). (2010). *The Healthcare Imperative: Lowering Costs and Improving Outcomes: Workshop Series Summary. Roundtable on Evidence-Based Medicine.* Washington, DC: Institute of Medicine. National Academies Press.

Zeng, W., Kim, C., Archer, L., Sayedi, O., Jabarkhil, M.Y., Sears, K. (2017). Assessing the feasibility of introducing health insurance in Afghanistan: A qualitative stakeholder analysis. *BMC Health Services Research, 17*:157. DOI 10.1186/s12913-017-2081-y.

12 Law and Health 4.0

Ambroży Mituś

Introduction

In recent years, the health sector has seen increasing implementation and development of numerous solutions for electronic data collection and exchange systems, and a proliferation of e-services. Nevertheless, it should be emphasised that e-visits, telemedicine (European Commission [EC], 2018), e-prescriptions, e-documentation (Milieu Ltd., Time.lex CVBA, 2014) or electronic cross-border health services (Directive 2011/24/EU; European Commission, 2019) do not constitute part of Health 4.0 as the term has come to denote revolutionary changes in healthcare.

In the near future, the development of technology will lead to the emergence of increasingly advanced health e-services, medical services, and products, including advanced personal medical diagnostic devices. This requires constant monitoring and analysis of legal and regulatory solutions in the healthcare sector, including in the area of ensuring interoperability among the products of this process (e.g. medical robots), their control systems (software) as well as a precise and detailed definition of the grounds and principles of liability of the manufacturer of a given device, its operating system's manufacturer, and the diagnostician and/or user. Ethical and health concerns are related to the discoveries in genomics, genetics, or nanotechnology, and require, inter alia, legal definitions of the limits of their application and use.

Due to the complexity and breadth of the subject matter, this chapter only highlights some of the challenges and issues that lawmakers are facing or will face in the future in connection with the development of technology, including artificial intelligence (AI) solutions used in medicine/healthcare. Some of them, such as ensuring data privacy and big data concerns, are already subject to analysis, while others, such as automated diagnosis, or even autonomous AI solutions require further legislative work. The aim of the chapter is to point out that, as humanity, we are probably only at the beginning, or even at the threshold of legal regulations concerning AI and its impact on various spheres of our lives, including such an important one as healthcare. For space considerations, a number of regulatory issues affecting human health, including food safety standards, have been omitted from consideration.

DOI: 10.4324/9781003144403-12

Artificial intelligence

Today, any significant advancement in medicine appears to be inextricably linked to the development of technology. In fact, AI has stimulated human imagination for the past two decades. This term, defined from a variety of viewpoints, is understood as: (a) a science that draws on intelligent human behaviour to devise complex algorithms subsequently used in combinations with other achievements (e.g. robotics) to generate 'intelligent' behaviour (the ability to learn and understand leading to the acquisition of knowledge used to make decisions and take action under changing circumstances) on the part of systems (e.g. voice assistants) or the devices constructed (e.g. robots) (cf. Ramesh, Kambhampati, Monson, Drew, 2004, p. 334); (b) technology modelled "on the brain's neural network, which uses multiple layers of information - including algorithms, pattern correlation, rules, deep learning and cognitive processing techniques - to understand the essence of data" (IBM, 2021).

The European Commission's first definition of AI was formulated in Communication COM(2018) 237 final (p. 1). They are systems

> that display intelligent behaviour by analysing their environment and taking actions - with some degree of autonomy to achieve specific goals (...). AI-based systems can be purely software-based, acting in the virtual world (...) or AI can be embedded in hardware devices (...).

The definition of the High Level Expert Group formulated in the document of 18.12.2018 and refined in the document made public on 8.04.2019 is commonly considered to be more exhaustive (see AI HLEG, 2019a, p. 6). The European Commission's first proposal for a normative definition of AI was included in the draft of the first regulation defining the legal framework for AI (COM(2021) 206 final). Article 3(1) of the proposed AI Act reads that AI system "means software that is developed with one or more of the techniques (...) and can, for a given set of human-defined objectives, generate outputs such as content, predictions, recommendations, or decisions influencing the environments they interact with" (COM(2021) 206 final).

AI systems already exist, to mention only voice assistants, speech and face recognition systems, robotic devices, or autonomous cars (cf. European Commission, 2020, pp. 1 et seq.). Building on the concept of electronic intelligent agents - itself the object of analysis more than two decades ago (see Do, March, Rich, Wolff, 1996, p. 2, after Jonkheer & Jansen, 1998, p. 21; Karnow, 1996, pp. 147–204; Singh, 2003, p. 639; Stosio, 2002, pp. 73 and 75) - an attempt can be made to identify the characteristics of AI (as self-learning technical systems) which include: a sui generis autonomy vis-à-vis its creators and users (once issued a command, AI systems are capable of taking further actions independently); a sui generis intelligence (they can understand and self-teach, to make logical inferences and act on them, and to adapt to changing circumstances); and a sui generis interactivity (they interact with a variety of subjects or data resources, such as patient medical records, diseases and medicines databases, etc.).

In order to operate effectively, AI needs access to information, preferably to large databases. Nowadays, we have huge collections of diverse and valuable data ready to be processed, which are referred to as big data (cf. Salas-Vega, Haimann, Mossialos, 2015, p. 287). In the area of health, this concept "refers to large routinely or automatically collected datasets, which are electronically captured and stored … for the purpose of improving health and health system performance. It does not refer to data collected for a specific study" (Habl, Renner, Bobek, Laschkolnig, 2016, p. 22). In the context of data, legal solutions must exist to ensure that such data are stored and accessed securely, and that patient data is kept confidential and private (cf. AI HLEG, 2019b, p. 17; Pentland, Reid, Heibeck, 2013, pp. 16–17). While there are fairly good data protection solutions in the EU (see Regulation (EU), 2016/679), it seems that their effectiveness must be monitored on an ongoing basis with a view to adapting them to challenges as they emerge. It is also necessary both to define data ownership and to establish rules for access to and use of such data (Habl et al., 2016, pp. 46–47; Pentland et al., 2013, pp. 17–18), including the interoperability standards of different datasets (e.g. clinical data, data from genomic experiments) (see Habl et al., 2016, p. 48).

Although AI is no longer science fiction but reality, it still appears to be subject to certain limitations. First, there are technical-technological issues - we are awaiting systems and solutions that could be called AI in the full sense of the term (i.e. fully autonomous, intelligent, and interactive) and be so widespread as to become commonplace in human life. Second, AI is subject to regulatory (legal) limitations. The main issues in this area include the responsibility for the operation and use of AI systems. While there is no need to enumerate the advantages and possible areas of application of AI, it is necessary to pay close attention to the principles of operation of a given system and/or device and its specific applications.

AI-based systems and solutions are by no means a recent creation; in fact, they have been present for several decades. It was only recently that the progress in the ability to create complex algorithms, the increase in computing power of the newly designed devices, and the existence of large amounts of data have resulted in a 'new quality' - a new level of advancement. It should also be noted that these changes go hand in hand with changes in society, where, along with technical development, people's attitudes to the outcomes of this development evolve. And while in the not so distant past being treated remotely was a cause for concern, today - probably also due to the SARS-Cov-2 pandemic - we are moving towards a standard of remote medical care. Likewise, while treatments and/or interventions performed by specialised robotic devices may still be feared by most, it is likely that as time goes on, more and more people will come to trust such solutions as free of the risk of human error. But does eliminating one risk inherent in humans eliminate another inherent in a highly specialised device and its software? After all, any robotic device may fail due to a design flaw, a glitch in its operating algorithm, or interrupted access to the virtual network (Internet) if it is indispensable to its proper functioning. Moreover, for any autonomous device there is the issue of anticipating its behaviour under certain critical conditions. These risks and the occurrence of untoward events may result from various reasons: system (software) errors, incorrectly issued commands or a wrong sequence of commands entered by the device operator. For example, the use of AI in medical diagnostics may give rise to errors in data processing and diagnosis (e.g. a mistaken entry in a database or erroneous attribution of disease symptoms may result in an incorrect diagnosis). Apart from the various types of errors, the security of data collected by systems or devices may also be compromised, and its correct operation may be interrupted by hackers. These and other factors can put a patient's health and life at risk. This raises a fundamental question: who and on what principles should bear responsibility for the negative effects of an AI system's - robotic device's intervention?

Liability

Addressing the issue of liability in the context of AI, wherever appropriate, I will refer to Polish regulations, which are quite similar to those adopted by other European countries. In principle, in the case of improper operation of an AI-based system, civil and criminal liability may be involved. Civil liability as a rule involves compensation for the damage to health that has occurred as a result of bodily injury or health disorder. On the other hand, in order for criminal liability to occur, the behaviour of the perpetrator must bear the statutory features of a prohibited act (criminal conduct) and culpability must occur.

In the case of medical treatment, liability for a medical error results from failure to observe the principles of due diligence on the part of physicians and other health professionals. The judicature defines the term due diligence in this context as "the exercise of due care that can be normally expected from the perpetrator given his/her ordinary ability to anticipate the consequences of his/her actions" (Judgment of the Supreme Court of 2.08.2001. II KKN 63/99; Judgment of the Supreme Court of 16.01.1974. III KR 311/73). This is, in effect, responsibility for an unintentional crime of consequence - improperly undertaken actions can lead to an effect in the form of damage to the patient's health or life. In order to impute liability for an unintentional crime to the perpetrator

> it is necessary (...) to ascertain that s/he was aware of the fact that his actions meet the criteria of a criminal act (i.e. s/he anticipated such a possibility) or that s/he did not anticipate such a possibility, although he could have anticipated it (...).
>
> (Judgment of the Supreme Court of 2.08.2001. II KKN 63/99)

Naturally, "the possibility to attribute the consequences of an act to the perpetrator includes only the normal (...) consequences of his conduct. (...) and these consequences must be linked to a culpable violation of these rules of due diligence (...)" (Judgement of the Supreme Court of 2.08.2001. II KKN 63/99; Judgement of the Supreme Court of 16.01.1974. III KR 311/73). The ruling of 16.01.1974 (III KR 311/73) states that a medical error can be considered punishable if it could have been avoided by the application of ordinary knowledge/skill and the physician's action was preceded by due diligence. In the Court's opinion, a one-off intervention caused by the urgency of the case - if it entails a mistake in diagnosis and faulty treatment - is not a punishable error as long as it does not meet the criteria of gross error. Moreover, according to the rules of law and the case law, the higher the professional qualifications of the physician, the more stringent criteria should be applied to his/her act of unintentional fault.

An important prerequisite for determining whether a physician will be held liable is whether his/her actions complied with the principles of medical knowledge and the art of medicine (lege artis). According to Art. 4 of The Act of 5 December 1996 on Medical and Dental Professions (2021), the physician "is obliged to practice medicine in accordance with the current medical knowledge, available methods and means of prevention, diagnosis and treatment of diseases, in accordance with the principles of professional ethics and with due diligence".

Applying the above remarks to systems referred to as AI requires identifying at least two distinct cases. In the first one, an intelligent robotic device remains under the direct control of a person (diagnostician/user), who authorises its actions or issues commands on an ongoing basis. In the other, the device operates without such human intervention; in other words, the moment its actions are authorised appears to be the same as when it is put to actual use. Such a device will continuously and autonomously retrieve data, update its system (software) and thus improve its operating procedures. This case includes systems whose operation (i.e. procedures and actions applied by the system or device) are known and predictable. However, more interestingly, it also includes situations in which the device, by analysing data and logically processing it, will itself decide on the best course of action at a given moment, all the while guided by built-in algorithms specifically devised to protect patient's health and life.

In the case of autonomous devices, their actions and messages generated are independent of the user. However, it should be noted that in the life cycle of a robotic device, it is not the device that makes the autonomous decision to act, but the human subject who wants to use it. It is still a tool in the hands of a person, which performs certain sequences of actions by reason of a prior general decision (command). The person who intends to use such an autonomous device agrees to it for a variety of reasons. In medicine, however, expected profit will not constitute the main reason. From a practical point of view, it will remain a secondary or even tertiary consideration, because a potential yet risky profit may transform into a high compensation payment for damage to health.

Accordingly, robotic devices operate by either executing commands that trigger sequential algorithms of action or require a one-time input of a complex algorithm that will initiate specific sequences of actions under designated conditions. But in both cases it is the human who decides: either each time a sequence of actions is to be activated or once at the moment of expressing the intention to use it. If a subject/user wants to activate a particular system or robotic device, s/he first manifests his/her intention to do so. By accepting the terms of use, s/he makes a kind of 'framework statement', the point of which is to agree to the interventions to be performed by the device. The responsibility for the actions of the AI system/robotic device cannot thus be attributed to the system/device itself. Under all circumstances, this liability will be borne not by the object - the AI system and the robot using it - but by the legal subject.

It appears that the issues of responsibility, including the attribution of actions to a person for the interventions performed by a robotic device acting as AI can be based on the concept of an electronic, 'automatic statement of intent' discussed in the literature two decades ago (see Stosio, 2002, pp. 62-63). Consequently, two fundamental cases apply to the use of AI systems and devices. The first one occurs when there is a certain time lapse between the act of will of the subject-user and the actual performance of actions by the device, but the user remains aware of all the actions taken. The second one is when the device takes actions on the basis of commands issued by itself (written in a binary format) as part of an algorithm input by its manufacturer/creator and the subject/user cannot anticipate or predict all the commands or actions that may be taken. As part of their operating system (software), such devices have a built-in broader or narrower inventory of possible behaviours, which are then concretised as demanded by circumstances. Given that we are dealing with an AI that understands, analyses, learns, etc. (which stems from its essence), it may also modify its software. But even if the outcome of the actions taken by the device is not directly related to the will of the person using it, it still operates for the benefit of that user, within the limits set by its software, and under the terms and conditions to which consent was given. Naturally, bearing in mind how a typical consumer or user familiarises him/herself with these terms and conditions (i.e. rarely or not at all), this issue becomes particularly important. These constitute just a handful of selected and in a sense classic problems that impact on the shape of regulatory (legal) solutions in this area.

As was already mentioned, AI cannot be attributed actual autonomy with respect to its user, as it only executes the algorithms provided and the commands entered by the latter. In my opinion, it cannot be treated as a legal subject, i.e. an autonomously and independently acting legal entity. For this reason, the existence of AI-based solutions raises fundamental questions about who should bear the consequences of its malfunction, since even such a sophisticated technology and systems based on it may not always work properly. Even simple devices operated and supervised by a physician, diagnostician or user are prone to error. The operators involved may issue commands and/or take actions on the strength of erroneous information provided to them by such a system or device. The question is whether or not such an action of the system or device resulted from a previous error made by the physician. Did the system correctly retrieve data from the right databases? What if the data pass through the interface of the device, but it fails to act on them or distorts them? The questions and concerns are many. Certainly, the patient must be informed of the risk of untoward event (risks), s/he must give appropriate informed consent, including specifically the consent to undergo treatment using a novel method.

Since it seems that at the moment the most common area of application of AI in medicine is diagnostics, one should attempt to answer the question of physician responsibility in this area. In the case of a diagnostic error resulting from faulty data collection or lack of basic knowledge/factual data, the physician cannot be held liable if s/he collected the data correctly or the error was not due to negligence or ignorance. Likewise, the physician will not be held liable if the patient's injury was solely due to an error on the part of the system/device of which the physician was unaware. However, the situation may be different if the physician did know about its malfunction and still risked using it. But is it really so obvious? Does a physician who decides to use an untested or malfunctioning device as a last resort to save a life deserve to be punished? Or maybe s/he should be rewarded instead?

Although the physician in charge of the procedure is also held responsible for the behaviour of others under his authority in the operating suite, it is difficult to extend his/her authority to AI, although the latter's actions may replace those previously performed by humans. It is also difficult to expect the physician to have non-medical skills, such as the ability to troubleshoot technical malfunctions, much less to tweak AI's complex algorithms. This gives rise to new areas of responsibility for the device manufacturer, the system (software) developer, and the medical facility, which should ensure that all its equipment operates correctly, even if only through proper maintenance and repair. Moreover, as was already mentioned, a device may malfunction due to intentionally harmful actions of external entities, such as hackers' attack via the Internet, a computer virus, etc. These dilemmas suggest that the legal framework for the operation of AI and associated liabilities can to a certain extent draw on the provisions used by the aviation industry.

In many areas of medicine, AI will play an important role, but it will likely take a long time before it becomes system in its own right capable of treating patients independently. People will continue to play a key role in complex medical procedures. Incidentally, policy documents at the moment emphasise the guiding role and direct supervision of humans over AI devices. Therefore, we will have to wait for the boundary between humans and machines (robots) to be really blurred. It should also be strongly emphasised that AI is not a substitute for a physician, but his/her ally, if only in the rapid filtering of relevant data from a veritable ocean of information/databases in order to make faster and more correct diagnoses.

The regulation of artificial intelligence

The cases and concerns discussed above are the proverbial tip of the iceberg in the regulatory sphere. AI is seen as a huge opportunity for civilisational development by both individual countries and international organisations, which take various regulatory actions in this area. Efforts to that effect are made, among others, within the framework of the Council of Europe or United Nations Educational, Scientific and Cultural Organization (UNESCO), which may provide the blueprint for future comprehensive regulatory solutions in the field studied. At the EU level, a variety of documents have been issued, especially policy documents (recommendations) and acts of relevance to the health sector. Examples include the following: Opinion of the European Committee of the Regions on 'Artificial Intelligence for Europe' (2019/C 168/03), OJ C 168/11; Opinion of the European Economic and Social Committee on 'Artificial intelligence - The consequences of artificial intelligence on the (digital) single market, production, consumption, employment and society' (own-initiative opinion) (2017/C 288/01), OJ C 288/1; Opinion of the European Committee of the Regions - White paper on AI - A European approach to excellence and trust (2020/C 440/14), OJ C 440/79; Opinion of the European Economic and Social Committee on 'White paper on Artificial Intelligence - A European approach to excellence and trust' (COM(2020) 65 final) (2020/C 364/12), OJ C 364/87; Commission Recommendation (EU) 2019/243 of 6.02.2019 on a European Electronic Health Record exchange format (Text with EEA relevance), OJ L 39/18; Opinion of the European Committee of the Regions on 'Digitalisation in the Health Sector' (2019/C 168/05), OJ C 168/21; Communication from the Commission to the European Parliament, the European Council, the Council, the European Economic and Social Committee and the Committee of the Regions - AI for Europe, Brussels (25.4.2018, COM(2018) 237 final).

In late 2020, the European Parliament adopted a number of AI-related resolutions, including on accountability (European Parliament, 2020/2014(INL)), and in 2021, on criminal matters (European Parliament, 2020/2016(INI)), among others. In the former, the European Parliament notes that the legal framework for civil liability must inspire confidence in the safety and reliability of products and services and must clearly assign liability. The latest proposal from the European Commission is the Regulation of The European Parliament and of The Council Laying Down Harmonised Rules on AI (AI Act) and Amending Certain Union Legislative Acts, Brussels (21.4.2021, COM(2021) 206 final).

Ethical issues concerning AI are specifically outlined in the Ethics Guidelines For Trustworthy AI developed by the independent High Level Expert Group on AI established by the European Commission in June 2018 (AI HLEG, 2019b). This document employs the term 'trustworthy artificial intelligence' to describe three important characteristics of a system equipped with it. Thus, AI: (a) should be lawful; (b) should be ethical; and (c) should be technically and socially sound (AI HLEG, 2019b, pp. 2 and 5). These characteristics complement and influence each other.

Any document addressing regulatory frameworks underscores people's guiding and supervisory role in relation to AI (see AI HLEG, 2019b, p. 2). All the AI regulatory frameworks must be human-centred. Undoubtedly, current and future legal regulations must be formulated so as to ensure that AI systems do not undermine human autonomy and prioritize respect for human dignity and freedom. It is the human being who decides, whereas AI cannot treat humans as objects, and thus cannot, e.g. collect data and classify humans by their genetic predispositions (cf. AI HLEG, 2019b, p. 4). Article 2 of the EU Treaty ("The Union is founded on the values of respect for human dignity, freedom, democracy, equality, the rule of law and respect for human rights") lays the groundwork for and promotes appropriate regulation of AI across the EU.

The EU has fairly good regulatory arrangements in the areas of data protection, product safety and liability, consumer rights protection, healthcare, medical devices, etc. that can be applied to AI. Nevertheless, some of them, if not now, will definitely need to be modified in the future. These modifications should be implemented on an ongoing basis from the EU level to ensure the smooth functioning of one of its core values, namely the EU single market. These solutions must also be supported by national standards and regulations. That is why regulatory activities in the field of AI are also undertaken by Poland (cf. Resolution of the Council of Ministers, 2020). Poland's public policy on AI development is comprised of four dimensions, i.e. international, ethical, legal, and technical and organisational standards (Resolution of the Council of Ministers, 2020, pp. 70-71). Although each of these dimensions stipulates the directions of regulation from the viewpoint of view of the Polish government, they can be applied more broadly to the internal regulations of each country. The legal dimension is supposed to: (a) provide a legal definition of AI; (b) prevent AI from acquiring legal personality; (c) establish due diligence as the basis for the liability for damages of AI producers, and strict liability as the basis for the liability of users (i.e. the imposition of liability on a party without a finding of fault); (d) distinguish the liability of end users from that of AI operators. As regards the technical and organisational standards, it is proposed, among other things to: (a) set technical standards; (b) mutually recognise certificates and compliance protocols; (c) introduce interoperability rules; and (d) introduce data management standards (Resolution of the Council of Ministers, 2020, p. 71).

Nanotechnology, genomics, and genetic engineering vs. the law

Nanotechnology is yet another area that will play an important role in Health 4.0. It concerns itself with building complex structures and devices on the scale of single atoms and molecules. This means that the possibilities of applying nanotechnology in numerous sectors of the economy and areas of human interest, including medicine, are enormous. Once it becomes possible to combine nanotechnology with AI, unimaginable prospects will open up.

The framework concept of nanomaterial for the purpose of legislation and policy-making in the EU is to be found in the Commission Recommendation of 18.10.2011 on the definition of nanomaterial (Text with EEA relevance; (2011/696/EU), OJ L 275/38). Whether or not something qualifies as such depends on the size of its constituent particles. Hence, according to the Commission Recommendations, a nanomaterial is "a natural, incidental or manufactured material containing particles (...) where, for 50% or more of the particles in the number size distribution, one or more external dimensions is in the size range 1 nm-100 n" (para. 2). However, other properties of nanomaterials, although they make them irreplaceable, may also render them toxic and harmful; that is why they are also sometimes called "the asbestos of the 21st century" (Orzechowska & Szymańska, 2016, pp. 67-68). Since nanotechnology presents a number of challenges in the context of human health, EU regulations are essentially concerned with requirements for identifying and communicating the hazards and risks associated with the use of nanomaterials. In medicine, this generally refers to medical devices, the formal framework for which is set by Regulation (EU) 2017/745 of the European Parliament and of the Council of 5.04.2017 on medical devices, amending Directive 2001/83/EC, Regulation (EC) No 178/2002 and Regulation (EC) No 1223/2009 and repealing Council Directives 90/385/EEC and 93/42/EEC (Text with EEA relevance) OJ L 117/1.

The regulatory challenges for nanomaterials are even greater than those for AI and are related to the diversity and properties of the products that qualify as nanomaterials. The main risks involve the safety of their manufacture and use, namely toxicity to human health. To illustrate the scale of problems and challenges associated with nanotechnology, which cannot be compared with any of the existing solutions that have been regulated so far, let us recall the regulatory challenges that accompanied human activity in the virtual space and the use of information and communication technologies. Initially, this sphere was regulated by issuing a variety of soft solutions (guidelines, etc.). Regulations did not anticipate potential behaviours; in many cases legislators only sanctioned the rules already devised and observed by users. However, these regulatory shortcomings were not acute, as many legal solutions could be applied by analogy with the traditionally existing ones. Nevertheless, it still seems impossible to say that all the aspects of this sphere have been regulated. Given that this phenomenon has caused so many problems and doubts, nanotechnology brings hitherto unimaginable challenges. Among others for this reason the Commission issued a Recommendation of 7.02.2008 on a code of conduct for responsible nanosciences and nanotechnologies research (notified under document number C(2008) 424) (2008/345/EC), OJ L 116/46).

Provisions that describe the world as we know it cannot be applied by analogy to nanomaterials for the simple reason that the latter have completely different properties. In this context, it appears that a register of manufacturers of nanomaterials will continue to remain an essential tool for overseeing their production and use (see Ponce Del Castillo, 2010, p. 9) supported by transparent reporting obligations, including the registration of nanomaterial products.

The toxicity risk posed by nanomaterial manufacturing and use requires the application of the maximum benefit - minimum risk principle. This involves weighing two values - the potential benefits and the negative effects of their use. In order, on one hand, not to stifle the innovative solutions seen in nanotechnology, and on the other, to ensure the necessary safety, regulatory instruments, apart from guidelines and standards, should be devised in a dialogue between public authorities and the key stakeholders in nanotechnology. The resulting regulations should be formulated with the common good in mind, where both the collective and the individual are given equal consideration. The solutions applied should bring benefits to society as a whole and its individual members.

The complexity, global reach of applications, and magnitude of risks are all valid arguments in favour of a supranational or even global regulatory framework that will serve as a reference for national legislation in the field of nanomaterials. It should be noted that EU legislation applies to nanomaterials used in food packaging, cosmetic, and biocidal products.

Another area that is already creating regulatory dilemmas is genomics and genetic engineering. Genomics is the science (field of molecular and theoretical biology) that studies genomes, i.e. the genetic sequences (DNA) of organisms, the genes in genomes, their functions, etc. The findings of genomic research are used, for example, to design and produce antibacterial preparations and vaccines. Thanks recent developments in this area, the number of sequenced genomes has exponentially increased. Genetic engineering, in turn, makes it possible to transfer fragments of DNA from one organism to another. This raises a number of both legal and ethical issues. It appears that first of all, the legal and ethical issues inherent in genomics and genetic engineering should be reduced to the basic ethical and normative postulate that genetic research/testing should always be carried out for the benefit of the individual and only for health purposes, and that the results produced should be disposed of after use. They should also be prevented from being exploited for other purposes, e.g. insurance. Any omission or irregularity in this regard is more likely than not to endanger human beings.

A key document which sets the regulatory framework in this area is the Convention for the Protection of Human Rights and Dignity of the Human

Being with regard to the Application of Biology and Medicine: Convention on Human Rights and Biomedicine, Oviedo, April 4, 1997. Its Article 2 underscores the primacy of the human being by stating that "the well-being of the human subject should take precedence over the interests of science and society".

Conclusions

AI, nanotechnology, genomics, and genetic engineering are the subject of interest of multidisciplinary sciences. Their development largely depends on advancements in information technologies, rapid access to large databases and information. In the field of AI and nanomaterials, we are dealing not only with individual challenges or legal and ethical problems but also with such basic issues as the lack of consensus on definitions (e.g. of AI), even though resolving them is crucial for determining the scope of subject vs. object regulation.

Undeniably, the law has a stabilising effect on a range of social relations, normative frameworks being fairly long-lasting guarantors of future behaviour. But it is also important to realize that it is not a panacea for all potential and actual irregularities and risks. The law will not always ensure that a novel solution works and is effective. It must be accompanied by other instruments to enforce the desired behaviours and social attitudes. Given the importance of AI, nanotechnology, etc. future legislation must be friendly towards ongoing research and further advancements in the field; it should facilitate progress and remove obstacles. Legal regulations must not only define what requirements should be met by certain solutions but also formulate prohibitions and specify what functionalities they should not have (e.g. AI systems should not question human commands). In medicine, patient safety is of paramount importance.

Taking into account the different areas and sectors of the economy where AI or nanomaterials-based devices/systems can be used, it appears that the scope and detail of regulation will fundamentally depend on the risks inherent in a given technology; for example, depending on the application, the risks of using AI in the healthcare sector may be negligible or substantial. Naturally, there will also be crucial issues to resolve, such as whether robotic devices should be given a special legal status (e.g. electronic persons) or whether robots should be empowered. Personally, I am against it, because this would entail too far-reaching consequences for human beings, which may open up space for unnecessary debates, e.g. on the insanity of a robot, the responsibility of a system, how to mete out punishment to an electronic device, etc.

Undoubtedly, the groups of issues discussed in this chapter demand generally applicable legislation (which will likely be created with some delay) and internal operating procedures, standardisation, and certification. In fact, the latter are the first solutions that put these phenomena into something resembling a regulatory framework.

The selected issues and doubts raised above do not mean that there are no regulations or documents at the level of individual countries, EU or international that could be applied to new, advanced technical and technological solutions. First of all, there are regulations concerning, among others data protection and data flow, product liability, medical devices, or health and safety at work. They can be found in fundamental regulations such as the Treaty on the EU, the Charter of Fundamental Rights of the EU, the Convention for the Protection of Human Rights and Fundamental Freedoms as well as in a number of other EU directives and regulations, not to mention various guidance documents (programs, recommendations).

Regardless of the above, it still seems reasonable to call for a precise definition of the responsibility of agents/entities involved in the life cycle of AI-based products that should include not only that of the manufacturer but also, among others, the entity that downloads or updates the software as distinct from the manufacturer of the hardware. Indisputably, AI regulations must specify, among other things: the requirements for AI systems, rules for the deployment of AI systems, and must allocate in detail and proportionately the responsibilities to AI providers and users. They must also introduce rules for the interaction of AI systems with people, rules for AI market monitoring and surveillance, and prohibit certain AI behaviours. It is also likely that regulations will need to be continually revised as technology evolves and new threats emerge from the Internet (cybersecurity), from the product itself when updated with faulty software (user safety), etc.

The law at the EU level must be consistent at least with basic EU policies and acts and must provide for effective enforcement measures. The draft regulation setting out the legal framework for AI presented by the European Commission on 21.04.2021 is to be welcomed.

The introduction of minimum requirements for AI systems in the form of an EU regulation under Article 288 TFEU will unify legal solutions in this area across the EU Member States. It should be noted that the draft act provides for the possibility to introduce individual national solutions within a prescribed range. Nonetheless, the proposed regulations need a fair amount of fine-tuning in terms of precisely defining the boundaries for risky AI applications, effective vindication of the rights of those affected, or streamlining bureaucratic requirements in favour of independent oversight of AI (Iwańska, 2021). The cited Polish government's AI development policy proposes further-reaching solutions than the draft EU regulation.

References

AI HLEG. (2019a). High-Level Expert Group on Artificial Intelligence set up by the European Commission. *A definition of AI: Main capabilities and scientific disciplines*; https://www.aepd.es/sites/default/files/2019-12/ai-definition.pdf (27.04.2021).

AI HLEG. (2019b). High-Level Expert Group on Artificial Intelligence set up by the European Commission. *Ethics Guidelines for Trustworthy AI*; https://ec.europa.eu/digital-single-market/en/high-level-expert-group-artificial-intelligence (27.04.2021).

Communication from the Commission to the European Parliament, the European Council, the Council, the European Economic and Social Committee and the Committee of the Regions - Artificial Intelligence for Europe, Brussels, 25.4.2018, COM(2018) 237 final.

Directive 2011/24/EU of the European Parliament and of the Council of 9.03.2011 on the application of patients' rights in cross-border healthcare. OJ L 88/45.

Do, O., March, E., Rich, J., Wolff, T. (1996). Intelligent Agents & The Internet: Effects On Electronic Commerce and Marketing. http://bold.coba.unr.edu/odie/paper.html.

European Commission. (2018). *Market study on telemedicine*. Luxembourg: Publications Office of the European Union; https://ec.europa.eu/health/sites/health/files/ehealth/docs/2018_provision_marketstudy_telemedicine_en.pdf (27.04.2021).

European Commission. (2019). *My Health in the EU. Digital exchange of ePrescriptions and Patient Summaries*; https://ec.europa.eu/health/sites/health/files/ehealth/docs/2019_ecrossborder_healthservices_qa_en.pdf (27.04.2021).

European Commission. (2020). *White Paper. On Artificial Intelligence – A European Approach to Excellence and Trust*, Brussels, 19.2.2020. COM(2020) 65 final.

European Parliament Draft Report, Artificial intelligence in criminal law and its use by the police and judicial authorities in criminal matters, 2020/2016(INI); https://oeil.secure.europarl.europa.eu/oeil/popups/ficheprocedure.do?lang=en&reference=2020/2016(INI) (27.04.2021).

European Parliament resolution of 20.10.2020 on a civil liability regime for artificial intelligence, 2020/2014(INL); https://www.europarl.europa.eu/doceo/document/TA-9-2020-0276_EN.html (27.04.2021).

Habl, C., Renner, A.T., Bobek, J., Laschkolnig, A. (2016). *Study on Big Data in Public Health, Telemedicine and Healthcare. Final Report*. Luxembourg: Publications Office of the European Union. DOI: 10.2875/734795.

IBM. (2021). https://www.ibm.com/pl-pl/watson-health/learn/artificial-intelligence-medicine (1.04.2021).

Iwańska, K. (2021). *Unia szykuje przepisy dotyczące AI: 5 problemów*. Pobrane z: https://panoptykon.org/wiadomosc/unia-szykuje-przepisy-dotyczace-ai-5-problemow (27.04.2021).

Jonkheer, K., Jansen, T. (1998). *Strategic Study. Intelligent Agents, Markets and Competition. State-of-the-Art Study on the Effects of Intelligent Agents in Markets*. Zoetermeer: EIM.

Judgment SN z 2.08.2001. II KKN 63/99. LEX nr 51381.

Judgment SN z 16.01.1974. III KR 311/73. LEX nr 21606.

Karnow, C.E.A. (1996). Liability for Distributed Artificial Intelligences. *Berkeley Technology Law Journal, 11*(1), 147–204. DOI: 10.15779/Z38ZD4W.

Milieu Ltd., Time.lex CVBA. (2014). Overview of the national laws on electronic health records in the EU Member States and their interaction with the provision of cross-border eHealth services. Final report and recommendations. Brussels. https://ec.europa.eu/health/sites/health/files/ehealth/docs/laws_report_recommendations_en.pdf (27.04.2021).

Orzechowska, A., Szymańska, R. (2016). Nanotechnologia w zastosowaniach biologicznych – wprowadzenie, *Wszechświat*, t. 117, nr 1-3, s. 67–68.

Pentland A., Reid T.G., Heibeck T. (2013). *Big Data and Health: Revolutionizing Medicine and Public Health: Report of the Big Data and Health Working Group 2013*. DOHA: World Innovation Summit for Health (WISH).

Ponce Del Castillo, A.M. (2010). *The EU Approach to Regulating Nanotechnology*. Brussels: ETUI aisbl. Pobrane z: https://www.etui.org/sites/default/files/Nano-working-paper.pdf (27.04.2021).

Proposal for a Regulation of The European Parliament and of The Council Laying Down Harmonised Rules on Artificial Intelligence (Artificial Intelligence Act) and Amending Certain Union Legislative Acts, Brussels, 21.4.2021, COM(2021) 206 final, 2021/0106 (COD); https://digital-strategy.ec.europa.eu/en/library/proposal-regulation-european-approach-artificial-intelligence (27.04.2021 r.).

Ramesh, A.N., Kambhampati, C., Monson, J.R.T., Drew, P.J. (2004). Artificial Intelligence in Medicine. *Annals of The Royal College of Surgeons of England*, 86/5, 334–338. DOI 10.1308/147870804290; https://www.ncbi.nlm.nih.gov/pmc/articles/PMC1964229/pdf/15333167.pdf (27.04.2021).

Regulation (EU) 2016/679 of the European Parliament and of the Council of 27.04.2016 on the protection of natural persons with regard to the processing of personal data and on the free movement of such data, and repealing Directive 95/46/EC (General Data Protection Regulation) (Text with EEA relevance. OJ L 119/1.

Salas-Vega, S., Haimann, A., Mossialos, E. (2015). Big Data and Healthcare: Challenges and Opportunities for Coordinated Policy Development in the EU. *Health Systems & Reform*, *1*(4), 285–300. DOI: 10.1080/23288604.2015.1091538.

Singh, R. (2003). Intelligent agents. In W. H. Bidgoli (Ed.). *Encyclopedia of Information Systems*, pp. 639–647. Elsevier. https://www.sciencedirect.com/topics/computer-science/intelligent-agent; https://www.sciencedirect.com/science/article/pii/B0122272404000940 (27.04.2021).

Stosio, A. (2002). *Umowy zawierane przez Internet*. Warszawa: Dom Wydawniczy ABC.

Resolution of the Council of Ministers (2020). Uchwała Nr 196 Rady Ministrów z 28.12.2020 r. w sprawie ustanowienia "Polityki dla rozwoju sztucznej inteligencji w Polsce od roku 2020". M.P. z 2021, poz. 23.

The Act of 5 December 1996 on Medical and Dental Professions (2021). Ustawa z 5.12.1996 o zawodach lekarza i lekarza dentysty. Dz.U. z 2021 r., poz. 790.

13 Human capital vs. Health 4.0

Alicja Domagała and Jacek Klich

Introduction

The Fourth Industrial Revolution leading to Health 4.0 directly affects human capital as a key component of the healthcare system, i.e. patients (the demand side) and health professionals, mainly physicians and nurses (the supply side). The aim of this chapter is to identify the key challenges that Health 4.0 poses to health professionals and to outline the key trends in this regard. These challenges emerge in the wake of changes in the position of patients in the healthcare system, resulting from their improved access to information, advances in information, and medical technologies (discussed in Chapter 5 on empowering the patient in the system). Below, we will show that these changes require redefining the relationship between health professionals and patients, as well as modifying medical education.

The demand side: the position of the patient in the healthcare system in the context of easy access to information

The unprecedented widening of access to information for both patients and health professionals as well as ongoing technological progress result in far-reaching changes to the operation of the healthcare system. The availability of information on diseases and treatment procedures on the Internet reduces the information asymmetry between the physician and the patient, which has existed for centuries. Moreover, patients are now involved in designing medical devices and applications used in therapy and/or rehabilitation (cf. Chapter 8). By using the Internet, patients can now verify medical diagnoses, compare medicines and treatments prescribed by physicians as well as share opinions on the qualifications and quality of services provided by a physician or clinic using blogs. This tool is rapidly gaining in popularity. Suffice it to say that if in the late 1990s, the number of websites containing health-related information ranged from 20,000 to 100,000 (Diaz et al., 2002, p. 180), by the end of the first decade of the 21st century the number of web-searches for medical information was estimated at millions per day

DOI: 10.4324/9781003144403-13

(de Oliveira, 2014, p. 327) and in 2019, Google already registered more than one billion health-related queries per day (The Medical Futurist, 2020).

Easy access to medical information promotes patient empowerment (Topol, 2012, pp. 33–58; Tubaishat, 2019) as do the changes in regulation and the expansion of patient rights, as was pointed out in Chapter 5 (Patient Empowerment in Health 4.0). Patient empowerment can be analysed in terms of M. Porter's model of five forces as an enhancement of customers' bargaining power, as was also noted in Chapter 11 (Financing Healthcare 4.0), where an increasing share of out-of-pocket spending by patients in total health expenditure in post-socialist countries is discussed. There are thus strong grounds to argue that we are dealing with a sustained, systemic shift in the balance between health professionals and patients in favour of the latter, which implies the need for appropriate changes on the supply side represented by the former.

The changes caused by the dynamic development of information technologies and the digitalisation of the healthcare sector as relevant to patients can be presented in subjective and objective terms. The subjective approach comprises patients' knowledge about diseases, prevention and health promotion, as well as their personal perception of health (self-diagnosis). The objective approach, on the other hand, reflects a parameterised evaluation of their health status, which is reflected in personal electronic medical records.

Easy and universal access to information for patients can also be considered in narrow and broad terms. The former boils down to access to medical information pertaining to the patients themselves (Lin et al., 2019), while the latter comprises all the information available to patients and physicians that can be used by either party when making decisions about treatment modalities and procedures.

Patient access to information in the narrow sense has been intensively studied for decades (Ross & Lin, 2003). The development of the Internet and data digitalisation mean that sensitive health data are collected and exchanged to an increasing extent, which causes problems both in sharing electronic medical records with third parties (family members, insurers, or police) (Drees, 2020) and in protecting them (Tubaishat, 2019; Fong, Fong, and Li, 2020, pp. 147–178).

Although patients enjoy increasing access to information, its underutilisation is still reported (Ancker et al., 2017; Alami et al., 2019). While the problem of patient access to information in the narrow sense does not lead to major disruptions in the physician-patient relationship, such disruptions may be present in access to information in the broader sense. This is due to the fact that patients may choose to rely on unreliable or sometimes outright misleading information posted on the Internet (e.g. on YouTube; cf. Goobie et al., 2019). Patients keen to take advantage of such information may misdiagnose themselves, refuse to seek professional consultation, chose to pursue treatment independently (self-medication), or even do nothing at all. All these options may have dangerous (Clark, 2020) or even tragic health consequences. Overuse of the Internet as a source of health information stemming from health anxiety may lead to cyberchondria also known as compucondria (White & Horvitz, 2009; Muse et al., 2012), which is a recognised mental condition (Starcevic et al., 2020). In its mild form, cyberchondria often complicates the physician-patient relationship.

On balance, however, the benefits of acquiring health knowledge from the Internet to patients (Wicks et al., 2018) or their caregivers (Kinnane & Milne, 2010; Bouju et al., 2014) seem to prevail. It is also worth mentioning that the increasingly intense human interaction with the Internet is of interest to researchers representing a wide variety of disciplines. This is evidenced by new specialties and emerging scientific journals. In the context of interest to us, examples include the *Journal of Medical Internet Research* (published since 1999), *Cyberpsychology, Behaviour,* and *Social Networking* (published since 1998) or the *Journal of the American Medical Informatics Association* (published since 1994).

It is also worth noting that some institutions (e.g. think-tanks, insurance companies) offer tips on their websites on how to select reliable sources of information. Platforms that use artificial intelligence to help patients self-diagnose (artificially intelligent self-diagnosing digital platforms) can also be considered as a form of assistance. Research shows that due to the diversity of these platforms and the wide range of diseases they cover, they are yet to be evaluated in-depth (Aboueid et al., 2019).

The supply side: challenges to health professionals due to patients' unrestricted access to information

As regards the supply side of the healthcare system, patients' mass and easy access to information poses new challenges to physicians and other health professionals. On the optimistic assumption that patients obtain reliable information from the Internet, including social media, and thus gain reliable knowledge about health and diseases, they become partners for the physician in the process of diagnosis and treatment. Research focussed on analysing the impact of information obtained by the patient from the Internet on the physician-patient relationship started several decades ago (Eysenbach & Diepgen, 1999; McMullan, 2006). The findings of a recent review study covering the period from 2000 to 2015 show that patients' search for medical information on the Internet can improve the physician-patient relationship as long as the latter chooses to discuss it with the former (Tan & Goonawardene, 2017). In this way, patients become partners in the treatment process (cf. Chapter 5 on patient empowerment and Chapter 8 on the role of patients in the co-creation process).

As concluded from the research evidence on these relationships, it was (Grandinetti, 2000) and is emphasised (Tan & Goonawardene, 2017) that physicians and other health professionals should help patients navigate the Internet resources by pointing out to authoritative and reliable sources of information and verifying their knowledge. This strengthens the argument for modifying the model of education and preparation for the medical and nursing professions.

At this point, let us note that another consequence for physicians and nurses resulting from such components of the Fourth Industrial Revolution and Health 4.0 as big data and the Internet of Things, namely the progressive personalisation of health services (discussed in more detail below). Currently, the SARS-Cov-2 pandemic has inspired discussions on the emerging new personalised health ecosystem (Spence, 2020).

Health 4.0 as a way to improve the use of available human resources and reduce the negative consequences of shortages of health professionals

Global population growth, population ageing, and the associated increase in demand for health and care services lead to an increased demand for trained health professionals. According to data presented by the World Health Organization (WHO) in its report *Global Strategy on Human Resources for Health: Workforce 2030*, the worldwide shortage of physicians, nurses, and midwives may total as many as 9.9 million in 2030 (WHO, 2016). Shortfalls of health professionals also pose a major challenge to European countries, and although the overall number of physicians and nurses has increased by around 10%–15% over the past 10 years, it is estimated that this is by no means sufficient to meet the growing needs of an ageing population. Adverse changes also occur in the age structure of the healthcare workforce in Europe, resulting in a steady increase in its average age. The uneven geographical distribution of physicians and difficulties involved in recruiting and retaining them in remote and sparsely populated areas is yet another daunting task for many countries, particularly in relation to general practitioners (GPs). Although in recent years, the overall number of physicians per population size has increased in most countries, the proportion of GPs has declined in many of them (OECD/EU, 2020). The supply of physicians in large urban areas is higher (which also reflects the concentration of specialist services), whereas shortages are particularly acute in rural and sparsely populated areas (Doty, 2019).

Countries are taking a range of measures to address the current and projected staffing shortages among others by implementing new technologies in order to maximise the efficiency of health service provision (Ono, Lafortun and Schoenstein, 2013). The tools offered by Health 4.0 permit a more efficient use of the available human resources through a better management of the working hours of health professionals. Wherever possible and feasible, new information and communication technology (ICT) tools should be implemented as they can play a very important role in such areas as electronic medical record keeping, telemedicine, clinical decision support tools, building links both among health professionals and between them and their patients. Thus, the implementation of new technologies offers a way to reduce inequalities in access to health services, overcome geographical barriers, improve the quality of those services, ensure the ability of sufficient medical resources, and optimise the treatment process itself. More importantly, the beneficiaries include numerous entities participating in the process of providing health services. The long list of benefits brought about by Health 4.0 in this respect includes improved treatment efficacy, time savings, increased patient satisfaction and safety, more accurate diagnostic process, improved physician-patient relationships and communication. According to some studies, physicians believe that digital solutions bring more benefits to patients than to the physicians themselves. This is mainly due to funding issues, the need to apply tried and tested tools, reliance on evidence-based studies, data management and accessibility (Győrffy, Rado and Mesko, 2020).

Telemedicine and human capital in healthcare: current state and future prospects

Telemedicine - a phenomenon introduced in Chapter 1 on the Fourth Industrial Revolution and the healthcare system, and discussed in more depth in Chapter 2 on the transition from telemedicine and e-health to Health 4.0 - not only overcomes the distance barrier between physicians and patients, but also contributes to increasing the quality of the services provided and to lowering their costs for the payer. At the same time, this form of service delivery offers solutions to reduce the waiting times for consultations by improving the effectiveness of physicians and nurses in terms of their workload and working time. The benefits thus accrue to patients, health professionals, healthcare entities, the payer, and the state that has the opportunity to ensure a better implementation of the citizens' right to equal access to publicly funded health services.

It is vital to identify the main implications of technological change for the future needs in terms of skills and competencies of health professionals. For the time being, there are no reliable or credible forecasts on how new technologies are likely to affect the labour market structure for health professionals. Research is currently being conducted to determine to what extent the health workforce is prepared to adapt to these changes. The report *Future Health Index 2020* (published in 2020) presents the findings of a survey conducted among the representatives of the younger generation of medical personnel (i.e. under 40 years of age), who in the next 20 years will constitute the majority of the global workforce in medicine and will bear most of the responsibility for the form and quality of health services. The said report is based on the results of a survey of 2867 younger generation professionals in 15 countries: Australia, Brazil, China, France, Germany, India, Japan, the Netherlands, Poland, Romania, Russia, Saudi Arabia, Singapore, South Africa, and the USA (Philips, 2020). The publication discusses their expectations of technology, training and job satisfaction, and describes their actual on-the-job experiences. The following are the main findings of the cited study in the context of the issue at hand:

- Young health professionals recognise four key gaps in their jobs, namely skills, knowledge, data, and expectations.
- Globally, some young healthcare professionals admit that they feel overwhelmed by the amount of digital medical data. Many opine that the reality of professional work does not meet their hopes or expectations.
- A total of 78% of healthcare professionals use at least one kind of digital solution in their practice or hospital.
- As many as 35% do not know how to take advantage of digital health data to make patient care decisions.

From a global perspective, the survey findings send a clear message to healthcare leaders and policymakers about the areas of most concern to the younger generation of health professionals. The three main areas to look at are

- Education and training (in healthcare management and administration, digital data processing and use, key principles of value-based care),
- Technology (investing in technologies that enable the exchange and sharing of digital data, improving work-life balance, improving work efficiency, and higher levels of interoperability), and
- Organisational culture (social recognition, commitment to the organisation, and flexible working hours).

The findings of the report *Future Health Index 2020* show that young healthcare professionals are ambitious and committed to the care of their patients. This generation, raised at the dawn of the fourth technological revolution, is naturally drawn to modern means of communication, digital methods of data processing and exchange, as well as mobile and Internet-based technologies. This is a cohort that uses digital solutions freely in their private and professional lives, seeks new knowledge and wants to improve their competencies, wants to be involved in the operational activities of their medical institutions, and is not afraid to take responsibility for shaping the healthcare system. It sees new technologies as an essential tool with which to transform healthcare, a way to provide appropriate and comprehensive patient care, as well as a factor that reduces stress levels and increases job satisfaction (Philips, 2020).

Conditions and barriers for using modern devices, techniques, and applications

Effective implementation of new technologies requires appropriate standards, accreditation procedures, and evaluation practices to certify and ensure the quality of the implemented solutions. Appropriate legal regulations for the provision of mobile health services and rules for the collection and processing of data resources in the context of observing the confidentiality requirements due should also be established (WHO, 2016, p. 19).

The most serious obstacles and potential barriers that hinder digitalisation efforts and the implementation of Health 4.0 solutions include the following: sometimes unfavourable social conditions (lack of trust or scepticism of part of the population towards ICT services due to low levels of IT literacy, especially among seniors and residents of non-urbanized areas), complicated legal regulations, and gaps/inconsistencies in regulations on financing telemedicine services. Moreover, the literature points to further barriers, such as increased workload (especially administrative) placed on health professionals, lack of resources and financial problems, insufficient familiarity with digital health technologies, lack of trained medical staff, misuse and misunderstanding of digital health technologies by patients, increased health disparities due to limited health awareness, problems with confidentiality and security of patient data, resistance on the part of some physicians (e.g. fear of losing control) or a work culture that is less than conducive to innovation (Brunner et al., 2018; Győrffy, Rado and Mesko, 2020; American Medical Associaction, 2020).

It is therefore advisable to consider potential actions that can be taken to overcome or remove the barriers to the digitalisation of health. They may include using evidence-based solutions, developing guidelines, ensuring accessibility to special dedicated training for staff, peer support and a supportive working environment, improving the quality, safety and effectiveness of digital health technologies, clarifying regulations that govern their admissible uses, or implementing easy and user-friendly solutions. It is also important to enhance motivation to implement IT innovations, promote positive attitudes and preferences of patients regarding digital health solutions, and build an innovation-oriented work culture.

In order to effectively implement Health 4.0 tools, it is also necessary to make appropriate changes in organisational management, including the promotion of digital leadership. The digital maturity of an organisation where 4.0 solutions are implemented requires it to adapt by developing relevant competencies, devising strategies and plans related to the implementation of new technologies, but primarily by advancing workplace culture.

As was mentioned above, the younger generation of health professionals is open to new technologies, however, it should be remembered that the current health system is dominated by older age groups. The average physician age is inexorably rising, nearly one in three of them being now 55 years old (OECD/EU, 2020). Generally speaking, physicians in older age groups tend to be less open to new technologies and require adequate support and training to be able to use them efficiently. Given the insufficient IT competencies of some older physicians, care should be taken to provide them with appropriate guidance and a friendly, supportive workplace environment that facilitates their smooth adaptation in order to enable them to use modern digital tools effectively.

The need for health professionals to improve their patient communication skills and, more broadly, their soft skills

Among the many important skills that an 'e-physician' should possess, three seem to be of particular importance: (1) digital literacy and a positive attitude towards digital technologies; (2) an awareness that the physician-patient relationship is changing into a partnership-based one; and (3) an empathic approach to patient treatment remains fundamental (Mesko & Győrffy, 2019).

Recently, e-health has been identified as central to current health reforms, which are expected to deliver more efficient, cost-effective care and better outcomes. In this context, healthcare professionals - both graduates and experienced staff - are increasingly expected to be ready to deliver e-health services in a variety of digital environments.

A study by Gray et al. on the educational needs of healthcare professionals necessary to implement digital health solutions found that a key factor that limits the e-health readiness of the current and future workforce is the lack of coordinated, formal education in the use of digital health technologies (Gray et al., 2014). Likewise, the participants in a European Health Parliament-initiated survey (2016), which involved 207 health professionals from 21 member states, when asked about their participation in digital skills training, overwhelmingly (61%) responded that they had not received such training. Of those respondents who confirmed having attended training dedicated to digital competencies, as many as 54% rated it as insufficient.

Digital competence development requires increased awareness and understanding of the purpose of e-health in the context of clinical practice as well as training in the use of technology. It is therefore necessary to integrate e-health education with clinical education, particularly in the professions of physician, nurse, midwife, and physiotherapist. A competence framework in e-health, once devised, will help identify the technical and IT skills needed for the development of human resources.

An important area in terms of the greatest impact of digitalisation is the care of the ageing population (it is estimated that the global population aged 60 or over will reach almost 2 billion by 2050). The growing demand for elderly care can be partly addressed by robotics and digitisation, which may assist in the delivery of certain care services and provide patient health monitoring. Due to the increasing proportion of elderly patients, adequate communication skills of physicians and patient involvement in prevention and treatment will become more important than ever. Furthermore, health professionals should be trained to diagnose, treat, educate, and monitor patients remotely.

On the one hand, physicians committed to digital technologies declare their enthusiasm to the potential and opportunities offered by new technologies, but on the other, experience a number of difficulties related to digital health (Győrffy, Rado and Mesko, 2020). Studies confirm that the popularity of digital tools has significantly increased in recent years among all physicians regardless of gender, specialty, or age (American Medical Association, 2020). However, it is important to bear in mind that physicians are often under pressure to integrate their medical practice with IT tools and stay abreast of new technologies, even though at work they are often forced to use low-quality, flawed or ineffective applications and technologies that actually reduce the amount of time they may spend with their patients (Mesko, 2017).

Some researchers point out that the empowerment of patients, the proliferation of digital health tools, and the biopsychosocial-digital approach to diseases have created a new role for physicians, who are only now slowly transforming themselves into guides for their patients in the maze of digital information and the complexities of the healthcare system (Mesko & Győrffy, 2019). The era of digital health not only means equipping patients with information, new tools and technologies, but also equipping physicians (e-physicians) accordingly with the time, capabilities, and technologies to fulfil the modern vision of the practicing health professional. As the practice of medicine becomes a collaborative process not only between healthcare professionals but also with significant patient participation, certain characteristics of both 'e-patients' and 'e-physicians' become comparable.

Thus, adapting to the current cultural changes initiated by digital medical technologies, the characteristics of the 'e-physician' may change from knower to seeker, from follower of established rules to creator, and from lonely hero to team player (Mesko & Győrffy, 2019).

Effective teamwork is essential since advances in science and technology make it virtually impossible to solve all the patient treatment problems by oneself. As knowledge and the treatment process become more globalised, so does the need to improve the ability to work in research and clinical teams.

Technicisation of medicine and artificial intelligence as a challenge to health professionals

Telemedicine has become an increasingly popular tool in the provision of health services in recent years, while a large-scale introduction of new Health 4.0 tools, such as artificial intelligence and robots, can be expected in the near future. In a survey of more than 11,000 people from 12 countries, as many as 55% declared that they were ready for physicians to be replaced by advanced technologies and robots equipped with artificial intelligence tools (PwC, 2017). When asked about the main reasons why they would like to undergo surgery or use a medical service provided by artificial intelligence or a robot, the survey participants primarily mentioned easier and faster access to medical services (36%) and speed and accuracy of diagnosis (33%). On the other hand, barriers included the lack of confidence in the ability of robots to make decisions (47%) and the absence of the human factor (41%).

Artificial intelligence tools can meaningfully support the diagnostic or therapeutic process and reduce the cost of health services. It also offers great opportunities to use historical data to diagnose new cases in support of the work of physicians and other medical specialists. The physician was, is, and will be the key person making the right decisions, but it seems that artificial intelligence solutions can support the physician's work, help eliminate certain errors, suggest the optimal course of action, and use the available resources and specialists' time more efficiently.

The ever-changing market, new patient expectations and needs mean that healthcare providers will have to make numerous adjustments to their organisations, otherwise they will suffer reduced profits and/or losing their market share. The changes mainly concern those areas of healthcare where new technologies are already available and the share of private financing is the largest. In particular, they will affect primary care services, outpatient specialist care, diagnostics, rehabilitation, and services for the elderly.

An analysis of Health 4.0 reveals that it has a two-pronged impact: on the one hand, it affects the development and progress in medicine, and on the other, it influences the management of medical institutions (especially hospitals). It is mainly physicians and nurses who face the challenges posed by Health 4.0, such as the need to continuously upgrade their clinical skills as well as to improve their competencies in interaction with patients using new digital technologies. Big data, cloud computing, virtual reality, artificial intelligence and many other emerging technologies are already finding their way into numerous healthcare applications. The expansion of digital ecosystems is having a significant impact on healthcare models (e.g. coordinated care), patient pathway management (through electronic medical records or telemedicine), new technologies and therapeutic devices. In principle, not only the delivery of medical services, but also the administration and management of healthcare can benefit from digitalisation and digital data flow support, computerised knowledge management and shared decision-making. Several countries have embarked on a race to catch up with the Fourth Industrial Revolution, while their health sectors are trying to adapt to Health 4.0 tools and solutions. Those capable of adapting their health systems more rapidly to the solutions and opportunities offered by Health 4.0 will be well ahead of those that fail to do so in the short term.

Conclusions

Healthcare digitalisation not only improves the work of health professionals but is also a prerequisite for building an efficient and patient-friendly healthcare system. The more advanced e-health services and tools are, the greater the synergy between them.

Telemedicine solutions (e.g. e-prescription, e-referral, teleconsultation/ remote consultation) proved to be extremely helpful during the SARS-Cov-2 pandemic, when face-to-face contacts between patients and health professionals had to be severely restricted.

Health 4.0 has already made spectacular inroads into patient care, but its further development is associated with new challenges. Digital health solutions may create a deeper relationship between the physician and the patient: informed and experienced patients are well equipped to share the burden of treatment, whereas technology can become a major tool in creating more engaged and responsible clients. Digital health is a tool that can improve communication in patient care and contribute to patients' trust by increasing their involvement in their own treatment-related decisions. In this context, the relationship between the health professional and the patient is being redefined into one in which the latter becomes a partner and an active participant in the treatment process.

The role of physicians is also changing: today and in the near future, they will have to perform more complex tasks, such as health IT, assisting in the digital orientation of patients and filtering information for them. In the era of digital health, physicians are guides, communicate efficiently with the patient and act as 'guardians' in managing information, collecting it and making safe and reliable contents available in the online space. In order to succeed in the ongoing shift from the hierarchical model of the physician towards a new physician-patient relationship in the 21st century, the future generation of physicians should be trained differently and prepared for all the changes described above. Medical curricula should emphasise the importance of health and prevention thanks to the latest advances in technology, whereas students must prepare themselves for a changing working environment, including their new role as a patient guide and proficient user of digital health technologies. The European Commission takes the view that training health professionals in the knowledge and use of digital health technologies should be central to the European agenda for digitisation of healthcare (European Health Parliament, 2016), and recommends that all Member States should establish mandatory, dedicated digital skills training programmes for healthcare professionals from early childhood education to ongoing and professional development programmes.

It should be the task of politicians and policy makers to create regulations that, on the one hand, require digital competencies for physicians in training and, on the other, motivate practicing physicians to acquire such competencies and reward them accordingly. These actions should be part of a concerted strategy to prepare societies for the new reality of the digital world.

The added value of this chapter is that it offers a more complete picture of the challenges posed by the dynamic development of technology to human resources in the healthcare sector, including the most important stakeholders representing the demand (patients) and supply sides (physicians and nurses) of the healthcare system. As was shown above, the prerequisite for effective implementation and use of the tools offered by Health 4.0 is their adaptation through the acquisition of new knowledge, skills, and experience by both above-mentioned groups.

References

Aboueid, S., Liu, R.H., Desta, B.D., Chaurasia, A., Ebrahim, S. (2019). The Use of Artificially Intelligent Self-Diagnosing Digital Platforms by the General Public: Scoping Review. *JMIR Medical Informatics* 7(2): e13445, doi: 10 2196/13445

Alami, H., Gagnon, M-P., Ahmed, M.A.A., Fortin, J-P. (2019). Digital Health: Cybersecurity Is a Value Creation Lever, Not Only a Source of Expenditure. *Health Policy and Technology* 8: 319–321, doi.org/10.1016/j.hlpt.2019.09.002

American Medical Association. (2020). Physicians' Motivations and Requirements for Adopting Digital Health Adoption and Attitudinal Shifts from 2016 to 2019. AMA Digital Health Research. Available at: https://www.ama-assn.org/system/files/2020-02/ama-digital-health-study.pdf (Accessed on 12 February 2021).

Ancker, J.S., Nosal, S., Hauser, D., Calman, N. (2017). Access Policy and the Digital Divide in Patient Access to Medical Records. *Health Policy and Technology* 6: 3–11, doi:10.1016/j.hlpt.2016.11.004

Bouju, P., Tadié, J-M., Uhel, F., Letheulle, J., Fillatre, P., Lavoué, S., Camus, C., Le Tulzo, Y., Gacouin, A. (2014). Internet Use by Family Members of Intensive Care Unit Patients: A Pilot Study. *Intensive Care Medicine* 40(8): 1175–1176, doi:10.1007/s00134-014-3371-z

Brunner, M., McGregor, D., Keep, M., Janssen, A., Spallek, H., Quinn, D., Jones, A., Tseris, E., Yeung, W., Togher, L., Solman, A., Shaw, T. (2018). An e-Health Capabilities Framework for Graduates and Health Professionals: Mixed-Methods Study. *Journal of Medical Internet Research* 20(5): e10229, doi:10.2196/10229

Clark, M. (2020, May 28). 9 Problems with and Dangers of Self-Diagnosis. https://etactics.com/blog/problems-with-self-diagnosis (Accessed on 4 February 2021).

de Oliveira, J.F. (2014). The Effect of the Internet on the Patient-Physician Relationship in a Hospital in the City of São Paulo. *Journal of Information Systems and Technology Management*. Revista de Gestão da Tecnologia e Sistemas de Informação 11(2): 327–344, doi:10.4301/S1807-17752014000200006

Diaz, J.A., Griffith, R.A., Ng, J.J., Reinert, S.E., Friedmann, P.D., Moulton, A.W. (2002). Patients' Use of the Internet for Medical Information. *Journal of General Internal Medicine* 17: 180–185, doi: 10.1046/j.1525-1497.2002.10603.x

Doty, M.M, Tikkanen, R., Shah, A., Schneider, E.C. (2019). Primary Care Physicians' Role in Coordinating Medical and Health-Related Social Needs in Eleven Countries. *Health Affairs* 39(1), doi: 10.1377/hlthaff.2019.01088

Drees, D. (2020). AMA: 10 Things to Know About Patient Access to Digital Health Records. Available at: www.beckershospitalreview.com/consumerism/ama-10-things-to-know-about-patient-access-to-digital-health-records.html (Accessed on 01 February 2021).

European Health Parliament. (2016). Digital Skills for Health Professionals. Committee on Digital Skills for Health Professionals. Available at: www.healthparliament.eu/wp-content/uploads/2017/09/Digital-skills-for-health-professionals.pdf (Accessed on 01 February 2021).

Eysenbach, G., Diepgen, T.L. (1999). Patients Looking for Information on the Internet and Seeking Teleadvice: Motivation, Expectations, and Misconceptions as Expressed in E-mails Sent to Physicians. *Archives of Dermatology* 135(2): 151–156, doi:10.1001/archderm.135.2.151

Fong, B., Fong., A.C.M., Li, C.K. (2020). *Telemedicine Technologies. Information Technologies in Medicine and Digital Health*, Second Edition. John Wiley & Sons Ltd.

Goobie, G.C., Guler, S.A., Johannson, K.A., Fisher, J.H., Ryerson, C.J. (2019). YouTube videos as a source of misinformation on idiopathic pulmonary fibrosis. *Annals of the American Thoracic Society* 16(5): 572–579, doi: 10.1513/AnnalsATS.201809-644OC

Grandinetti, D.A. (2000). Physicians and the Web. Help your patients surf the Net safely. *Medical Economics* 77(5):186–188, 194–196, 201.

Gray, K., Dattakumar, A., Maeder, A., Butler-Henderson, K., Chenery, H. (2014). Advancing E-Health Education for the Clinical Health Professions. Available at: http://clinicalinformaticseducation.pbworks.com/w/file/fetch/74500403/PP10_1806_Gray_report_2014.pdf (Accessed on 12 February 2021).

Győrffy, Z., Rado, N., Mesko, B. (2020). Digitally Engaged Physicians about the Digital Health Transition. *PLoS ONE* 15(9): e0238658, doi: 10.1371/journal.pone.0238658

Kinnane, N.A., Milne, D.J. (2010). The Role of the Internet in Supporting and Informing Carers of People with Cancer: A Literature Review. *Support Care Cancer* 18(9): 1123–1136, doi: 10.1007/s00520-010-0863-4

Lin, S.C., Lyles, C.R., Sarkar, U., Adler-Milstein, J. (2019). Are Patients Electronically Accessing Their Medical Records? Evidence from National Hospital Data. *Health Affairs* 38(11), doi: 10.1377/hlthaff.2018.05437

McMullan, M. (2006). Patients Using the Internet to Obtain Health Information: How This Affects the Patient-Health Professional Relationship. *Patient Education and Counseling* 63(1–2): 24–28, doi: 10.1016/j.pec.2005.10.006

Mesko, B. (2017). Health IT and Digital Health: The Future of Health Technology Is Diverse. *The Journal of Clinical and Translational Research* 3(S3): 431–434, doi: 10.18053/jctres.03.2017S3.006

Mesko, B., Győrffy, Z. (2019). The Rise of the Empowered Physician in the Digital Health Era: Viewpoint. *Journal of Medical Internet Research* 21(3): e12490, doi: 10.2196/12490

Muse, K., McManus, F., Leung, C., Meghreblian, B., Williams, J.M.G. (2012). Cyberchondriasis: Fact or Fiction? A Preliminary Examination of the Relationship Between Health Anxiety and Searching for Health Information on the Internet. *Journal of Anxiety Disorders* 26(1): 189–96, doi: 10.1016/j.janxdis.2011.11.005

OECD/EU. (2020). *Health at a Glance: Europe 2020: State of Health in the EU Cycle*; Paris, France: OECD Publishing.

Ono, T., Lafortun, e G., Schoenstein, M. (2013). Health Workforce Planning in OECD Countries: A Review of 26 Projection Models from 18 Countries. OECD Health Working Papers, No. 62, OECD Publishing, Paris, doi.org/10.1787/5k44t787zcwb-en

Philips. (2020). Future Health Index 2020. The Age of Opportunity. Empowering the Next Generation to Transform Healthcare. Available at: https://www.philips.com/a-w/about/news/future-health-index/reports/2020/the-age-of-opportunity.html (Accessed on 8 February 2021).

PwC. (2017). What Physician? Why AI and Robotics Will Define New Health. Available at: https://www.pwc.com/gx/en/industries/healthcare/publications/ai-robotics-new-health/ai-robotics-new-health.pdf (Accessed on 8 February 2021).

Ross, S.E, Lin, C.-T. (2003). The Effects of Promoting Patient Access to Medical Records: A Review. *Journal of the American Medical Informatics Association* 10: 129–138, doi: 10.1197/jamia.M1147

Spence, P. (2020) Five Trends Driving the Emergence of the Personalised Health Ecosystem, Avaiable at: https://www.ey.com/en_gl/life-sciences/five-trends-driving-the-emergence-of-the-personalised-health-ecosystem (Accessed on 5 February 2021).

Starcevic, V., Berle, D., Arnáez, S. (2020) Recent Insights into Cyberchondria. *Current Psychiatry Reports* 22: 56, doi:10.1007/s11920-020-01179-8

Tan, S.S.L., Goonawardene, N. (2017). Internet Health Information Seeking and the Patient-Physician Relationship: A Systematic Review. *Journal of Medical Internet Research* 19(1): e9, doi: 10.2196/jmir.5729

The Medical Futurist. (2020, December 10). Available at: https://medicalfuturist.com/top-10-online-medical-resources (Accessed on 4 February 2021).

Topol, E. (2012). *The Creative Destruction of Medicine. How the Digital Revolution Will Create Better Healthcare.* New York: Basic Books.

Tubaishat, A. (2019). The Effect of Electronic Health Records on Patient Safety: A Qualitative Exploratory Study. *Informatics for Health and Social Care* 44(1): 79–91, doi: 10.1080/17538157.2017.1398753

White, R.W., Horvitz, E. (2009). Experiences with Web Search on Medical Concerns and Self-Diagnosis. *AMIA Annual Symposium Proceedings 2009*, 696–700.

Wicks, P., Mack Thorley, E., Simacek, K., Curran, C., Emmas, C. (2018). Scaling PatientsLikeMe via a "Generalized Platform" for Members with Chronic Illness: Web-Based Survey Study of Benefits Arising. *Journal of Medical Internet Research* 20(5): e175.

WHO. (2016). *The Global Strategy on Human Resources for Health: Workforce 2030.* Geneva, Switzerland: WHO.

14 The role of civil society organisations in Health 4.0 service delivery

Examples from Poland

Agnieszka Pacut and Kamila Pilch

Introduction

Civil society organisations (CSOs) are one of the stakeholders in the health system, alongside the state, the private sector, communities, and individuals (WHO, 2002, 2013, 2018). They make an important contribution to the health system by participating in public service delivery, policymaking, and governance. In practice, CSOs pursue a broad range of activities, especially in the direct delivery of disease prevention and health services, advocacy, setting standards, promoting community partnerships, mobilising resources (Greer et al., 2017) as well as testing and disseminating innovative solutions. Health CSOs are recognised as important actors at the local, national, and international level (McCoy & Gafton, 2020).

In recent years, the range and modes of delivery of health services have undergone complex transformations. They are due to changes in the public sphere that have resulted in reduced opportunities for applying hierarchical solutions to social problems and the development of mechanisms for multi-level governance of public affairs (Pollitt & Bouckaert, 2011). Not without significance are the transformations of the social sphere resulting from increasing citizens' expectations for the quality and accessibility of public services as well as the belief held by the key actors that it is more and more necessary to form coalitions of public, private, and civic organisations to achieve the agreed goals (Evers, 2005; Mitton et al., 2009; Stewart, 2013). An important rationale for change in the health system is the Fourth Industrial Revolution, which is the main point of reference in this book. The use of advanced information technologies affects the way the state, society as well as the economy operate, including health, healthcare, and global health (World Economic Forum, 2019). This leads to a new approach to healthcare known as Health 4.0 (discussed in more detail in Chapter 1 on the Fourth Industrial Revolution and the healthcare system).

In view of the above, the aim of this chapter is to identify the challenges to the activities of CSOs arising from the opportunities offered by the new solutions (Health 4.0) that emerge in the area of healthcare.

DOI: 10.4324/9781003144403-14

The considerations given here are theoretical and empirical in nature and are divided into three parts. First, the concept of CSOs and their importance in meeting social needs in the area of health, including in the context of Health 4.0, are outlined. This is followed by a discussion of qualitative empirical research - a series of case studies of Polish CSOs which implement programs involving the use of technology in the delivery of health services. The final section reviews and summarizes the findings of this research.

Civil society organisations in health

The term CSOs denotes grassroots, private, non-commercial forms of civic self-organisation as distinct from the public and commercial sectors. According to the structural-operational approach, these activities are pursued by a group of organisations that are formal, private, non-profit-distributing, self-governing, and voluntary (Salamon & Anheier, 1992). The UN statistical agency uses the term 'third sector' or 'social economy sector', and includes non-profit institutions, cooperatives, mutual societies, social enterprises, and voluntary work. It emphasises the legal diversity of these groups, the lack of government (or public sector) control over their activities and the provision of goods and services for free or at economically insignificant prices (United Nations et al., 2018). Both CSOs and other terms used in the literature (non-governmental organisations [NGOs], third sector, independent sector, social economy) are operationalised in different ways (Vakil, 1997), but they invariably refer to a diverse group of social actors (pressure groups, interest groups, activist organisations, professional, and voluntary bodies) that independently pursue common goals for the public good (Martens, 2002).

Studies conducted by the WHO identify four groups of (non-state) actors involved in the provision of health services and solutions (WHO, 2018):

- NGOs - non-profit entities operating in the public interest independently of government. They include foundations, associations, civil society groups and networks, disease-specific organisations, and patient groups.
- Private-sector entities - profit-making commercial enterprises, including private-sector operators and business associations representing enterprises, and international associations - not-for-profit private-sector entities representing the interests of their members (commercial enterprises, business associations).
- Public benefit organisations (charities, foundations) - non-profit entities whose assets are derived from donors. Their income is allocated for socially useful purposes.
- Academic institutions - entities engaged in the pursuit and dissemination of knowledge through research, education, and training.

In view of the purpose of this inquiry, the discussion below will focus on the activities of the first group, i.e. non-governmental organisations, which include foundations, associations, civil society groups, and networks.

D. Sanders, R. Labonte, F. Baum, and M. Chopra point to at least four not mutually exclusive ways of involving civil society in health research and service delivery, identifying the roles they play (Sanders et al., 2004):

- Sponsors (primarily disease charities)
- Users
- Generators (providers)
- Actors

In its report, the WHO identified five health system functions, in each case highlighting the role played in them by CSOs (WHO, 2001):

- Health services (providing services, improving the availability of services)
- Health promotion and information exchange (disseminating health information, conducting and using health research, helping to change public attitudes)
- Policy setting (representing public interests in policy, negotiating public health standards, increasing public support for policy)
- Resource mobilisation and allocation (financing health services, increasing community preferences for resource allocation, organising community co-financing of services)
- Monitoring quality of care and responsiveness (monitoring the responsiveness and quality of health services, giving voice to marginalised groups, promoting equity, advocating for patient rights on quality of care issues, communicating and negotiating patients' complaints and claims)

M.J. Roy, R. Baker, and S. Kerr identify four areas related to interventions undertaken by grassroots organisations in the area of health improvement and well-being (Roy et al., 2017): personal care services, arts and creativity, work integration, and community development. Activities in these areas are related to mental health, physical health and impact on social determinants (ibid.). Organisations provide services to beneficiaries to improve their health and living standards by engaging in a variety of projects (Figure 14.1).

In terms of the general functions of civic organisations, their health-related activities can be summarised as consisting of (Greer et al., 2017):

- Policymaking (evidence and agenda-setting, policy development, advocacy, mobilization, consensus-building, watchdog activity, accountability)
- Service delivery to the public and members
- Governance of health and healthcare (setting standards, self-regulation, social partnership) (Kickbusch & Gleicher, 2013)

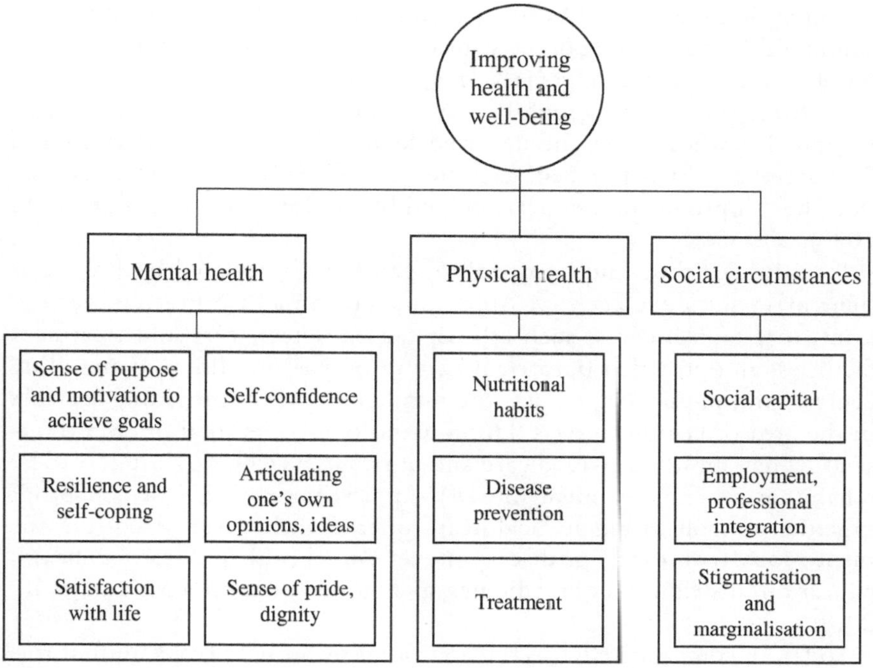

Figure 14.1 CSO interventions related to health and wellbeing.

Source: Own study based on Roy et al. (2017).

Health 2020 - the European policy for health and well-being in the 21st century - emphasises the need for improved intersectoral and interdepartmental governance in the area under analysis (Greer et al., 2017; Kickbusch & Gleicher, 2013; McQueen, 2012; WHO, 2013). The new governance model should involve individuals and community groups, as reflected in *The whole-of-society approach in Health 2020* (WHO, 2013). This concept assumes that the involvement of the whole society, including the private sector, NGOs, communities or individuals (cf. Chapter 5: Patient Empowerment in Health 4.0) should complement public policies, thus enabling more effective promotion, protection, and delivery of health and well-being services (Chapter 8: Co-creation in Health 4.0). In this chapter, we shall focus on exploring the provision of e-health solutions.

CSOs in Poland and their role in healthcare

In Poland and in other Central and Eastern European countries, CSOs have played a major political role in restoring pluralism, democracy, and civil society. Now their main objectives include: to address social needs which cannot be met by the state or the market, combat social marginalisation and exclusion, mobilise the initiative of individuals and groups, stimulate social discourse, innovation, and freedom at all levels of the social structure, social control of the functioning of the state and business, as well as facilitate institutional and systemic changes (Hausner, 2006).

In 2018, there were about 101 thousand non-profit organisations in Poland. Healthcare was the declared focus of 4.2% of associations and foundations, which pursued activities in such fields as disease prevention, health promotion, education, and blood donation (Borysiak et al., 2020).

In 2016, 3.9 thousand non-profit organisations declared healthcare as their main statutory activity. Approximately, 85% of NPOs ran various kinds of establishments, such as hospitals, hospices, care and treatment facilities, and provided outpatient care in outpatient clinics, counselling centres, and physicians' offices (the number of NPOs providing services in the area of healthcare was 0.6 thousand out of the total of 28.5 thousand). They mostly provided care and nursing services (50%) followed by rehabilitation and treatment (36.4%). Approximately, 15% of non-profit organisations operating in healthcare offered their services outside the institutional context (e.g. disease prevention, health promotion, health education, distribution of medicines, and blood donation) (Banduła et al., 2018).

So far, in comparative terms the non-profit sector has played a minor role in the provision of healthcare services in Poland in institutionalised form - 2% of facilities were run by the civil sector, 13.4% by the public sector, and 84.6% by other actors. NPOs provided services to 2 million recipients, mainly people with disabilities, dependents, the terminally and chronically ill, children, and young people (Banduła et al., 2018).

Under contract with the National Health Fund, associations and foundations provided 1.3 thousand services in the area of outpatient care (e.g. clinics, counselling services, and physicians' offices), rehabilitation and therapy as well as long-term care. Most of these services (0.8 thousand) were provided by associations and the remaining 0.5 thousand by foundations (Borysiak et al., 2020).

The ways and forms of service provision in healthcare are subject to change as a result of the impact of the Fourth Industrial Revolution (see Chapter 1: The Fourth Industrial Revolution and the Healthcare System). The ensuing profound transformations can be observed both in developed and developing countries (Luna et al., 2014, p. 3) and are associated with the widespread use of new equipment and technologies, including communication technologies (cf. Chapter 3: Technologies Enhancing Health 4.0). This revolution removes barriers between man and machine (Ćwiklicki et al., 2020, p. 1), and in broadly conceived healthcare, it translates into the possibility to use Industry 4.0 technologies (such as big data, the Internet of Things, cyber-physical systems, 5G, and others).

A survey conducted in Poland by the Digital Poland Foundation reveals that the vast majority of the respondents (92%) consider health as an area where new technologies should be used (Digital Poland Foundation, 2019, p. 84). A total of 89% of the respondents are ready to wear wristbands to relay their health data, whereas 34% would agree to be operated on by a robot. The groups most open to new technologies in medicine include men, younger people, and residents of large cities. In the cited report, the authors present forecasts on the future use of new technologies in healthcare in the short and long term (Table 14.1).

The use of modern technologies in the provision of health services reflects the transformation of the entire system of healthcare and disease prevention. A study conducted by the authors identified a knowledge gap related to the impact of the Fourth Industrial Revolution on the activities of CSOs in the area of health, especially the perceived benefits and barriers in the delivery of Health 4.0 solutions.

Table 14.1 Forecasts on the use of new technologies in health

Short-term forecasts	*Long-term forecasts*
E-prescriptions; electronic repeat dispensing service. Automatic checks which nearest pharmacy stocks the needed medicine. Mobile apps enabling users to purchase medicines remotely.	Telemedicine, teleconsultations, smartwatches, or devices that monitor vital functions, alert and enable real-time communication with physicians 24/7.
E-booking system in medical facilities complete with information on waiting time.	Faster diagnosis and symptom recognition thanks to artificial intelligence and machine learning.
Central Electronic Patient Record System and Central Vaccination Register.	Digitalisation of patient data, services, insurers, service providers, diseases, imaging studies, test results enabling real-time analysis and prediction of health status of both individuals and whole populations.
Longer waiting times for consultations; increasing costs of private healthcare.	Common and inexpensive genome testing for every patient. Possibility to copy and transplant genes.
Central system of approvals for the use of medical data, transplants, and transfusions.	Delivery of medicines using drones.
System of information on diseases and medicines, self-service assistance and answers to queries and problems of sick people.	New kinds of insurance based on health, lifestyle, and diet monitoring etc.
E-prescriptions to purchase medicines in other EU countries.	Surgeries performed remotely or by robots without physician supervision.
	Prevention is better than cure: real-time monitoring, research using artificial intelligence, machine learning.
	Tailored diets, well-being, Food 2.0 (meat, milk, egg substitutes and test-tube foods).
	Software-only therapies

Source: Own study based on Digital Poland Foundation (2019).

Methodology of the study

The aim of the study was to identify the challenges posed by the Fourth Industrial Revolution to CSOs operating in the area of health.

The following specific questions were formulated in the research process:

- What is the rationale for the use of modern technologies in health services delivered by CSOs?
- What are the outcomes of actions taken by CSOs?
- What problems have been identified by CSOs in the delivery of solutions using the latest technologies?

The study was exploratory in nature (Denzin & Lincoln, 2018). Even though it presents a narrow and fragmentary perspective illustrating the experiences of Polish CSOs, it may serve as a useful reference point for other Central and Eastern European countries (Sześciło, 2017).

Due to the nature of the questions, the study was conducted using qualitative research tools (individual in-depth interviews, IDIs) among Polish CSOs that employ state-of-the-art technologies to achieve their statutory goals in the area of healthcare. The interviews were conducted in the first quarter of 2021 via the Zoom platform. Individuals who were considered to have special insight into the subject in question (purposive selection; cf. Creswell, 2014) were approached. An overview of the research process is show below (Figure 14.2).

The first step of the process involved identifying those CSOs in Poland that use modern technologies. The search yielded a list of existing projects in the area studied, which were subsequently categorised according to the adopted criteria:

- CSOs and other entities involved
- Area of intervention (prevention, diagnosis, analysis, treatment, telerehabilitation, e-documentation, monitoring, etc.)

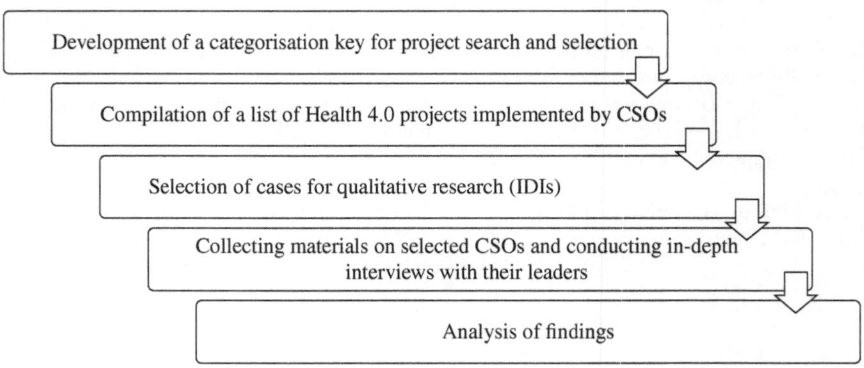

Figure 14.2 Overview of the research process.

Source: Own study.

- Project status (pilot, implementation, ongoing, completed)
- Recipients (project target groups)
- Type of service
- Technology used
- Scope of the project (local, national)

The database of organisations and projects implemented by them was then divided by the tools (technology) used, the target group, and the type of service provided in an attempt to diversify the group of the respondents. Respondent characteristics are presented in Annex 1. Next, in-depth interviews were conducted with six representatives of CSOs. The responses obtained were supplemented by a review of materials on the studied organisations and the projects implemented by them. The results were then coded and processed using NVIVO software, which supports qualitative data analysis.

The study results

The study is discussed in three thematic sections (rationales, outcomes, and barriers to implementing new solutions using the latest technologies by CSOs) and illustrated with quotations from the interviews. Each quote is assigned a respondent number (e.g. R1; cf. Appendix 1).

Rationales

The starting point of the study was to find out about the circumstances and rationales for the use of modern technologies by CSOs in achieving their statutory goals related to health protection and promotion. The reasons for the use of new technologies varied among the studied group of organisations. The *internal* ones resulted from the perception of the importance of new technologies in life, individuals interests of the founders and employees, their recognition of the need to professionalise in order to achieve their statutory goals more effectively as well as the needs of a given CSO itself.

> From the very outset at the Foundation, we assumed that we would use new technologies. It is natural for us that we want to move with the spirit of the times. Such is the world we live in and we need to use these tools. Because they allow us to reach different groups.
>
> (R3)

This was supported by personal interest in new technologies of those involved in the organisation's activity.

The decision to use new technologies was informed by the needs of CSOs in the area of knowledge and information management. For the respondents, access to modern software and working tools meant in practice gaining new insights into the behaviour of their beneficiaries. This enabled them to deliver better targeted interventions.

> … In our work and, more broadly, in our philosophy, the organisation is constantly seeking better solutions for the rehabilitation and employment support of our charges … The market cannot do without technology, but it is also the future of therapy, including groups such as our charges.
>
> (R1)

New technologies were also perceived as a tool to enable development and provide actual support for the organisation's beneficiaries in finding gainful employment. Virtually all the respondents believed that new technologies should be implemented in the day-to-day functioning of their organisations:

> New technologies enable us to move forward in different areas of our interest. Thanks to them we can really do a lot to assist people with disabilities. You can't leave these people in backwater areas, where absolutely nothing happens. They first become isolated at school, and then in society … New technologies provide opportunities to change this situation.
>
> (R3)

The current way of providing healthcare and/or disease prevention services - be it by governmental institutions, medical institutions or organisations - was recognised as ineffective or inadequate to the needs. This is exemplified by the following statement:

> Problem areas or trends that are emerging [were identified] on the basis of interviews with all the medical staff, parents, and patients … and then an extensive report was compiled as far as the hospital of the future is concerned, in which we identified areas particularly prone to change … areas where technologies are beginning to emerge or those that lack innovation, process optimisation, etc.
>
> (R5)

The interest in new solutions was also influenced by *external* factors - cooperation with other entities from Poland and abroad, unmet needs of beneficiaries, and public programmes in support of social and technological innovations. The cooperation of CSOs with other entities - commercial or social ones - sparked interest in new technologies and services, and encouraged the respondents to prepare projects based on them.

Inspirations on the kind of technology to apply in the projects carried out by the respondents often came from the observation of trends and systems used abroad:

> During extensive research on innovations in the field of healthcare, we found a description of one such system and started to do further research on how effective it actually was. These are mainly inspirations

> from foreign hospitals, especially from Western hospitals (…) we started to look at the situation in Poland … and how we can implement such pilot projects in order to have tangible results so that we can talk to the National Health Fund about spreading such innovations to other hospitals.
>
> (R5)

The rationale behind the use of modern technologies to achieve statutory goals also resulted from the unmet needs of CSO beneficiaries. Respondent 2 (R2) mentioned a number of systems available on the market intended for persons with vision impairment, but considered them inadequate to the needs and expectations of potential recipients. These needs inspired them to design an original smartphone tool/app to improve the coping skills of vision-impaired people in their families as well as social and professional lives.

> A vision-impaired person who wants to use the currently available apps has to rely on volunteer help. And this is generally OK, but in a home environment. (…). Good intentions alone are not enough … Another issue is the availability of these volunteers and the quality of their help.
>
> (R2)

People's needs in the area of healthcare and health promotion identified by R3 involved knowledge deficits, among others, in the diagnostics and treatment of rare diseases, systemic forms of support, treatment and rehabilitation or social attitudes promoting the adaptation of people with disabilities to new working environments.

> We try to go out into the world and respond to the needs of different groups. People often call us with very basic questions, because they cannot get information about rehabilitation, funding, etc. People need knowledge. It's not like they just go to the right website and search by themselves. With us, on the website or in the app, they have everything organised in one place.
>
> (R3)

In the group studied, an important stimulus to act was provided not only by unmet needs but also by the feelings and expectations of the beneficiaries as regards the scope of assistance and the ways in which it could be delivered. For vision-impaired people as recipients of R2 activities, it was important to receive support covering different aspects of their social and professional functioning. But they found it equally important that such support should ensure the subjectivity and autonomy of its recipients, and should be provided as a professional service, not as an aid.

CSOs' interest was also attracted by programmes for the promotion of innovative solutions offered by public and/or social institutions. The respondents mentioned programmes to encourage social innovation intended to address the problems faced by dependent and socially excluded individuals. For many of them, they offered an opportunity to devise new forms of activity, including those involving the latest technologies.

It is worth noting that the rationales and motives presented above were intertwined, and CSO representatives attributed varying importance to them.

Outcomes

The respondents were positive about the organisational and social outcomes achieved thanks to projects which involved the application of modern technologies. They contributed to time savings for the CSOs' staff and beneficiaries, while improving the efficiency of their operation.

> As soon as we introduced this system in our organisation and when it really started to work, when people started to use it, well, our interpreters [of sign language] didn't have to go outside so often to interpret; so thanks to this interpreting process in general, we can help more people (…) so there more things can be done, which is just as well, because they tend to grow in numbers.
>
> (R6)

Innovative solutions also served to professionalise support for beneficiaries, improve the services offered as well as expand the organisations' range of activities. They created real opportunities for them to provide support to more people, including new target groups. Moreover, most the respondents highly appreciated their positive experiences with new technologies in supporting their beneficiaries in the area of health. They provided an incentive to look for novelties and to use technology on an ongoing basis.

> It is worth doing, investing in unconventional projects, including those using technology. The more eclectic our approach to the needs of people with disabilities, the more effective our work becomes. And technological innovations serve this purpose.
>
> (R1)

Barriers to implementation

The analysis of the respondents' experiences of implementing and developing projects using modern technologies in health promotion and care revealed four problem areas: technological, financial, organisational, and social. The organisations studied were unable to develop such complex technology on their own. Due to its specialist nature, they had to purchase it on the market.

> Of course we had to find a technological partner, because we wouldn't have been able to do it on our own, we didn't have the right people who could introduce such technology, besides, maintaining such a system in this technological context is time-consuming, labour-intensive, and you need to have the right knowledge. We decided to look for a partner who would run this system with us, found one, and we have been working with him from the very beginning … but these technological challenges are still there, because technologies keep developing, they keep changing.
>
> (R6)

Quite often, the non-standard product needed was simply unavailable. At other times, it required taking into account specific needs and/or limitations of individual beneficiaries, which cannot always be anticipated or taken into account by software writers. As a result, the respondents complained about the prototypical nature of the devices they used both in terms of design and functionality.

> We had a lot of technical glitches with the app … What bothered me was, above all, that the app should be universally accessible and, of course, meet the needs of vision-impaired people.
>
> (R2)

All the organisations raised the issue of funding, citing it as a key success factor. As almost none of them had sufficient means to implement innovative projects independently, hence they were forced to seek external funding. Its sources included public institutions (mostly European Union's contribution), commercial entities, private donors, and sponsors. Finding the funds to cover the costs of invention, purchase the technology, and tide themselves over the kick-off stage required hard work and great creativity on the part of all the organisations. Still, it was even more challenging to find financial backing to continue the projects in question, including the evaluation and upgrading of the tool, promotion of the solution or the provision of funding for the project implementers - the CSO staff.

> The problem of finances, how to fund this project so that it may go on. An IT project such as an app requires constant financial backing for it to be efficient and operable … libraries, the so-called data libraries, for example, need to be regularly updated … it would be best to do it at least once a year, and preferably every six months to make sure that this app runs correctly, well, it would be nice to have money for promoting it, we tried to get it here, too, but, well, we didn't succeed … now projects could start to support those innovations that are already underway … it is difficult for us to get to these new incubators with our project, because it is not new.
>
> (R4)

The lack of funds at this stage prevented some the respondents from continuing their projects.

The problems experienced by CSOs in using new technologies also had an organisational aspect, which was associated with the shortage of human resources that could join the project and support its implementation not only in organisational but also in substantive terms. When putting together a team, one must take into account the interest of its prospective members in new technologies, their organisational skills, and their current workload.

> People [members of the association] work in different institutions and … we don't work at the association on a daily basis … the time factor, however … the fact that we don't work here full-time, because then it would be different, then I could focus more, at least on looking for funds.
>
> (R4)

The respondents pointed out that effective project implementation, including the safety of the people involved, requires educating the beneficiaries and organisations' representatives in operating modern technology devices. The device in question must take into account both the skills and limitations or dysfunctions of beneficiaries. Moreover, random people off the street can hardly play the role of assistants (partners) on the part of an organisation.

> The digital skills of society in general, but especially among the elderly … are far from great, so we had to start training up deaf people so that they are not afraid to communicate via the Internet, so that they try to take advantage of the fact that they can really deal with issues effectively … all the time, we are working on [partners and beneficiaries] to convince them that this way of communication is really good, you can use it and you can do what you need as quickly as possible.
>
> (R6)

An organisational problem that makes it difficult to scale up innovative projects and ensure their sustainability is the insufficient scope and intensity of cooperation between CSOs and public policy makers. One of the functions of CSOs recognised in the literature is to test innovations and to be the agents of change (Kramer, 1981). The CSOs studied have implemented innovations on a micro scale, but due to their limited capacity they have been unable to disseminate their achievements or ensure their sustainability on their own.

> NGOs function as if they were street musicians. For example, we find a solution and we are unable to disseminate it throughout Poland due

> to the fact that by definition it is a microinnovation and the scale of our activity is small. There just has to be someone higher up to take this idea further and spread it to other organisations.
>
> (R2)

The use of new technologies and the resulting changes in the provision of health services requires a change in the organisation of activities not only on the part of CSOs or their beneficiaries but also on the part of partners (such as health centres and hospitals). In this context, the respondents mentioned the need to convince their partners that changing procedures offers a long-term potential for improvement.

> The first challenge is to persuade the medical staff, that is, the people, to change. People who work in hospitals, who have relied on well-known and established practices for years, it is difficult to convince both the staff and the patient, because they are afraid of it. Their fear comes from ignorance, lack of interaction with such technology
>
> (R5)

One respondent commented on an important issue related to a technical solution used to improve a certain medical service, namely the risk that beneficiaries (patients) would become overly dependent on it:

> [It is imperative] not to make the patient dependent on [a piece] of technology … if we are dealing with such an absorbing technology and such interesting content, it may lead to a situation in which the patient will be unable to undergo the procedure without this technology, but we want to equip the patient with a tool for creating positive associations with the procedure itself, so what we are going to do is to develop content to educate the patient.
>
> (R5)

A list of factors associated with the implementation of Health 4.0 systems and solutions by CSOs, including the rationales, outcomes, and identified problems, is presented in Figure 14.3. However, the limitations of the analysis resulting from the specificity of the methodology applied must be borne in mind. As was noted at the outset, our research was exploratory in nature, and the use of qualitative techniques to collect research material means that the results obtained cannot be generalised or treated as statistically significant. Moreover, due to the purposive selection of the sample, the findings and conclusions are based solely on the analysis of the group studied. In this context, it would be interesting to carry out quantitative research, which would permit a statistical validation of the relationships identified in our study.

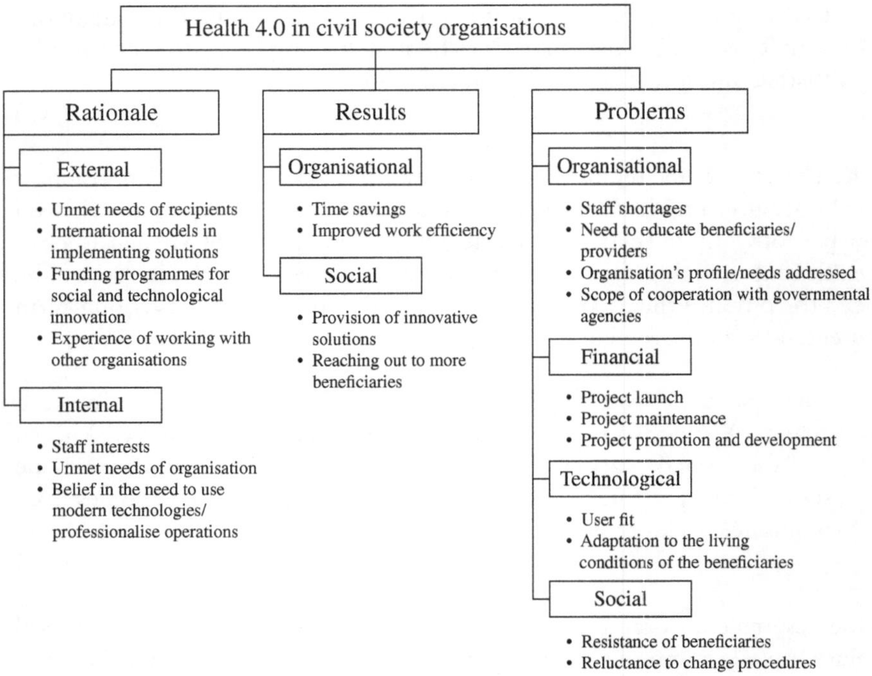

Figure 14.3 Components of implementing Health 4.0 solutions in CSOs.

Source: Own study.

Discussion of research findings

The term 'e-health' was used for the first time by Mitchell in 1999. Since then, researchers looking at the experiences of implementing solutions that draw on modern technologies in the delivery of health services have shown both the benefits and the barriers or challenges associated with them. This chapter focuses on one group involved in the delivery of health services, namely CSOs. The aim of the study was to identify the benefits and challenges faced by these organisations in carrying out projects in the area of interest. From this perspective, it is interesting to compare our findings and conclusions with those reached by other researchers who deal with e-health. Thus, as regards the benefits that may accrue thanks to the implementation of modern technologies in the provision of health services, it seems that they are universal in relation to all entities that provide e-health services. The observation that the positive impact of technology on efficiency may translate into better patient care is supported by the available research on electronic health records (Bell & Thornton, 2011; Buntin et al., 2011; Chaudhry et al., 2006; Kumar & Bauer, 2011; Wildenbos et al., 2016). It is worth emphasising that due to the context in which the CSOs operate (including the limited financial and organisational resources), of particular importance are the social benefits associated with the possibility to provide services based on modern technologies. The respondents underscored the fact that the needs of their actual and potential beneficiaries are quite specific and it is for this reason that the latter turn to them for help (due to the limited possibilities to obtain it from others). e-Health thus not only has a positive impact on the effectiveness of CSOs' operations but also permits them to provide innovative solutions to people who otherwise would be unlikely to take advantage of them.

Introducing change and innovation is invariably fraught with difficulties. In e-health, these are discussed in relation to the development and subsequent use of the analysed systems and solutions. Researchers consider them both in terms of specific disease groups (e.g. in the area of mental health this issue was addressed by: Batterham et al., 2015; Hadjistavropoulos et al., 2017; Kip et al., 2021) and meta-analyses on barriers to e-health implementation (Ross et al., 2016; Schreiweis et al., 2019).

The study discussed above helped us identify e-health-related challenges that representatives of Polish social organisations encountered when implementing projects in the area under consideration. Our findings complement those available in the literature. In this context, it is worth mentioning the conclusions drawn from the literature review conducted by B. Schreiweis, M. Pobiruchin, V. Stotbaum, J. Suleder, M. Weisner, and B. Bergh on the benefits of and barriers to e-health projects (Schreiweis et al., 2019). The authors compiled a list 76 barriers described by researchers, which can be subsumed under three main categories: individual, environmental, and technical (ibid.). Ten most common ones are listed below (ibid.):

- Limited knowledge of e-health
- Lack of necessary equipment
- Problems with funding
- Cognitive barriers
- Security
- Motivation
- Accessibility
- Solutions not tailored to the needs of intended recipients
- Confidentiality
- Lack of fit with organisational structures
- Excessive workload

Not all the barriers described in the literature on social organisations were identified by Polish respondents; nevertheless, the most pressing problems undoubtedly comprise insufficient financial resources and excessive workload. These appear to be the universal characteristic features of the environments in which most CSOs operate (and affect not only with the provision of health services using new technologies). The respondents also noted the presence of cognitive barriers mostly due to the fear of new technologies, especially on the part of beneficiaries. However, it is worth noting that in the projects analysed for the purposes of our study no mention was made of lack of motivation or limited knowledge about e-health. Accordingly, it can be concluded that CSOs not only have a positive attitude towards e-health projects but also actively seek information about the possibilities to implement them in their activities.

Conclusions

In this chapter, the concept of Health 4.0 was discussed in the context of the activities of CSOs as an important stakeholder group in health service delivery and advocacy, policy development and standard-setting in healthcare and public health (WHO, 2001). The authors identified the rationales, outcomes, and problems with implementing the promises of the Fourth Industrial Revolution by the CSOs. So far, this topic has been poorly recognised and rarely addressed by researchers.

The findings discussed above testify that CSOs can successfully apply a wide range of technologies in pursuit of their statutory objectives in health protection and promotion. New technologies offer them numerous opportunities to address the health needs of their beneficiaries in a more professional, innovative, and effective manner. This chapter comments on the various goals and undertakings carried out by non-profit organisations in the field of healthcare, a number of technological tools (e.g. smartphone apps, biometric wristbands, virtual reality devices), and the target groups that use them (people with disabilities, including vision-impaired people, adults with autism spectrum disorders, children, employers, and others). All this points to the huge potential of modern technologies to meet the needs of citizens-patients and charges of NGOs.

In order to ensure that the implemented projects are effective, the tools should be matched to the skills as well as the limitations/dysfunctions of the intended beneficiaries. As important as inventing and implementing a modern technology-based solution or service is its periodic evaluation and updating, but its sustainability tends to depend to a great extent on the availability of sufficient funds.

In the context of Health 4.0, the following challenges identified by representatives of CSOs should inform the perspective of public decision makers:

1 The civil sector should be supported in using information and communication technologies (ICT) tools, artificial intelligence, and other modern solutions more widely in ways which, apart from being effective, are also ethical and safe for beneficiaries.
2 CSOs can play an important role in testing and disseminating innovative health solutions based on modern technologies, while their easy access to target groups (beneficiaries) encourages pilot projects. The positive

image of CSOs offers great opportunities to promote and strengthen the legitimacy of such solutions. CSOs use new technologies to empower their beneficiaries, foster their independence, and improve the latter's well-being by developing their ability to tap into the information resources held by the electronic media, use other ICT tools and platforms devised specifically for healthcare applications.

3 CSOs' in-depth knowledge of the needs of their target groups (patients, beneficiaries), including ways to meet them effectively using modern technologies as well as their ability to rapidly identify and diagnose social problems are the reasons why their potential should be utilised in research and development works initiated by public policy makers, commercial entities, academic circles, and their partnerships in the area of health. Given the expertise and competencies of CSOs, they should be routinely involved in setting research priorities and selecting tools with which to support the recipients of health services.

The findings of this study fill the knowledge gap in the area of CSOs' experiences in the provision of e-health services by comparing and contrasting the challenges and benefits of e-health projects as described in the literature with those of the representatives of Polish CSOs. An analysis of their perspective helps us gain an insight into the specificity of their operations and to formulate recommendations on their role in the delivery of Health 4.0 solutions.

References

Banduła, K., Borysiak, K., Jajkiewicz, I., Jarębska, K., Kazanecka, M., Makowska-Belta, E., Sekuła, T., Stasiak-Jaśkiewicz, U., & Wilk, R. (2018). *Rola sektora non-profit w dostarczaniu usług społecznych w latach 2014–2016/The role of the non-profit sector in provision of social services in 2014–2016*, Warszawa-Kraków: Główny Urząd Statystyczny.

Batterham, P. J., Sunderland, M., Calear, A. L., Davey, C. G., Christensen, H., Teesson, M., Kay-Lambkin, F., Andrews, G., Mitchell, P. B., Herrman, H., Butow, P. N., & Krouskos, D. (2015). Developing a roadmap for the translation of e-mental health services for depression. *Australian & New Zealand Journal of Psychiatry, 49*(9), 776–784. https://doi.org/10.1177/0004867415582054

Bell, B., & Thornton, K. (2011). From promise to reality: Achieving the value of an EHR. *Healthcare Financial Management: Journal of the Healthcare, 65*, 50–56.

Borysiak, K., Dąbrowski, D., Fediuk, A., Jajkiewicz, I., Jarębska, K., Kielińska, E., Knapp, A., Kowalska-Żak, K., Makowska-Belta, E., Organek, L., Sadłoń, W., Sekuła, T., Stasiak-Jaśkiewicz, U., Główny Urząd Statystyczny (GUS), & Urząd Statystyczny (Kraków). (2020). *Sektor non-profit w 2018 r./The non-profit sector in 2018*, Warszawa-Kraków: Główny Urząd Statystyczny.

Buntin, M. B., Burke, M. F., Hoaglin, M. C., & Blumenthal, D. (2011). The benefits of health information technology: A review of the recent literature shows predominantly positive results. *Health Affairs, 30*(3), 464–471. https://doi.org/10.1377/hlthaff.2011.0178

Chaudhry, B., Wang, J., Wu, S., Maglione, M., Mojica, W., Roth, E., Morton, S. C., & Shekelle, P. G. (2006). Systematic review: Impact of health information technology on quality, efficiency, and costs of medical care. *Annals of Internal Medicine*, *144*(10), 742. https://doi.org/10.7326/0003-4819-144-10-200605160-00125

Creswell, J. W. (2014). *Research design: Qualitative, quantitative, and mixed methods approaches* (4th ed.), Thousand Oaks: SAGE.

Ćwiklicki, M., Klich, J., & Chen, J. (2020). The adaptiveness of the healthcare system to the Fourth Industrial Revolution: A preliminary analysis. *Futures*, *122*, 102602. https://doi.org/10.1016/j.futures.2020.102602

Denzin, N. K., & Lincoln, Y. S. (Red.). (2018). *The SAGE handbook of qualitative research* (5th ed.),Thousand Oaks: SAGE.

Digital Poland Foundation. (2019). Technologia w służbie społeczeństwu. *Czy Polacy zostaną społeczeństwem 5.0?*, Warszawa: Fundacja Digital Poland. https://www.digitalpoland.org/assets/publications/spoleczenstwo-50/technologia-w-sluzbie-spoleczenstwu-czy-polacy-zostana-spoleczenstwem-50.pdf

Evers, A. (2005). Mixed welfare systems and hybrid organisations: Changes in the governance and provision of social services. *International Journal of Public Administration*, *28*(9–10), 737–748. https://doi.org/10.1081/PAD-200067318

Greer, S. L., Wismar, M., & Kosinska, M. (2017). What is civil society and what can it do for health? *Civil society and health: Contributions and potential*. Copenhagen: WHO Regional Office for Europe,.

Hadjistavropoulos, H. D., Nugent, M. M., Dirkse, D., & Pugh, N. (2017). Implementation of internet-delivered cognitive behavior therapy within community mental health clinics: A process evaluation using the consolidated framework for implementation research. *BMC Psychiatry*, *17*(1), 331. https://doi.org/10.1186/s12888-017-1496-7

Hausner, J. (2006). Organisacje pozarządowe—Trzeci sektor współczesnego społeczeństwa. *Zeszyty Naukowe Akademii Ekonomicznej w Krakowie*, *714*, 5–21.

Kickbusch, I., & Gleicher, D. (2013). *Governance for health in the 21st century*. Copenhagen: World Health Organisation, Regional Office for Europe.

Kip, H., Oberschmidt, K., & Bierbooms, J. J. P. A. (2021). e-health technology in forensic mental healthcare: Recommendations for achieving benefits and overcoming barriers. *International Journal of Forensic Mental Health*, *20*(1), 31–47. https://doi.org/10.1080/14999013.2020.1808914

Kumar, S., & Bauer, K. (2011). The business case for implementing electronic health records in primary care settings in the United States. *Journal of Revenue and Pricing Management*, *10*(2), 119–131. https://doi.org/10.1057/rpm.2009.14

Kramer, R. M. (1981). *Voluntary agencies in the welfare state*. Berkeley: University of California Press.

Luna, D., Almerares, A., Mayan, J. C., González Bernaldo de Quirós, F., & Otero, C. (2014). Health informatics in developing countries: Going beyond pilot practices to sustainable implementations: A review of the current challenges. *Healthcare Informatics Research*, *20*(1), 3. https://doi.org/10.4258/hir.2014.20.1.3

Martens, K. (2002). Mission impossible? Defining nongovernmental organisations. *Voluntas: International Journal of Voluntary and Nonprofit Organisations*, *13*(3), 271–285. https://doi.org/10.1023/A:1020341526691

McCoy, D., & Gafton, J. (2020). Civil society and global health politics. In W. C. McInnes, K. Lee, & J. Youde (Red.), *The Oxford handbook of global health politics* (pp. 365–385). Oxford University Press. https://doi.org/10.1093/oxfordhb/9780190456818.013.22

McQueen, D. V. (Red.). (2012). *Intersectoral governance for health in all policies: Structures, actions and experiences*. Copenhagen: WHO, Regional Off. for Europe.

Mitchell, J. (1999). *From tele-health to e-Health: The unstoppable rise of e-health*. Department of Communications, Information Technology and the Arts.

Mitton, C., Smith, N., Peacock, S., Evoy, B., & Abelson, J. (2009). Public participation in healthcare priority setting: A scoping review. *Health Policy, 91*(3), 219–228. https://doi.org/10.1016/j.healthpol.2009.01.005

Pollitt, C., & Bouckaert, G. (2011). *Public management reform: A comparative analysis: New public management, governance, and the neo-Weberian state* (3rd ed). New York: Oxford University Press.

Ross, J., Stevenson, F., Lau, R., & Murray, E. (2016). Factors that influence the implementation of e-health: A systematic review of systematic reviews (an update). *Implementation Science, 11*(1), 146. https://doi.org/10.1186/s13012-016-0510-7

Roy, M. J., Baker, R., & Kerr, S. (2017). Conceptualising the public health role of actors operating outside of formal health systems: The case of social enterprise. *Social Science & Medicine, 172*, 144–152. https://doi.org/10.1016/j.socscimed.2016.11.009

Salamon, L. M., & Anheier, H. K. (1992). In search of the non-profit sector. I: The question of definitions. *Voluntas, 3*(2), 125–151. https://doi.org/10.1007/BF01397770

Sanders, D., Labonte, R., Baum, F., & Chopra, M. (2004). Making research matter: A civil society perspective on health research. *Bulletin of the World Health Organisation, 82*(10), 757–763.

Schreiweis, B., Pobiruchin, M., Strotbaum, V., Suleder, J., Wiesner, M., & Bergh, B. (2019). Barriers and facilitators to the implementation of e-health services: Systematic literature analysis. *Journal of Medical Internet Research, 21*(11), e14197. https://doi.org/10.2196/14197

Stewart, E. (2013). What is the point of citizen participation in healthcare? *Journal of Health Services Research & Policy, 18*(2), 124–126. https://doi.org/10.1177/1355819613485670

Sześciło, D. (2017). *Zmierzch decentralizacji?: Instytucjonalny krajobraz opieki zdrowotnej w Europie po nowym zarządzaniu publicznym*. Warszawa:, Wydawnictwo Naukowe Scholar.

United Nations, Department of Economic and Social Affairs, United Nations, & Statistical Division. (2018). Handbook of National Accounting: Satellite account on non-profit and related institutions and volunteer work, Series F No.91, Rev.1, New York: United Nations.

Vakil, A. C. (1997). Confronting the classification problem: Toward a taxonomy of NGOs. *World Development, 25*(12), 2057–2070. https://doi.org/10.1016/S0305-750X(97)00098-3

WHO. (2001). *Strategic alliances. The role of civil society in health* [Discussion Paper No. 1]. Geneva: World Health Organisation.

WHO. (2002). *WHO's interactions with civil society and nongovernmental organisations: Review report*. Geneva: World Health Organisation.

WHO. (2013). *Health 2020: A European policy framework supporting action across government and society for health and well-being*. Copenhagen: WHO Regional Office for Europe.

WHO. (2018). *Handbook for Non-State Actors on Engagement with the World Health Organisations*, Geneva: Word Health Organization.

Wildenbos, G. A., Peute, L. W., & Jaspers, M. W. M. (2016). Impact of patient-centered e-health applications on patient outcomes: a review on the mediating influence of human factor issues. *Yearbook of Medical Informatics, 25*(01), 113–119. https://doi.org/10.15265/IY-2016-031

World Economic Forum. (2019). Strategic Intelligence, https://intelligence.weforum.org/topics/a1Gb0000001RIhBEAW?tab=publications

Appendix 1 Characteristics of the CSOs studied

Designation	*Legal form*	*Main statutory objectives*	*Technology used*	*Area of activity*	*Target group*	*Organisation size*
R1	Foundation	To help children and adults with disabilities, their families, and to develop systemic solutions to improve their quality of life.	Biometric wristbands	Diagnostics, analytics	People with disabilities	Large
R2	Association	To support the advancement of people with disabilities; to improve their situation in the family, society, and the labour market.	Smartphone app	Monitoring	Vision-impaired persons	Large
R3	Foundation	To help people in need, at risk of social exclusion, their families and carers in the field of treatment, therapy, care, and education.	Smartphone app, website	Prevention, diagnosis, dissemination	People with disabilities, their families, carers; employers	Small
R4	Foundation	To provide innovative solutions to improve the comfort of the medical staff, reduce patient stress, to speed up procedures and change the hospital experience as a whole.	Virtual reality	Treatment	Cancer patients (4–11 years of age)	Large
R5	Association	To organise activities for people with different disabilities; to protect and promote health; to provide education; to provide information; to shape positive attitudes towards people with different types of disabilities.	Smartphone app	Monitoring, dissemination of information	Dependent persons	Small
R6	Association	To associate, integrate and rehabilitate deaf people and those with impaired hearing; to jointly resolve their problems; to equalise developmental, educational, professional and social opportunities.	Communication platform	Monitoring, dissemination of information	Hearing-impaired people	Large

Source: Own study.

15 Recommendations for implementing Industry 4.0 in the healthcare system

Marek Ćwiklicki, Jacek Klich, and Michał Żabiński

Introduction

The issues of Health 4.0 raised in this book inform a number of recommendations for those who provide and benefit from its solutions. In this chapter, we underscore the need for a holistic and iterative approach to implementing the achievements of the Fourth Industrial Revolution in the national healthcare systems. First, we review the main problems and concerns in the development of Health 4.0 and then formulate recommendations which draw on the deliberations presented so far in this book as relevant for the main groups of stakeholders in healthcare, i.e. the government, non-governmental organisations (NGOs), patients, health professionals, and health managers. We conclude by pointing out the critical role of government in this area.

Threats and problems in the development of Health 4.0

The process of implementing Health 4.0 solutions is gathering momentum, but its actual pace seems to greatly depend on the wealth of a given economy (Slakey & Davidson, 2019). The vast majority of research findings on new Health 4.0 solutions comes from highly developed countries, as they require the commitment of substantial financial resources (Marino & Lorenzoni, 2019). Moreover, access to Health 4.0 services is contingent on Internet access, and in this area huge inequalities persist. While developed countries boast the Internet access rate of 81%, in developing ones only 17.5% of the population enjoys such access (Lopes et al., 2019).

The four key drivers for the development of Healthcare 4.0 are

a international harmonisation of quality standards for services, technologies, and solutions in the healthcare and medical industries (Iizuka & Ikeda, 2019),
b development of legislative pathways that promote efficient verification and implementation of new solutions in the national healthcare systems (Castro e Melo & Faria Araújo, 2020; Iizuka & Ikeda, 2019),

DOI: 10.4324/9781003144403-15

c development of 5G infrastructure (Latif et al., 2017; Schulte et al., 2020; Yang & Gu, 2021), and
d building specialised/professional digital competencies among health professionals and general ones among society at large (Castro e Melo & Faria Araújo, 2020).

Another important factor that hinders the implementation of new technologies in Health 4.0 is the lack of international standards, which significantly reduce transaction costs. The adoption of such standards as part of Health 4.0 and the establishment of mutual recognition agreements for national product release procedures, not to mention the potential harmonisation of compliance standards, are key to streamlining the pace of Health 4.0 development (Iizuka & Ikeda, 2019).

A critical component of Health 4.0 is 5G network infrastructure; without it, the full potential of digital health technologies cannot be realised (Latif et al., 2017; Lee et al., 2020). The possibility of fast, stable transmission of large amounts of data is a prerequisite, without which the discussed technologies cannot be used on a widespread basis. Thus, the slow pace of development of relevant infrastructure is a serious limitation to the implementation of the idea of Health 4.0 (Latif et al., 2017; Yang & Gu, 2021).

Technology can help us solve certain problems, but, paradoxically, its implementation can be limited by exactly the same issues. For example, information technology and the Internet of Things (IOT) may allow us to increase the public's awareness of the challenges inherent in healthcare and thus positively affect the level of public education in the area of basic issues related to health promotion and prevention, i.e. health perception. However, a fundamental factor that determines whether or not the positive effects resulting from the availability of new technology and new devices can indeed accrue is the process of acquiring the ability to use them (Sapci & Sapci, 2019). In the era of technologies based on internet access, these competences are referred to as 'digital literacy'. It may appear trivial and obvious to someone who takes advantage of the possibilities offered by the IOT on a daily basis; however, as research shows, digital illiteracy and hence the lack of skills to use the tools based on new technologies pose a very real threat of digital exclusion - a serious problem and limitation as we strive to bring these technologies to widespread use in the healthcare system (Dunn & Hazzard, 2019; Napoli & Obar, 2014).

Data security also presents a serious challenge. How data is stored can be an issue - as was shown by the fire at one of OVHcloud's data centres in Strasbourg on March 10, 2021. According to Netcraft, as a result of two server rooms burning down, including one completely, 3.6 million websites running on 464,000 domains were temporarily disabled, including bank sites, online stores, and e-government portals. As a consequence, many customers who had no backup systems in place suffered partial or complete database loss (Mutton, 2021). This high-profile example provides a good illustration of an important problem known as the 'Quantified Planet': Internet technologies based on continuous communication, real-time data sharing, aggregation, and processing lead to a state extreme global connectivity within a single highly integrated system. The storage of huge amounts of different data from different systems that need to communicate with each other in one place raises serious security risks, which range from data loss, theft, leakage, or corruption, to their misuse, e.g. to enhance authoritarian power. It may also lead to knowledge unification: This risk is particularly intriguing, as it points to the problems inherent in a monopoly in the market of ideas, including, but not limited to reduced competition, dwindling number of new ideas, research directions, and scientific experiments (Özdemir, 2018).

Recommendations for the main stakeholders

Government (state authorities)

Applying the criterion of importance to the four categories of stakeholders in the health system identified in this chapter, it can be shown that government (state author) should be the first and most critical recipient of the recommendations. Despite a certain erosion of its position and influence in the wake of globalisation (Jessop, 2005), it remains the only institution that can provide an effective counterweight to the growing role of international organisations and transnational corporations. Recommendations for government apply to both the Health 4.0 development drivers mentioned above and the issues addressed in the individual chapters of this book. They include the following:

- It should create a networked Health 4.0 information system in order to collect and process information on the effects of Industry 4.0 as relevant to healthcare. Both the existing resources (universities, research institutes, and think tanks) and newly created agencies and institutions can be employed for this purpose. The principles of operation of these entities should be based on cooperation with healthcare stakeholders (defined more broadly than in this chapter). The system should serve, among others, to monitor the impact of Industry 4.0 on public health, provide a basis for health policy, and counteract fake news and misinformation in the area of health.
- Based on knowledge and information aggregated in this way as part of the Health 4.0 information system, government should conduct, both of its own accord and with the help of NGOs, long-term campaigns promoting the concept and solutions in the field of Health 4.0 with a view to raising public awareness of the fact that all social groups need to use these systems and solutions.
- In building such a system, government must create an appropriate infrastructure (including 5G) to enable the use of big data technologies and guarantee its safety.

- Alongside the above activities, government should have an efficient institutional system for developing and improving the digital skills of citizens, including health professionals and patients.
- Government should initiate and support actions intended to verify and introduce new solutions in the medical industry (including, above all, the pharmaceutical industry, medical devices, and applications) and healthcare.
- In all these efforts, the principle of preserving social cohesion should apply, understood (above all) as preventing certain social groups from gaining advantage in access to the most modern services and health procedures only (or mainly) on the basis of income or easier access to financial resources.
- Perhaps the greatest challenge for government arising from Industry 4.0 in the context of Health 4.0 involves creating legal regulations for human enhancement procedures and ensuring their effective enforcement. As above, they should be based on the principle of preserving social cohesion.

All these recommendations should be taken up and implemented by government in cooperation and agreement with other countries, whether within the framework of economic integration (e.g. the European Union) or on a global scale (World Health Organization [WHO]).

Non-governmental organisations

NGOs, acting as intermediaries between technology providers and society, should be actively involved in technology development. Being well acquainted with potential users - after all, some of them are not only clients but also founders of such organisations - they can more effectively engage social groups exposed to digital exclusion. The elderly and the disabled described in this book have the opportunity not only to receive support from these organisations but also, and more importantly, to be consulted by an entity intimately familiar with their needs. The intermediation of NGOs will contribute to increasing the scale of impact of solutions devised with elderly or disabled people in mind.

Recommendations for this group of shareholders in the healthcare system are as follows:

- The intermediary role of NGOs means that in order to be successful, they should accurately recognise the social needs of their clients and tailor their solutions accordingly. This is associated with the development of Health 4.0 technologies as part of the co-creation model discussed in this book.
- These organisations should try to ensure the security of the data stored and processed by health information systems. Representing the users of

such systems, i.e. patients, NGOs are an important, though by no means a dominant, component of the healthcare system in the context of Health 4.0.

- Apart from representing patients, NGOs should consider initiating legislation in the field of data security, taking into account patients' data privacy, as well as in the field of counteracting exclusion and marginalisation of selected social groups.
- The above recommendation also applies to their initiation of and involvement in consultations to create quality standards for the provision of health services using information technology.
- NGOs can play an intermediary and educator role for society in terms of developing knowledge about and desirable attitudes to the solutions offered by Health 4.0. This recommendation stems from the need to disseminate neutral and objective information and to combat digital exclusion and digital illiteracy.
- These organisations can also initiate the development of novel niche technologies. As sponsors, they should ensure financial backing for such projects, which, in turn, entails tapping a variety of sources for funding.

Patients

Patients are the focus of the healthcare system as recipients of medical services as well as a source of information about the expectations of new therapies, innovations, etc. As is shown in this book, they should be more broadly involved in the entire system. The following recommendations apply to this group:

- The primary guideline for patients related to the personalisation of solutions is to try to use advanced medical solutions on their own or with the help offered by patient support organisations. Patient empowerment, as was mentioned in this book, facilitates the delivery of medical services. In particular, this recommendation concerns the elderly, which also means that they need to be supported in using medical devices, i.e. in improving their digital skills. It is also necessary to develop their habits to effectively use new technologies in everyday life, which requires both support in terms of training and building social acceptance/support for such attitudes.
- Due to the high unit cost of using Health 4.0 solutions, it is recommended that patients should participate in associations and groups, which contributes to economies of scale and lowers the costs medical services supported by technology. Participation in more complex medical procedures that require access to advanced medical technology involves contact with specialists. The latter can be found precisely in organisations formed with a view to providing services using such equipment.

- Considering the technologies described in this book, access to medical resources via the Internet should be considered the easiest to use and the most straightforward. Thanks to Internet activity one may not only consume online contents but also actively participate in the provision of health services, hence the recommendation to familiarise patients with this form of communication.
- Participation in more complex medical procedures that require access to advanced medical technology involves contacts with specialists. Hence the suggestion to cooperate with NGOs mentioned previously.

As discussed in the chapter on co-creation, the role of patients is changing, which is also reflected in the above recommendations. Taking an active role in the development processes depends not only on the patients' predispositions - it is necessary to encourage them to do so, which is also the responsibility of the other stakeholders mentioned in this chapter.

Health professionals and healthcare managers

Health professionals and managers of healthcare institutions (regardless of the level at which they operate) are directly confronted on an ongoing basis with the impacts of Industry 4.0 and Healthcare 4.0, and it is them who in the first place determine how the patients perceive and evaluate those effects.

Recommendations for health professionals:

- Health professionals should recognise and accept the systemic change in the patient's position and build their relationships with the latter accordingly. The patient is no longer a passive recipient of services over whom the physician has a huge information advantage.
- The patient should be perceived as a partner in the processes of diagnosis and treatment. In view of the widespread use of the contents available on the Internet and related to diagnosis and treatment, health professionals (above all physicians) should improve their skills of persuasion and influence so as to effectively implement the next recommendation, which is
    - to expand the classical functions of a health professional to include that of a patient's guide through the healthcare system (above all, in relation to the treatment process and the sources of reliable information about health and illness available on the Internet).
    - While performing the classical task of updating their knowledge on new medicines, medical devices, and treatment methods, health professionals should carefully follow new solutions in the field of digital technologies and the possibilities of their use in medicine. This presupposes that health professionals themselves possess the appropriate digital skills.

Recommendations for healthcare managers:

- Monitor and use data from Healthcare 4.0 information systems for potential implementation in the healthcare facilities they run.
- Recognise, support, and reward entrepreneurial attitudes among employees of the facilities they manage.
- Help health professionals to acquire and improve digital skills and motivate them to continuously update their knowledge in the area of modern medical technologies.

Conclusions

The Fourth Industrial Revolution poses enormous challenges for governments in terms of financing and organising their healthcare systems. Governments must increasingly monitor stratification in access to health services and prepare to regulate and supervise the use of the latest advances in biomedicine, genetic engineering, and nanotechnologies as applicable in medicine. The recommendations for the main stakeholders of the healthcare system in the context of Health 4.0 have several points in common. For example, the recommendation to encourage more active patient participation in high-tech projects corresponds with the recommendation for health professionals to modify their perception of the patients' role. This testifies to the interdependence of activities pursued by various agents in providing medical services that implement Industry 4.0 solutions in the healthcare system.

References

Castro e Melo, J. A. G. de M. e, & Faria Araújo, N. M. (2020). Impact of the Fourth Industrial Revolution on the health sector: A qualitative study. *Healthcare Informatics Research*, *26*(4), 328–334. https://doi.org/10.4258/hir.2020.26.4.328

Dunn, P., & Hazzard, E. (2019). Technology approaches to digital health literacy. *International Journal of Cardiology*, *293*, 294–296. https://doi.org/10.1016/j.ijcard.2019.06.039

Iizuka, M., & Ikeda, Y. (2019). Regulation and innovation under Industry 4.0: Case of medical/healthcare robot, HAL by Cyberdyne. *Working Paper Series UNU-MERIT*. https://doi.org/10.13140/RG.2.2.35788.97928

Jessop, B. (2005). The Future of the State in an Er of Globalisation. In A. Pfaller & M. Lerch (eds.), *Challenges of Globalisation: New Trends in International Politics and Society (pp. 13–26)*. London: Routledge, Taylor & Francis Group.

Latif, S., Qadir, J., Farooq, S., & Imran, M. (2017). How 5G wireless (and concomitant technologies) will revolutionize healthcare? *Future Internet*, *9*(4), 93. https://doi.org/10.3390/fi9040093

Lee, P., Casey, M., & Wigginton, C. (2020). Private 5G networks – Enterprise untethered. *Deloitte Review*, *27*.

Lopes, J. M., Marrone, P., Pereira, S. L., & Dias, E. M. (2019). Health 4.0: Challenges for an orderly and inclusive innovation [commentary]. *IEEE Technology and Society Magazine*, *38*(3), 17–19. https://doi.org/10.1109/MTS.2019.2930265

Marino, A., & Lorenzoni, L. (2019). *The impact of technological advancements on health spending: A literature review* (OECD Health Working Papers No. 113; OECD Health Working Papers, Vol. 113). https://doi.org/10.1787/fa3bab05-en

Mutton, P. (2021, March 10). *3.6 million websites taken offline after fire at OVH datacenters* [Netcraft]. https://news.netcraft.com/archives/2021/03/10/ovh-fire.html

Napoli, P. M., & Obar, J. A. (2014). The emerging mobile internet underclass: A critique of mobile internet access. *The Information Society, 30*(5), 323–334. https://doi.org/10.1080/01972243.2014.944726

Özdemir, V. (2018). The dark side of the moon: The Internet of Things, Industry 4.0, and the quantified planet. *OMICS: A Journal of Integrative Biology, 22*(10), 637–641. https://doi.org/10.1089/omi.2018.0143

Sapci, A. H., & Sapci, H. A. (2019). Digital continuous healthcare and disruptive medical technologies: M-Health and telemedicine skills training for data-driven healthcare. *Journal of Telemedicine and Telecare, 25*(10), 623–635. https://doi.org/10.1177/1357633X18793293

Schulte, A., Majerol, M., & Nadler, J. (2020, July). Narrowing the rural-urban health divide. Bringing virtual health to rural communities. *Deloitte Review, The essence of resilient leadership. Business recovery from COVlD-19*(Issue 27), 79–93.

Slakey, D. P., & Davidson, I. (2019). Robotic surgery: An example of uncoupling the economics of technology. *Health and Technology, 9*(1), 25–29. https://doi.org/10.1007/s12553-018-0249-z

Yang, F., & Gu, S. (2021). Industry 4.0, a revolution that requires technology and national strategies. *Complex & Intelligent Systems*. https://doi.org/10.1007/s40747-020-00267-9

Index